Living
with Dying

Living with Dying

A Loving Guide for Family and Close Friends

David Carroll

McGRAW-HILL BOOK COMPANY

New York   St. Louis   San Francisco   Auckland   Bogotá   Guatemala   Hamburg
Johannesburg   Lisbon   London   Madrid   Mexico   Montreal   New Delhi
Panama   Paris   San Juan   São Paulo   Singapore   Sydney   Tokyo   Toronto

1234567890 DOCDOC 898765

ISBN 0-07-010098-5

LIBRARY OF CONGRESS CATALOGING IN PUBLICATION DATA

Carroll, David, 1942-
  Living with dying.

    1. Death.   2. Death—Psychological aspects.
3. Terminally ill.   4. Terminal care.   5. Children and
death.   6. Bereavement. I. Title.
HQ1073.C37   1985   306'9   84-15462
ISBN 0-07-010098-5

Book design by Chris Simon

Acknowledgments:

I'd like to thank the following people for their help in making this book possible: Dr. Margaret Meyers; Virginia Barrett; Hannah Carroll; Dr. Robert Solid; Dr. Mark Rickover; Lester Hume; Dr. Harry Moody; Rene Maughn; and especially Kenneth Stuart for his support in the editorial end of things.

To Charles,
and to the rest of us
—may we all die before we die . . .

Contents

CONTENTS

Foreword

In recent years there has been much theoretical speculation about caring for life-threatened patients resulting in the formation of guidelines for caregivers in the allied health professions and for family members. This book offers more than theoretical speculation, providing readily understandable and clearly expressed information about the psychosocial issues raised when "living with the dying." It offers anecdotal illustrations of appropriate responses to major problems and questions that arise during crisis situations.

The many dimensions of chronic, critical, and life-threatening illness should be handled utilizing medical technological advances, sophisticated caregiving techniques, and perceptive, sensitive activities. As patients encounter the various roles they are forced to play within today's complex medical environment, they may experience depersonalization and alienation in the attempt to conform to what has been mandated for them as the path to recovery. Patients are referred to a large number of specialists who have only limited—although important—connections to them and their family members. Frequent breakdowns in communication leave patients and family members in a state of confusion, abandonment, and ignorance. The leadership role assumed in past years by the family physician is now an anachronism, as patients are "subdivided" among the various medical specialties that extend their chances for survival.

Among the most significant factors in psychosocial caregiving for the dying are commitment to the prevention of isolation of patients from family and community, support of coping mechanisms that reinforce a positive quality of life, and enrichment of interpersonal relationships, even when days are few and hours short.

This book offers guidance for those involved in a thanatological context—not only patients and professional caregivers, but also family members and friends. Although some aspects of life may be compromised negatively by irreversible change, the satisfaction derived from knowing how to maintain compassionate human contact with loved ones can be a bridge to personal growth and enduring solace.

Dr. Austin H. Kutscher
President
The Foundation of Thanatology
Columbia-Presbyterian Medical Center
New York, New York

November 14, 1984

Introduction

After many years in the closet, death has emerged as a part of life. Over the past twenty years a plethora of books, seminars, and personal accounts devoted to the process of dying have been produced. However, few of these efforts have been directed at those people whose involvement counts the most—the family and friends of the dying and the dying person undergoing the awesome process of entering one of "death's ten thousand different doors."

This book fills that gap and is a welcome change. It is readable, pays attention to the practical problems and issues surrounding death, and most importantly, provides guidelines in dealing with them. Following awareness of an impending death, there are always questions, and this book raises them in the sequence in which they are most likely to occur. It then proceeds to answer these questions in an informative, reassuring, and practical way. It is a book that will be of active help for those involved in the death of a loved one.

Information from professional and technical literature on death and dying is combined in these pages with knowledge derived from life experiences. In addition to practical matters that range from bill paying to funeral planning, questions which are seldom addressed are raised in this book on such topics as: sex and the dying person, suicide, dealing with difficult or dishonest doctors, "pulling the plug" on life support machines, negotiating with a funeral director and choosing a cemetery, helping the very young dying child, pathologic grieving, speaking about death to children, and negative feelings on the part of the family toward the dying patient. All are openly and honestly discussed. Definitions of death and the grieving process are also provided. In addition, services available to assist the dying and their caregivers are described. The last section of this work provides a list of useful books on the subject of dying, with annotations about the content and value of each.

Family and friends of the dying have need of information and direction which, if not provided, lead to frustration, isolation, and extended grieving. Sooner or later all of us will experience the dying of a family member or close friend. As the ancient saying has it, "while men live, the whole world is too small—when they die the grave is large enough." This book, while it cannot prevent the occurrence of grief and death, provides real support and honest answers for the bewildering moment.

Virginia Barrett, R.N., ME.d.

1

Talking with the Dying about Death

When Is One Actually Considered to Be Dying? As Opposed to Simply Being Very Sick?

Although there admittedly can be a fine line between a condition of great sickness from which one will possibly, or even probably, recover and a condition of terminality from which the chance of recovery is minimal, there are several criteria that can be used to define the state of impending death.

The first criterion applies when a person develops a disease generally considered to be incurable. Then death may be imminent or it may not. It may be close at hand or it may be months, even years away. Whatever the schedule involved, the moment one comes down with a fatal illness the active process of dying has started.

The second criterion is when, due to massive bodily damage caused, say, by an accident, a person is judged to have little chance of survival.

The third criterion applies when a person's vital organs begin to fail. The cause can be old age, sickness, or a combination of the two.

1

Is There Any Way of Telling for Certain If a Sick Person Will in Fact Die?

No, at least not with anything approaching complete certainty. There are countless numbers of people who have been at the brink of death and returned. There are countless numbers who have died inexplicably from seemingly minor ailments and wounds.

What about Statistics? Aren't Records Available That Disclose Recovery Probabilities for Various Accidents and Diseases?

One can rely on statistics only up to a point. These are, after all, only numbers calculated according to collective probabilities and they do not take the personal idiosyncrasies of the individual into account. It is well worth remembering in matters of death and dying that there is only one absolute: We are all going to die. There are nothing but uncertainties after that, because we do not know when.

If a Patient Is Diagnosed as Suffering from a Terminal Ailment, Should a Doctor Tell the Patient That He or She Is Dying?

Probably no issue concerning death and dying is more widely discussed and elaborated on than this one. Entire books have been penned on the question, and the debate still goes hotly on. The reasons for the recent preoccupation with this difficult topic, both among medical professionals and the public at large, stem largely from our culture's uninformed attitudes towards death along with the resultant tendency to label matters such as these morbid, irrelevant, and in bad taste. As has often been pointed out, death has become the unmentionable obscenity of the modern age, just as sex was once the target of fascinated loathing and knee-jerk censorship in a previous era.

Thus it has been assumed for many years, both by the hospital staff and by the family of a dying person, that the sick person should at all costs be kept in the dark concerning his or her approaching annihilation. It was for the person's own good, everyone agreed. A dying person who knew the truth was assumed to be unable to bear it. It was easier this way for everyone.

Over the past decade or so, the pendulum has taken a swing. Many professionals today feel that it is better to tell dying persons the truth, and better to tell them quickly, before a complex net of lies and half-truths begins to entangle everyone involved. This is all well and good, of course, and there are many testimonials to the fact that *open awareness*, as it is called—that is, having knowledge of one's impending death, as opposed to *closed awareness*, which is not knowing—is a better system all around. Yet, as doctors and patients have found out, there are many subtleties and unpredictable elements involved in this delicate question, and very few absolute rules.

If Someone Is Dying, How Can the Truth Be Hidden from the Person After a Certain Point, Anyway?

Usually it cannot, unless the person chooses not to know, which is not infrequent. If those administering to the dying person are skilled at dissimulation, however, the deception can be carried on for a surprisingly long period of time.

What Laws, If Any, Determine Whether Doctors Must Tell Patients That They Are Dying?

There are no such laws, and in all likelihood there never will be. Neither doctors nor members of a doctor's staff are under legal obligation to inform a patient that his or her condition is terminal. If a doctor withholds this information and a patient sues the doctor for so doing, the patient's chances of winning the case are miniscule.

Why Do So Many People Today Feel That Patients Should Be Told That They Are Going to Die? Why Is Knowing Necessarily Better Than Not Knowing?

This question of why it is better to tell is perhaps best answered by describing a typical situation in which a person has *not* been told that she is dying.

Begin with the relationship between the patient and her family. Closed awareness by its very nature is a deception, and thus brings with it many brittle and disturbing contingencies. For instance, if family members choose to keep their relative in the dark concerning the seriousness of her condition, they must rehearse and act out a complicated masquerade to this effect. The scene is set mainly at the hospital. Here the family's first obligation is continually to keep up false appearances with cheery smiles and bright words. Sincere, convincing discussions are acted out with the dying person concerning her future, as if the fact that she had a future was a foregone conclusion. Even as the evidence in the mirror says otherwise, the patient must be assured that she looks wonderful today, that her health is returning with noticeable vigor—everyone can see it! Rarely is the disease itself mentioned or the suffering that accompanies it. When the patient brings up the matter, there is a sudden silence in the room and the subject is quickly changed. The patient is assured in a perky voice that all will soon be okay.

How exhausting this playacting soon becomes! Even under the best of circumstances, to feign happiness is a difficult task. Unless the sick person is totally insensitive, she begins to sense that something is wrong. "Why do my friends whisper in the hall when they come to see me?" she wonders. "What do those little looks mean? Why are the lesions not getting any better? If everything is so rosy, why do people treat me so solicitously, why am I being babied in such a silly way? Why does my daughter have swollen eyes when she visits? Why is my husband bringing me all those flowers? Why is everybody so damned *nice* all of a sudden!"

On the one hand, the dying person's family is constantly bombarding the patient with verbal assurances, while a mass of puzzling, contradictory cues are simultaneously being communicated through their body language: looks of anxious concern, fist-clenchings of worry, postures of dejection and sadness, voice tones of insincerity strangely mingled with grief. When the patient asks what is going on, everyone laughs nervously and tells her that she is just tired. Best to get some sleep—she'll feel better tomorrow.

After enduring this stilted behavior for some time, after noticing that her ailment is not, in fact, getting any better, and after realizing that there are precious few signs that she is about to be discharged from the hospital, the patient begins to despair and may even question her own state of mental health. "Who is crazy, them or me?" Who can she trust? It is difficult to be sure. So she turns to the medical staff for answers.

Here, however, an even more elaborate game is being played, this one featuring players of consummate skill and vast experience, each pitted against a person who is singularly unprepared for such an encounter—because, of course, she has never died before—a person without resources, without allies, without knowledge that a game is being played in the first place. The family at least has an investment in being involved with the dying person. The medical staff has an investment in *not* being involved and will often go to elaborate lengths to keep things this way.

According to the unspoken rule among most hospital staffs, the doctor is the only person with the authority to tell this patient that she is dying. The staff is under an obligation to follow the doctor's lead. As a result, the nurses, and to a lesser degree the rest of the staff, must begin the orchestration of a deceit equal in complexity to that practiced by the family, one designed to keep the patient ignorant of the truth until (1) she discovers it for herself, (2) she is informed of the fact by her doctor, (3) she learns of it through some other source, or (4) she dies.

To begin with, the nurses must confine themselves to the most superficial interchange with the patient. If a sincere, meaningful relationship is established, the truth might be revealed. A wall comes literally built into the system.

It becomes important to construct a false medical report, one designed to convince the patient that her disease is curable and that her recovery is imminent. The patient is, of course, anxious to be informed regularly of her progress and the staff is obliged to labor diligently to reinforce the original false report with equally false supporting data and sham daily medical updates. Details of this matter must be implemented with great care and even a certain amount of creative bluff. One false move could arouse suspicions.

An equally energetic effort is made to draw the patient's attention away from her serious symptoms and focus them on false improvements. High hopes must be raised. The staff may hint that the patient will soon be returning home, that this new medicine will definitely do the trick, that the latest lab tests show important improvements. A conspiracy of misdirection is created.

This is a difficult trick to carry off, of course, and must be supported by everyone in the patient's environment. This means that those peripherally responsible for the patient's welfare must be impressed into the deception together with the health care regulars, the dietician, and the orderly, and soon a web of illusions enfolds not only the dying person but also everyone else, even other patients who have somehow learned the dark secret. They, too, become parties to the lie.

Ultimately, as often happens, the staff may come to feel guilty about this trickery. Few people enjoy lying, even if it is done in the name of a greater good. If nothing else, it is exhausting. Yet even if the staff wishes to change their tactics in midstream, they can scarcely announce to the patient that they had been kidding all this time, and that, surprise, surprise, the patient is, after all, dying from a fatal disease. Moreover, such a disclosure delivered out of the blue will almost certainly guarantee complete loss of the patient's trust. The fact is that once the juggernaut of closed awareness is set in motion, it continues on by its own momentum. It is like a ball rolling downhill. It cannot be called back.

Yet all the time that this sad charade is being played out, the reality of the situation remains that the patient *is* dying, and it thus becomes increasingly difficult to perpetuate the ruse. More and more, conversation with the patient must be kept to a minimum lest the truth slip out, and all dangerous subjects must be avoided. If the dying person asks too many questions, the nurses are obliged to cut her off or ignore her question.

They are obliged to change the subject, treat the question as a joke, refer her to the doctor, or tell another lie. Since, as the expression goes, "the liar forgets his lies," these cover-up answers gradually lose their consistency and a collection of contradictory explanations piles up. The explanation of the night nurse is different from the explanation of the day nurse; the explanation of the orderly is different from the explanation of the attending physician.

What's more, the ever-increasing intensity of the patient's medical treatment begins to give the lie to the optimistic diagnoses. She continually undergoes a bewildering battery of new and sometimes painful tests. Without preparation or explanation she is moved from one room to another. New prescription follows new prescription, and sometimes whole regimens of pills are prescribed simply to negate the harmful side effects of the primary medicines.

The patient feels increasingly miserable. The medicines do not seem to be taking effect and no longer does anyone mention her discharge from the hospital. Each day brings greater weakness and pain, yet try as she may, she cannot learn the results of all those tests. The hospitalization drags on, and her doctor becomes less and less available even as her condition seems to grow worse. No matter how she begs to be enlightened about what it all means, she receives only frozen smiles, implausible explanations, promises that it will all turn out fine, and increased inattention.

When the situation finally gets unbearable the patient may, in desperation, try to force the issue. She may suddenly ask the nurse or doctor point-blank if she is dying, attempting to catch them off-guard; she may throw a scene and demand to be told what is taking place; she may try to sneak a look at her records; she may announce that she is dying and watch how the staff reacts; she may try to check out of the hospital; she may attempt to pry the truth from one of the new nurses or from her neighbor in the next bed. The hospital staff, well trained at fending off such attempts, rebuts her assault by stepping up the conspiracy of silence. They may label the patient as a troublemaker and leave her more to herself than before.

After Being Exposed to So Many Hints and So Much Ambiguous Behavior on the Part of Both Family and Medical Staff, It Would Seem That Any Normal Patient Would Start to Guess That Her Condition Is More Serious Than Others Are Letting On.

According to a ground-breaking study on the subject of death awareness by Barney G. Glaser and Anselm L. Strauss (Glaser and Strauss, 1965), patients suffering from a fatal disease move through several distinct stages of awareness.

In the first stage the patient believes that nothing is seriously wrong, and others encourage this illusion.

After a while the symptoms become obvious, however, and patients move into a condition that Glaser and Strauss refer to as *suspected awareness*, a kind of netherworld between knowing and not knowing, an awareness that is neither open nor closed. The patient suspects that she is sick, all right, perhaps very sick. But she doesn't know for certain, and she's not sure she wants to find out. Suspected awareness in many ways is the worst of all crosses for the dying patient to bear. The person no longer enjoys the bliss which ignorance provides, and yet she cannot gain the relief that full disclosure brings. She hangs in the limbo of it all, and few there are that will cut the line.

"Somewhere between open acknowledgment of death and its utter repudiation," writes Avery Weisman (Weisman, 1972, pp. 65, 66), "is an area of uncertain certainty called *middle knowledge*. . . . As a rule middle knowledge tends to occur at serious transition points, such as when a patient begins the descent to death, undergoes a setback, or finds obvious equivocation among people on whom he depends. . . . Middle knowledge is marked by unpredictable shifts in the margin between what is observed and what is inferred. Patients seem to know and want to know, yet they often talk as if they did not know and did not want to be reminded of what they have been told. Many patients rebuke their doctors for not having warned them about complications in treatment or the course of illness, even though the doctors may have been scrupulous about keeping them informed. These instances of seeming denial are usually examples of middle knowledge that herald a relapse. When a patient with a fatal illness suddenly becomes unable to draw plausible inferences about himself, slipping back into an exacerbation of denial, it is often a sign that the terminal phase is about to begin."

If a Person Finally Learns for Certain That He Is Dying, Will He Always Let On to Others That He Knows?

If the people surrounding him have an investment in keeping awareness closed, or if the patient prefers not to confront the feelings that disclosure would arouse, the patient may adopt a posture that Glaser and Strauss term *mutual pretense*. In this case the patient knows the truth. And the others know the truth. And he knows that they know, and they know that he knows— and nobody says a word.

This reciprocal ritual is common when a patient wishes to continue on good terms with the medical staff and not alienate them by bringing up the forbidden fact. Or when the patient believes that his family could not take the truth (just as, ironically, they think *he* cannot take the truth), and so all participants willingly act their parts, talking as if the patient has a future, as if he will soon be healthy again, as if life is as it has always been. While conversations between the patient and others may vaguely allude to the seriousness of the disease, and while patient and doctors delicately talk around the subject of the patient's death, saying what has to be said by inference, direct discussion of dangerous topics is avoided and there is an unspoken agreement on both sides not to confront the issue point-blank. If by chance the truth is let slip, or if, for whatever reason, the true situation is mentioned, it is incumbent on all parties to pretend that nothing was ever said and to continue with the charade as before. Glaser and Strauss give, by example, the case of a nurse who walks into the room when a patient is crying, and then pretends that she doesn't see what is happening or with a skillful comment makes it seem that she believes the patient is crying for a trivial and unrelated reason.

Aren't There Advantages to Mutual Pretense?

As Glaser and Strauss remark, mutual pretense can provide a measure of dignity and privacy to a patient, and with some members of the family it may reduce embarrassment and emotional strain. At the same time, pretense of any kind in the matter of death more or less guarantees that the patient will be forced into nonintimacy with both family and staff, that she will be deprived of the needed chance to speak candidly with others concerning her feelings, and that the general atmosphere of pretending will cause extensive strain and tension on all involved.

In What Ways Do Patients Usually Learn That They Are Dying?

There are dozens of possible ways. As mentioned, it is far more common today than in past decades for a physician to be honest with a person concerning a diagnosis. The consequences of closed awareness have proved so unpleasant for so many years that many health care professionals now prefer to clear the air from the beginning.

Therefore, it is usually the doctor who is the first to disclose the truth. However, sometimes the doctor will defer to the family; a close relative such as a daughter or a brother may be the one to bring the news. In practice, the doctor often tells the family before telling the patient, and together they work out terms whereby the patient will be informed. Chaplains are also frequent bearers of the news.

When awareness is kept closed this is a different story, of course. In such a case, a patient might learn the facts from any number of random sources: by accident, by inference, by overhearing a conversation, by tricking a nurse. R. A. Kalish (Kalish, 1970) has compiled a list of the various channels by which the dying discover the truth of their condition. These include:

- Direct statements from the physician
- Overheard comments of the physician to other people

- Direct statement from other personnel, including aides, nurses, and technologists
- Overheard comments by staff to each other
- Direct statements from family, friends, chaplain, lawyer
- Changes in the behavior of others toward the patient
- Changes in medical care routines, procedures, and medications
- Changes in physical location
- Self-diagnosis, including reading of medical books, records, and charts
- Signals from the body and changes in physical status
- Altered responses by others toward the future

What Is the Best Way to Tell a Person That He Is Dying?

The best way is to have the patient ask *you*—not the other way around. When it is clearly evident that a person is suffering from a fatal illness but he asks no questions, this probably means that he is not ready to know. When he *is* ready he will bring the subject up himself. Up to that time it may be better judgment—*may* be, we say, for each situation requires individual discretion—to allow the person to initiate the subject himself.

Another hint may be taken from the wise physician. Instead of revealing the whole truth in one sharp blow, the physician opens the gates of truth slowly, a little at a time, suggesting that this symptom implies this possibility, refusing reassurance when leading questions are asked, stressing the treatments that are available but not implying that they will necessarily work, inviting the patient to frame his own questions, and then answering them with gentle candor. The patient hears what he is ready to hear. Gradually the truth is made clear. A wise physician knows the value of timing, of body language, of letting the patient go at his own pace and setting his own agendas for awareness. As Avery Weisman points out, "Truth is not so bitter that it must always be downed in a single gulp, nor is it so poisonous that we must avoid it completely" (Weisman, 1972).

When answering a patient's question about his chances for

survival, a patient's diagnosis and a patient's prognosis must both be taken into account. The *diagnosis* is the name of the disease and its degree of advancement. The *prognosis* is an estimate of the seriousness of the disease and whether the patient will get well. The person may be told specifically what ailment he is suffering from. Once informed he will usually draw his own conclusions. At no time should the patient be told that he is dying per se, only that he is very sick. Moreover, to specify precise amounts of survival time, to inform a person that he has exactly three months to live, for example, is a risky practice and, what's more, a fallacious one, as those countless numbers of "terminal" patients who have outlived their physicians will testify to.

In other words, there is no set formula. The rules of thumb are:

1. Let the sick person bring up the subject first. Let him be the one to tell you.

2. Be cautious, gentle, and circumspect. It is not so much the exact words that you use but the *way* you tell him.

3. Avoid telling a person that his disease is invariably fatal or that he has so-and-so number of weeks until the end. All any of us knows in these matters are probabilities, and these are far from being inevitable.

4. Proceed at the person's own pace. Let him ask as much as he wants to know at a given time. Do not give him more than he asks for.

What Do You Do If a Person Asks You If He Is Dying?

The best way of answering such a question is to reflect it back to the patient. If he asks if he is dying, you might say, "Why do you ask?" or "Do you *think* that you are dying?" If he says yes, you might ask him why. At this point chances are that he will continue on his own and speak about what is on his mind.

If a Doctor Refuses to Tell a Patient That He Is Dying, Do Others Have the Right to Tell the Patient the Truth?

The doctor is in charge. It is the doctor who decides if and when a patient should be told, and it is wrong to countermand this decision. Perhaps the doctor knows something that you don't. There may be sound reasons for withholding the information. By no means should others take it upon themselves to go behind the doctor's back and set the patient straight. Such behavior may cause complications worse than those which already exist.

What If the Patient Wants to Know and the Doctor Will Not Give Him a Straight Answer?

Every patient has the right to know how sick he is. If the doctor is evasive, the patient should seek out other informed persons, such as the social worker, the nurses, or the chaplain. The patient should insist on receiving a clear, unequivocal report on what disease he is suffering from, how advanced the disease has become, the probabilities for survival, and the available alternatives.

If the Signs Are Obvious That a Person Is Dying, Should One Assume That the Patient Knows Even If She Has Not Been Told?

No, do not assume anything. If nothing else, spending time with the dying reveals the lengths to which people will sometimes go to deceive themselves. However, at a certain point most people will know that they are suffering from something serious. The thought of death may have occurred to them and they may even have discussed it with others. This is by no means a guarantee that they understand the full seriousness of the situation.

Do Most People Want to Know They Are Dying?

Many surveys have been taken to establish the answer to this important question. Almost invariably the majority of those questioned reply that, yes, they would prefer to know. Of the group that Herman Feifel queried in 1963 (Feifel, 1963), 82 percent said that they wanted to know. A survey by August Kasper a few years earlier (Kasper, 1959) revealed that from 77 to 89 percent preferred the true facts. Even among physicians a majority did not wish to have such information withheld (Feifel et al., 1968). The general estimate is that at least 75 percent of people would prefer open awareness to closed.

What about Persons Who Show No Signs That They Know They Are Dying, or Who Show No Interest in Finding Out?

If much physical deterioration is evident and if the person seems oblivious to it or seemingly uninterested, assume that the person is in a state of denial. Some people, on the other hand, know quite well how sick they are but refrain from speaking about it, feeling that it would be too upsetting for others. The rule of thumb is to allow the patient to bring up the subject, not to inaugurate it oneself.

If a Person Knows That She Is Dying and Wishes to Talk about It, Are There Any General Guidelines a Listener Can Go By When Having Such Discussions?

The most important thing *is* to listen—carefully. Paying attention is in many ways more important than giving advice or making comments. The person may raise questions, it is true, but really what she wants is to speak about her feelings and to do so with someone who is attentive, sympathetic, and honest.

There are, at the same time, several things to avoid when speaking to the person concerning her impending death. Do not tell her that she is being morbid or gloomy. Nothing will make her clam up faster. Do not try to joke her out of her depression or belittle her pain. Expressions such as "Come on, now, you're going to outlive us all" or "I know it's tough, but at least try to smile" are perceived as impatient put-downs, and usually they are. Further, do not change the subject she has brought up, even if it is an unpleasant one. Avoid intellectualizing. Speak to her as you would speak with any normal person, without a maudlin tone of voice and without undue sympathetic nods, smiles, and pauses.

Look the person directly in the eye. When she tries to articulate what is difficult to put into words, ask direct questions, ask for examples and more information, help her to formulate her thoughts by summarizing what she has said, then feed it back to her for confirmation. Help her to put her ideas into concrete language. Let her dwell on the details if she wishes, even if they are intimate or gruesome.

Often a patient will talk around the major issues, speaking in metaphors, in suggestions, in figurative language. Instead of speaking about her sick body she may refer to her "broken-down house"; instead of talking about her incontinence she may refer to "the old running hose." If she is more comfortable with such symbolic language, speak back in the same idiom. Usually, both of you will know when you are communicating, even if the language is highly indirect. One elderly woman suffering from an incurable liver ailment held long discussions with the hospital therapist concerning her love of the sea, how each raindrop came from the ocean, rose to the sky, fell to earth, and then returned to the great waters. Both parties were clearly aware that the individual raindrop the woman spoke of was herself.

Be directive only insofar as it helps lead the person in the direction she wants to go. Otherwise, let her set the goals. Avoid argument, confrontation, or talking too long about your own theories and opinions. You are on delicate ground. Jarring or challenging words will usually cause a loss of trust. Draw the person out but allow her to go at her own speed. Do not force things that are not ready to be said. At the same time, if there are particular practical problems to be addressed, these should be aired and conclusions reached as efficiently as possible.

Once a Patient Is Told That He Is Dying, Does This Guarantee That He Will Accept the Fact?

No, it does not necessarily mean that the fact has been accepted. If the person withdraws into a posture of denial, he is indicating that he prefers at present not to confront his probable death. Perhaps at a later date he will. The important thing is that he be given the opportunity.

Might Telling a Person She Is Suffering from a Fatal Disease Cause Her to Suffer a Breakdown or Even Go Mad?

That is what people once thought, or at least said they thought. But all evidence points in the opposite direction—that patients who are honestly informed of their situation respond with relief and occasionally a sense of thankfulness, especially if they have, until now, been kept in the dark about their diagnosis. Only on the rarest occasions will someone fall entirely to pieces, and then only for a limited period of time. Usually, people are glad they have been told.

How Soon After the Diagnosis Should a Person Be Told?

By most estimates, the person should be told as soon as possible. The alternatives are to string the person along with generalities that give him no real answers, or to lie.

What If the Person Cries Uncontrollably When He Receives the News?

He probably will. Let him. Most people who learn they are dying pass through suffering and depression. It is inevitable. The rationale behind keeping the secret of death is that it will spare a person pain. But a dying person *must* feel pain, in one way or the other. Except in the rarest occasions, it is inescapable.

The question then is: What kind of pain must he feel? By consensus, the pain one undergoes when told the truth about death is preferable to the pain one feels when lied to, confounded, patronized, and ignored—as in closed awareness.

Does the Attitude, Manner, and Timing of the Person Who Bears the News of Death Affect the Way the Patient Will Respond?

People who have been informed of their death in an offhanded, cold, or brusque manner tend to deny more than those who are eased into the knowledge and given immediate follow-up support. This is especially true if the news is delivered by a stranger, or if it is given at an inappropriate time.

Is It Possible to Give Too Much Information to a Dying Person concerning the Seriousness of His Condition?

Usually, only the basic facts are necessary in the beginning. Later the particular medical details will reveal themselves as a matter of course. Unless he specifically asks for it, do not bombard the person with information on medical protocols, on the technicalities of possible treatments, or on the statistics of the prognosis. One can overexplain to a dying person just as one can underexplain.

What about Forcing Open Awareness on a Patient?

This is a cruel and unnecessary practice. By no means should a person be forced to accept what she is not ready to accept. This type of action can, in fact, ignite the very pathologic breakdown which people are so afraid will take place during normal disclosure. For example, a woman who had recently turned 50 years old was admitted to a hospital with suspicious spots on her lungs. The doctors quickly identified cancer, but the woman was told that her diagnosis was unclear and that exploratory surgery was necessary. Several days before the operation a well-meaning but insensitive x-ray technician decided that he would set the woman straight, and he did so by telling her to go home, look at her reflection in the mirror each night, and repeat loudly to herself: "I have cancer, I have cancer, I have cancer!" This disclosure came so unexpectedly, and was delivered in such an abrupt, uncaring manner that the woman became hysterical and had to be kept under sedation for several days.

If a Person's Condition Is Uncertain and the Doctors Do Not Know If He Will Live or Die, Should the Person Be Told That He Is Getting Better?

He should simply be told the truth: that his condition *is* uncertain and that at this point it is impossible to say what the outcome will be.

What If a Person Wants to Talk about Her Death but Is Shy or Afraid to Bring the Subject Up?

It usually doesn't take much to get such people to open up. Statements like "You look as if you've got something heavy on your mind today?" or "It hasn't been easy here for you, has it?" are good for openers. Once you signal your interest and willingness to listen, the person will usually talk.

What about Talking to Strangers?

Surprisingly, the dying are sometimes more willing to talk to strangers about their intimate hopes and fears than they are to their own families. Usually, this is because the family is unavailable or uninterested or unwilling to face what the person has to say.

Sometimes One Feels Awkward around a Dying Person, Especially If He Wants to Talk about His Death. If One Hasn't Been Trained in Talking with Patients, How Do You Know What to Say to Him? How Can You Avoid Saying the Wrong Things?

It is not as difficult as you might think. The best method is to let the dying person carry the conversation and to follow his conversational leads. If he wants to talk about God, let him talk about God. If he wants to talk about pain, then talk about pain. If he wants to discuss the Pittsburgh Steelers, follow suit. Ask questions. Put out leading statements and let him lead the conversation. Repeat back to the patient a particular word or phrase that he has just used and let him elaborate on it. Offer no interpretations or judgment unless they are requested, and even then do so with a minimum of comment. You might also suggest that the person may be feeling such-and-such a way about an issue, and then let him accept or reject this lead, as he wishes. That is what it is all about, allowing the person to say what he wants to say.

If he asks you questions about life and death, answer according to what you believe. No doubt you have your own thoughts on these subjects. Speak to him as you would to anybody else. He'll appreciate it. Don't assume that he expects you to say profound things or that he thinks you'll come up with cosmic answers. He knows that no one has the answers. But that does not stop him from having the questions.

As to saying the wrong things, if the person knows the truth about his condition, there aren't many wrong things that *can* be said. Exercise simple tact, of course, and learn the full extent of the person's awareness before discussing details. If you say something that is obviously out of place, the person will understand. Dying persons are often far more tolerant than their healthy brethren. Apologize and continue. Some people, you will notice, are aggressive about discussing their condition one minute and tentative about it the next. This is a natural behavior pattern among dying persons, but it can be surprising and puzzling for an unprepared listener. Again, it is best not to launch into heavy material right away but to let the other person set the pace and intensity.

When Is Open Awareness Not Advisable?

Such times include when a person is in an unstable mental condition, when a person has just received an enormous shock such as the amputation of a limb or the loss of a loved one, and when a person has explicitly let it be known that she does not *want* to be informed about the implications of her diagnosis. In most instances those who are not ready to know will not know. They will be spared by their own denial devices.

2
Coming to Terms with Death: Stages of Acceptance

How Do People React to a Diagnosis of Terminal Illness? Do They All React the Same Way?

How people come to terms with the prospect of their own death is one of the most frequently discussed topics in the field of death and dying, and one of the most debated. The well-known pioneer in the field of thanatology, Elisabeth Kübler-Ross, in her famous book *On Death and Dying* (Kübler-Ross, 1969), was among the first to popularize the notion that there are a series of identifiable psychological stages that a person passes through in the process of coming to terms with his or her own death. She based her analysis on the experience of keeping watch by the bedside of more than 200 dying men and women and of conducting lengthy interviews with these people concerning their most intimate anxieties and expectations.

Some persons have accepted Kübler-Ross's map of the dying process without argument. Others have argued the point silly. The discussion still goes on, with Kübler-Ross standing in the background, having had her say and allowing her case to rest.

What Are the Five Stages of the Dying Process Defined by Elisabeth Kübler-Ross?

Briefly, these five stages are:

1. *Denial*:   refusal to accept the evidence that one is dying.

2. *Anger*:   bitterness over the fact that it is *me* who has been singled out by fate.

3. *Bargaining*:   an attempt to postpone death or to alter its schedule by self-imposed (and often unreasonable) contracts, negotiations, pledges, and promises. These can be made to one's self, to one's god, or to one's fate. An example might be: "I can't afford to die until I've made provisions for the children." Or: "When I finish my novel, then I'll be prepared to go."

4. *Depression*:   despair and hopelessness in the face of death's inevitability.

5. *Acceptance*:   a final, often peaceful, and occasionally joyous acknowledgment of one's ultimate situation.

Could You Go into These Stages in a Bit More Detail?

Yes. In fact, we will look at them in depth. Kübler-Ross's ideas, although perhaps open to interpretation (she herself makes no claim for their infallibility), still offer one of the best blueprints yet devised for understanding the dying process.

The first category is denial. This, simply, is the refusal to accept the fact that one is dying. To understand this very human reaction is to understand many things concerning the way dying people behave.

When, for instance, someone brings news that a close friend has suddenly been killed, our first response is disbelief. The person who brought the news must be misinformed. Perhaps our friend is badly hurt, even maimed. But dead? Or in daily matters, when a job is suddenly terminated, when something precious is lost, the tendency is to deny: "Is this really happening to me?" Denial, in short, is a counter-reaction to any shock or trauma, a common and fundamental coping maneuver that allows one to escape, at least momentarily, from pain.

Small shocks cause small denials. But news of impending death can set off a reaction that may continue for weeks or months, sometimes even up to the moment of death itself. Many people have literally denied their death into the grave. Denial can take on a spectrum of forms, not all of them identifiable as denial per se. For example, the ailing person may begin to haunt libraries and bookshops, becoming an expert on his particular disease, searching medical books for passages that offer the smallest hint that his condition will not be fatal. He may seek out costly specialists for a second opinion, and then for a third and a fourth and a fifth, meanwhile clinging to the assurances of well-meaning but ignorant friends who promise that everything is going to turn out "just fine."

Unrealistic plans are made, a trip around the world is proposed, a new business venture is begun, as if to give the lie to one's diagnosis by a display of frenzied energy. Previously skeptical persons, those who prided themselves on their reasonableness, find themselves searching for miracle cures, believing every rumor, undergoing bizarre and often painful unorthodox therapies. Enormous hopes are pinned on medical cures which are, as ever, just around the corner.

Those caught up in denial may also minimize their condition, assuring everyone that they are in the hospital just on a routine visit, just to make sure. Patients with heart conditions step up their Sunday rounds of golf or insist on continuing their strenuous routine of exercise and sauna baths at the gym. Surveys show that among people who have been directly informed that they are suffering from terminal cancer or incurable heart disease, almost one-fourth deny suffering from any ailment whatsoever, and a certain percentage of these deny that they received such a diagnosis in the first place.

Conversely, just as a person may search hectically for a miracle cure, so she may turn against the very doctors who have administered her sentence of death. This person may condemn the medical community at large, her doctor in particular, and insist that she has been misdiagnosed and cheated in the process—all those doctors want to do is operate!

Friends and relatives, of course, invoke their own smoke-screens. From many reports we know that long after dying patients have accepted their own death, they carry on the masquerade of ignorance to appease friends and relatives who choose not to know the truth. Talk may thus go on at the bedside between patient and visitor concerning plans for next year's Christmas party, or for a summer vacation in the mountains, all with the unspoken knowledge that none of these events will ever come to pass. The family, for their part, feels that they are soothing the dying person; the dying person, in turn, thinks that she must humor the family lest they make a scene. Where the denial originally begins becomes a kind of chicken-and-egg question. Once such a stone has been set in motion it is not so easy to stop its forward movement.

Are There Different Kinds of Denial?

Denial is highly personalized according to the temperament of each person. It can be categorized only in the most general terms. Broadly speaking, a person might deny in any of the following ways:

1. Absolute denial. This is a flat-out refusal to believe what one has been told. As mentioned earlier, almost one-fourth of those informed that they were suffering from cancer and heart disease refused to accept their diagnosis, and some blocked out the fact entirely. This indicates that people who otherwise seem stable can exhibit sudden pathological responses to news of terminal illness. Such people can, for instance, wipe out the memory of weeks, even months spent in the hospital staring with blank eyes at anyone who mentions the event. At times it may even seem that the person is losing his mind, but the truth is that each person has his own tolerance for bad news and his own methods for digesting it.

A case in point is Lamont. An aging theatrical producer, Lamont was informed directly by his doctor, in front of several attending relatives, that he was suffering from an incurable cancer of the lungs and that he had only a few months to live. Lamont, who at this moment in his career was busily putting together a retrospective of his most successful theatrical revues, took the news without flinching, made a brave speech to everyone in the room that he was not ready to die, that he would fight this thing to the end, and that he would live to see his new show in lights. Several days after the affair, however, visiting relatives were amazed to find that when they referred to Lamont's courageous attitude and to his "situation," he returned their remarks with uncomprehending looks and an abrupt change of subject. In a short while it became clear that Lamont had blanked the event from memory, and that in his estimation he was quite ready to go home.

2.   Fluctuating Denial. Today a young man sits on the side of his bed talking frankly to his parents. He now understands that he has only several more weeks to live. He is putting his papers in order, he tells them, and making last minute amendments to his will. A good number of tears are shed at this meeting, long-overdue embraces are exchanged, and a sigh of relief goes out on the part of the youth's parents: at least now the terrible secret need no longer be kept.

A day later the dying man's parents come again, but this time they are intercepted in the hall by the man's wife. She warns them that her husband has been making plans all morning for the courses he will be teaching during the upcoming spring term—he is a teacher at a prep school—and that he keeps talking about his hopes to work with the lacrosse team this season if he is feeling up to it. The patient, it is clear, chooses to slip in and out of a state of denial. What he can bear to face one day he cannot bear to face the next.

People under stress of death often change in their capacity to deal with the truth. Sometimes this capacity may be puzzlingly inconstant, emerging and vanishing from hour to hour like the sun through the clouds. A dying patient may carry on long discussions with the night nurse or even the janitor, making it quite clear that he is aware of the seriousness of his disease. Then, in front of family members or friends, he does a complete about-face, chatting away, quite sincerely, about personal plans that extend far into the future.

The ego is in many ways a wise and kindly governor. It knows its own limitations; it knows when to shut down. If a moment arrives when it can no longer endure bad news, it mercifully sets up a dividing wall between itself and the world, and protects its integrity. The amount of avoidance a dying person practices is exactly the amount he needs in order to function on a bearable level.

3. Modified Denial. A person may acknowledge part of the truth, but a truth tailored to suit particular needs. She may, for instance, admit to being very sick but not to being terminally sick. She may twist medical opinion, taking a physician's statement that "We'll do everything we possibly can" as a promise of cure. She may inform friends "They're not giving me radiation treatment. I think that must mean I don't have cancer." This type of avoidance behavior allows a person to acknowledge that something is wrong, perhaps seriously amiss, but not amiss enough to constitute a crisis.

The Degree of Denial Can Change Constantly, Then?

Yes, denial adapts itself to each situation. It modifies itself according to the person's needs.

And Denial Is Not Necessarily Harmful?

Sometimes it can be a needed protection, especially when a person's ego strength is not sufficient to tolerate the knowledge of death. Furthermore, although the process of denial appears to be based on self-delusion, in reality it may ultimately tend toward the opposite condition—toward acceptance. One day a patient prefers not to know any of the truth. The next week she admits to being sick, but only temporarily. Some weeks after this the seriousness of her situation is openly admitted, although hope may last, quite properly so, to the end. An inner psychic process is at work here, one in which the dying person opens up slowly and organically to her own mortality. It is a process which should by no means be tampered with or artificially hurried along.

So Denial Can Play a Positive Part As Well As a Negative Part?

Denial itself, although it can certainly become a pathological means of avoidance, is often a necessary part of the saying-goodbye process. It is not inherently good or bad.

The realization of imminent death, it should be understood, triggers a flood of fundamental fears: fears of abandonment, of physical suffering, of helplessness, of identity loss, of extinction. Denial stands as a brave if temporary buffer between these primal ghosts and the ego, serving as the finger in the dike, holding off the process of recognition long enough for the person's unconscious mind to prepare for it.

In the end most people do come to terms with their dying and do pass beyond the stage of denial. Many people, perhaps most by all reports, die peacefully, accepting their end. Before this moment arrives, denial can be a needed ally in a time when allies are in short supply.

Should a Patient Be Discouraged from Denying, or Encouraged?

It depends on how ready a person is to know. Very often part of a person wants to know, but another part will not allow it. If you feel that it is appropriate to break through another's denial barrier, do it with discretion. Words are not always the most efficient vehicle. Try nonverbal communication instead: body language, voice tone, gestures, silence. In this way a dying person can be told much which could turn oppressive or banal or incomplete when put into words.

For example, try remaining silent or making no positive response when the patient speaks about his plans for the future. If he asks you direct questions on the subject, you can simply tell him you do not know. A look can say a lot—so can looking away, a shrug, a raising of the eyebrows, or a shaking of the head. If the person wants to read this silent language, he will. If not, he won't.

Still, it is a tricky dance and should be entered into only after much thought and preparation. Over the past years it has become the trend to criticize the use of deception when dealing with dying patients. It is urged that doctors and family be as honest as possible with dying patients concerning their chances of survival. Although in most ways this frankness is a healthy sign, there can be a tendency to carry things too far. At this point it can be said that denial has its place in the dying process, especially in the beginning, when it gives one time to come to terms with the situation; and that it should not be violated by those who wish to rush things, placing what they consider the "truth" above the emotional tolerance and hence the psychological welfare of the dying person.

When Can Denial Become Dangerous?

It is most dangerous when a person has suspicious symptoms which she ignores or puts off having examined by a physician. It is also dangerous when one is advised to alter his lifestyle in matters of diet, sleep, exercise, and so on, due to a specific ailment and then ignores the advice, insisting that nothing is wrong, that the doctor is an alarmist, that there is no harm in carrying on as before.

But What Part Does Courage and a Positive Attitude Play in All This? Isn't It Better to Refuse to Give Into Death, to Insist on Fighting It to the End?

Refusing to give into death is not the same as pretending that disease has no power and death no sting. A person may be fully aware of his sickness with all the implications and still set out to beat it. This is considerably different from announcing that the doctors do not know what they are talking about or claiming that "no disease can ever get me." The first attitude knows all the facts and faces them squarely. The second bends the facts through the glass of denial, distorting them until the disease itself is unrealistically minimized and the person's own powers are exaggerated out of proportion.

If a person is told that he is suffering from a fatal disease— say cancer—and that he has only five months to live, and this person insists on using all his resources, both inner and outer, to fight back, this is a wonderful sign and may in fact help defeat the cancer. We know, for example, that the biochemical balance of the body is heavily influenced by a patient's psychological attitude toward his ailment, and that people who remain optimistic, hopeful, and open-minded—as opposed to those who roll over and die once the diagnosis is in—have a statistically greater chance for both remission and recovery.

Do Others besides the Dying Patient Deny Death?

Indeed they do, each in specific ways: the nurses, the doctors, the family, the friends. Almost everybody. Few of us can look death in the eye without flinching. ("We cannot look squarely at either death or the sun," remarked the French wit, La Rochefoucauld.)

In What Particular Ways, and for What Reasons, Might Members of the Medical Staff Deny Death?

Ordinarily, the job of a doctor is to make people well, to heal. Such is the basis of all lessons taught to health care professionals, and such is the inspiration behind the art that makes medicine a noble calling.

Yet, in the event of terminal illness assignments are not always clear. The science of healing, although of course never entirely abandoned, now takes second place to the art of nurturance. Doctors, having had little instruction in the nurturing arts (most medical schools do not teach courses in helping the dying die), and having always viewed themselves as healers rather than comforters, pass the burdensome task of administering to emotional needs over to those "better suited" for the task—the nurses.

The nurses, in turn, while often more thoroughly trained to deal with the drama that a terminal situation brings, have their own problems with acceptance of death and with the establishment of professional involvements with people they know will quickly be passing away. So they, too, develop both a set of defenses and a coping system that will ultimately place a wall between themselves and the dying.

Most medical staffs and, for that matter, most hospitals, are geared toward eradicating pain and disease rather than preparing a human being for an easeful death. Medical professionals are taught to see death not only as an enemy but as a kind of interloper, an accident of nature which, had we just a little more knowledge, just a little more technology, might be corrected forever. Consequently, when the chance of saving a life becomes an improbability, and when no amount of skill or knowledge can prevail against nature, the staff, instead of accommodating themselves to the patient's new needs, may withdraw from him—he is, in a certain way, breaking the rules by "refusing" to be healed—and abandon the dying person to the three-minute daily look-in visit, and to the depersonalized comfort of the hypodermic needle.

Does This Mean That Doctors Fear Death More Than the Average Person?

There is no way of being sure about such a matter, although many scholars and professionals, including Herman Feifel, one of the pioneers in the field of death and dying, has maintained (Feifel, 1963) that people may choose the profession of medicine to gain power over their own death fears. Studying the issue, Feifel concluded that doctors showed considerably more terror of death than either a test group of healthy people and—this is interesting—a group composed of the sick and dying. Feifel also found that doctors thought less about death than did the other groups, developed fears of death at a younger age, and tended to be more negative in their general attitudes toward death. When asked how they would react to the death of another person, most physicians said "It would make me reflect on my own mortality," while the majority from the other two groups claimed that it would make them "feel bad" or "sorry."

What Are Other Examples of a Doctor's Denial?

Examples include removing oneself from the dying patient, delegating responsibilities for the patient's care to others, keeping a patient too heavily drugged, keeping a patient in isolation, and concentrating on prolonging the patient's life rather than preparing the patient for death. There are also examples which are not identifiable as denial per se: for instance, discussing the patient's condition in front of the patient as if he were not there at all. As Avery Weisman and Robert Kastenbaum remark: "On a surgical ward even a renowned scholar might be reduced to the status of his diseased organ. He would be, say, a carcinoma to his doctor, a complaining voice to his nurse, an open mouth to the dietician, and an unpaid bill to the front office" (Weisman and Kastenbaum, 1968, p. 49). Other denials might include minimizing a patient's complaints, blaming the patient for the fact that he is not improving, refusing to discuss the patient's diagnosis with the patient, keeping hope open for a cure when none exists, and lying to the patient concerning his condition.

How Would a Doctor's Denial of Death Interfere with Her Professional Doctor-Patient Relationship?

The doctor might harbor feelings of anger or resentment toward the patient. The patient, to her frustration, will simply not get well no matter what is prescribed. Such feelings and attitudes are, of course, entirely unacceptable from a social and professional point of view. So the doctor vents her angers at the staff, say, or at the patient's family, and proceeds to ignore the patient completely or to become estranged in her relationship with him.

If a Doctor or Nurse Does Discuss a Patient's Condition in Front of the Patient, What Can the Patient Do about It?

Several things. One, she can request that the doctor and nurse stop doing it at once. Two, the patient can request that she at least be included in the process, and that since it is her body they are discussing, the conference be made into a three-way conversation. If the attending professionals insist that the information is too technical, the patient can request that she at least be informed of the gist of the conversation, especially if it seems to involve serious matters.

What about a Doctor Who Seems to Become *Too* Involved with a Patient? Can This Also Be a Form of Denial?

In an oblique way, yes. It has been observed that doctors fall into two distinct avoidance patterns when faced with the imminent death of their patients. The first is indifference, the second is overconcern.

In the latter case, when a physician becomes too involved with a patient, we often witness situations where the doctor enters into the patient's suffering, where he becomes intimately involved with the mourning family, where he takes upon himself responsibility for the fact that the patient does not improve. It becomes a kind of mea culpa on his part.

Although passing for empathy, such a stance is more often an acting out of the physician's own terror. "The dying person is me," writes E. Mansell Pattison, speaking of the doctor who indulges in what he calls "exaggerated compassion" (Pattison, 1977, p. 15), "but then the miraculous occurs, for when the dying is dead I am still alive. I have beaten death after all. Such professionals often become personally and professionally overinvolved in the life of the dying person. I have seen these persons angrily denounce any distance or detachment they see in others who work with the dying. How can you have compassion if you are not totally involved? Here, dying is made acceptable through professional *subjectification*."

Along these same lines, it should also be said that a doctor who is overly optimistic about a patient's chances of recovery from a normally fatal illness, must also be looked upon with a suspect eye. The guideline is this: If through hints, inferences, and intonations a physician implies that a fatal disease is not *that* serious, and if he promises a cure for a disease that everyone knows is incurable, one may have grounds to assume that the doctor is being both impractical and evasive, if not directly dishonest.

Why Do Doctors Run So Many Tests on People with Incurable Diseases?

Some do it out of a sense of professional conscience, to make certain that they leave no possible stone unturned. Some do it as a kind of clinical habit, simply because that is what you are supposed to do when such-and-such a patient has such-and-such a disease. A few do it because testing generates much extra income for many people, including, of course, themselves.

If One Has Been Self-Honest during Most of His Life, Will He Tend to Face the Reality of Death More Easily and More Directly?

Perhaps not more easily but probably more directly. The consensus among those who attend the dying is that people's style of death usually mirrors their style of life. If a man or woman has spent most of his or her time on earth running from unpleasant situations or repressing disagreeable truths, chances are they will do the same when the time comes to die. If a person has met life head-on and has not indulged in too much self-deception, chances are that person will have an easier time of it at the end. As Laurens P. White remarks in an essay on death and the physician (White, 1977), "In short, it appears that the great majority of humans have a degree of denial which is appropriate to them; that it forms an integral, if occasionally variable, part of the way they deal with illness, and if necessary, with impending death."

Can One Expect to Find Both Denial and Acceptance Occurring within the Same Person?

Dumont and Foss have devoted a book-long study to this question (Dumont and Foss, 1972). According to the authors, a dying person will commonly swing back and forth between these opposites, because in times of crisis human reason and human emotion work in opposition.

On the one hand, the physician is announcing that a patient has only several months to live. The physician has no axe to grind; her opinion is based on empirical evidence and scientific conclusion. At the same time, something inside the person is saying, "No, not me, not me!" And he refuses to accept the diagnosis. Death thus finds itself accepted on an intellectual level but denied on an emotional one. In some cases these two sides can never be reconciled, and a person vacillates between *yes* and *no* until the end.

So It Is Unrealistic to Expect Consistency in Any of These Matters?

Yes, it is unrealistic to suppose that anyone looking down the long, grim gun barrel of their own death will not waver between extremes. As a general rule, denial can be expected as an early reaction to news of one's impending death. Acceptance ordinarily comes later. Actually, however, there is no fixed schedule.

Is Anger a Form of Denying Death or of Accepting It?

It can be either. Anger is the second stage in Kübler-Ross's five-stage model. It comes, she maintains, after the initial period of "No, not me!" has waned. It is replaced now by the forlorn cry, "Why me!"

On the one hand, anger can be a covert avoidance mechanism. On the other, it can mean that a person is finally willing to look the affliction directly in the eye and perhaps even take a swing at it.

Then Anger Is a Good Sign?

It can be, especially when demonstrated by a person who has hitherto refused to look obvious realities in the eye. Usually, it is neither bad nor good but simply part of a larger process.

Who Is the Patient Usually Angry At?

The doctor. The family. The hospital. The nurses. The ailment. The accident. Oneself. God. The world. Fate. Luck. Other people. Those who will survive.

Isn't Anger Also Aimed at Particular Persons for Particular Reasons?

Yes, and sometimes for good reasons. Anger is not always subjective. Sometimes the doctor *has* been too negligent. Or the nurse really *is* nasty and pays no attention when she should. This is a perfectly correct reaction and has little to do with the stage of anger we are discussing.

What Kind of Anger Does Kübler-Ross Mean, Then?

The anger that Kübler-Ross speaks of has a particular flavor to it. It is often irrational. It is often inappropriate. It can be aimed at anybody and can erupt at any time. It lasts longer than normal anger and has a certain unnecessary intensity behind it.

Isn't It True That Some Dying Patients Have a Tendency to Turn People into Scapegoats with Their Anger?

This is a tendency that patients must continually watch for in themselves. In dire situations it is especially easy to make others bad guys: The doctor doesn't know her job, the woman in the next bed talks too much, the occupational therapist is all thumbs, the family doesn't visit enough (or too much). Just as it is human nature to idealize our helpers—we are as apt to make our doctor into an impossibly epic figure as we are to throw mud at her—so it is a simple matter for those confined to the monotony of the hospital room to turn small problems into large ones, and to see faults in others where none exist.

Is a Dying Person Always Angry?

Almost always, but not always in ways that are directly identifiable. The anger can be turned inward. A person will talk of how useless and meaningless life has been. The anger can be beamed onto seemingly unrelated things such as the political situation or traffic on the street. It may come out in snide comments or in sudden irritabilities.

Should One Try to Calm a Person Who Seems Angry?

Is the aim to produce a "good," well-behaved patient who represses all her terrors in order to please other people? Or is it to help the person deal with what faces her?

The Anger Is Natural, Then?

It can be. How would you react if you were told that your days were numbered? On the other hand, if the patient seems inordinately aggravated, if the anger goes on and on, if the anger turns into violent behavior, perhaps professional help is in order. Each situation is different.

What about People Who Are Usually Angry Anyway?

They will probably be good and angry now, and may well stay that way up to the end. For such people, anger is a highly efficient coping mechanism, the best of all defenses against frustration. It has worked before; it will probably work now. For such people anger may be a kind of terrible blessing.

Can't Anger Be Indulged in Just Out of the Need to Be Noticed?

Anger is a reaction to pain. Something is wrong and the person is telling you so. In this case something enormous is wrong and the reaction is proportionately large. Remember, the person is not just filing an idle complaint. He is *dying*! Even if he is the type of person who has for many years made a habit of gaining attention through displays of anger, the fact of his present situation makes things somehow different. It gives his complaints a different significance, a different importance. Death makes some things all right that wouldn't otherwise be all right.

What about Friends and Family? Don't They Also Exhibit Anger?

Very much so, and sometimes toward the patient herself. Expect it. It would be unnatural if a part of each of us did not shake a fist at the dying person for leaving us, and for putting us through the inconvenience and heartbreak of death. The friends and family of a dying person must work very hard to realize that the negative feelings they harbor toward the dying person are not secret at all. Just ask anyone who has been through the process.

Do Other Antagonistic Emotions Usually Accompany Anger?

There can be many, such as jealousy, irritability, meanness, a pouting silence, dissatisfaction, unfriendliness, and so on. They are, in a certain way, all forms of the same thing.

Isn't This Very Difficult for Others to Take?

Yes, it is. The period of anger is the most trying of all times for the family and for the staff. The sick person projects resentment onto anyone in her vicinity. Provocation need only be slim.

How Should One Behave toward a Dying Person If He Demonstrates Unreasonable Anger Reactions?

Friends and family find themselves in a predicament. They care a great deal for the dying person. Yet he may become so impossible that they feel themselves secretly wishing that he would get it over with—or at least shut up!

These guilt-provoking thoughts are difficult to express, especially in light of the fact that the person is sick and hence (it is supposed) not responsible for his actions.

Then the situation may be made worse when the ill patient uses his ailment as leverage, taking advantage of the fact that others will now be more tolerant of his idiosyncrasies. Who, after all, is going to tell a dying person to knock it off and behave himself?

The stage of anger is consequently a trial for all involved. "Why don't you spend more time here at the hospital?" the patient moans continually to his friends and family, and his complaints become a self-fulfilling prophesy: they finally do stay away, no longer able to tolerate his tirades against their truancy.

Family and friends, for their part, then become racked with guilt. Perhaps they *haven't* been attentive enough. If perchance the loved one dies during a time when they are alienated from him, the guilt that follows can haunt for a lifetime.

How then to deal with an angry dying patient?

With compassion, concern, creativity—and common sense. First, the patient should not be muffled or ignored, no matter how sharp his resentment. On the other hand, neither should he be allowed to demolish everyone at hand. Being in a terminal state gives an individual the special privilege to be blunt—but not cruel. It gives him special allowances—but not unlimited ones. You as the bedside companion have a right at the appropriate time to step in and say: "Hold it! Wait a minute! That hurts! That's enough!"

In many cases gentle but direct confrontation is the best way to quiet a person whose anger has become too extreme. In fact, without exercising a bit of necessary verbal self-protection, the friend or family member may find it increasingly difficult to return to the bedside, and the patient will suffer accordingly. Although tensions build quickly during crisis situations, a carefully handled showdown, tempered perhaps with a touch of humor, can prove a welcome cathartic for everyone involved. Indeed, do not forget the dazzling power of humor to make strong medicine more palatable. No situation is without its absurd side or its frivilous moments. In the midst of confusion, suffering and even horror, humor above all things can, with a well-timed wink, remind people that the human spirit has the power to prevail over all the tragedy of this very tragic world.

Showdowns notwithstanding, it is the job and the duty of loved ones to be compassionate and to grin and bear the patient's agitations with good humor. Harsh words spoken over a deathbed are not forgotten, and often not forgiven. The dying person should be allowed to exercise any means possible to deal with his tumult—pillow pounding, cursing, screaming, and especially crying. It is important to get the poison out. More important, though, is to discover what the patient is really angry about. Frequently, it is not death itself that is so hated but the realization of wasted years, of projects unfinished, of the fact that you, the family, the x-ray technician—all of us—are walking around safe and sound while he, the dying person, has only the next wave of pain to look forward to plus the final *coup de grace* from the angel of death.

In this sense, discussion, dialogue, constant conversation with the dying person is a necessary and soothing balm. Encourage him to speak about whatever he wishes. There are no secrets now, no taboos. No subjects should be barred. Each person has his own lexicon of fears. If these fears are not brought into the light and discussed, they will be pressed into other vehicles of negativity, anger being first among them.

One of the Most Difficult Aspects of Putting Up with a Patient's Anger Is When That Anger Is Directed at the Very People Who Are Trying to Help.

Perhaps the person is putting you on trial: how much can you take, she wonders, before you run out, before you desert her, like luck has deserted her, like God has deserted her. There are few enough opportunities in this life to exhibit utterly unselfish care and concern. This may be one of them.

From another standpoint, why shouldn't the person be angry at you? You are alive and whole. She is about to die. All your efforts to please her and serve her may be viewed as patronizing charity.

This stage too shall pass. Listen to what the person says, even if it is abusive, and try to read between the lines. This may be the first time in the person's life that she is willing to come to grips with certain unpleasant truths concerning herself, others, and life. The process may be a difficult one. What begins as a burst of negativity may end in a burst of cleansing understanding.

Remember, too, that the person may be trying to *tell you something with her anger*, something in your relationship that needs telling before death. Something you should listen to. For example, a dying child may be hostile to those around her, not by natural inclination but due to frustration toward her parents' neglect. A dying husband may be sullen toward his mate out of frustration over their lack of intimacy at this late hour, or for old hurts which show no signs of being resolved. Sometimes a negative emotion covers up a positive hope which cannot find its proper expression. The real meaning of the word *patience* becomes especially apparent during two moments in a person's life: the death of a loved one, and one's own death.

It Seems That Part of the Reason the Person Is Angry Is That She Feels Out of Control.

This is very important. There are few more humiliating experiences than helplessness. The sick person feels at the whim of everyone. Even her body functions won't obey her. She soils her clothes. A nameless hospital functionary carries her from bed to bathroom. Bells ring all day and all night. High-tech medical machines are wheeled in and out. Tests are administered without explanation. Faceless people perform undefined managements on her body. Is there anything that makes people more frustrated than being deprived of mastery over their own organisms?

Do Some Patients Remain Angry Up to the Time of Their Death?

Some, but not many. Very few pass their last hours in anger. By this time they are usually beyond it.

Do Some Patients Stay Angry for Prolonged Periods of time?

Yes, some stay angry. The length of time they remain this way is often a correlate of their life circumstances. Young people tend to remain angry longer than old people. Affluent, important people maintain anger longer than those who have been given less control over their fate. People in the midst of great projects, creative enterprises, or large business deals are more resentful than those who feel that their life work is done. Relatedly, those who report that their lives have been full and meaningful tend toward peaceful resignation more easily than those who see life as signifying nothing. Parents are often exceedingly angry at being yanked away from their families; bachelors, widows, and widowers seem to pass through their anger more quickly. The nature of the ailment itself also plays a part. Someone dying of a slow, painful malady is more likely to be belligerent than a person whose death is swift and painless. People suffering from degenerative diseases or from the effects of deforming accidents are more apt to display anger than those dying from kinder causes.

Is There Anything Else That One Can Say to Dying People to Help THEM Understand THEIR Anger?

Elisabeth Kübler-Ross (Kübler-Ross, 1974, p. 21) suggests an interesting way of dealing with the inevitable question, "Why me?" She replies to the person that she doesn't know "Why you" but that another question might be raised in its place: "Why not me?" Because, of course, we all must die.

What the person is really asking, she maintains, is: "Why is it happening to me *now*?" Her suggestion is to let the person bring up the query, then respond to it with all the rage she can muster, expressing the feelings and thoughts which have up till now been repressed. These will provide clues about how to give the person further help.

Very often a person comes to the realization that though she will perhaps soon be dead, she is still alive *right now*, today, and that the truly wise action is to make every moment count. "Because they [the dying person] have a limited time to live," Kübler-Ross writes: "Very often they live with more intensity, with different values, and enjoy life more because they do not always plan for tomorrow and next year, the way healthy people do."

When a Person Enters the Third Stage of the Dying Process—Bargaining, As Kübler-Ross Calls It—Does This Mean That the Dying Person's Anger and Denial Have Lessened?

At least the denial has lessened. To be in a position of bargaining means that the dying person can now at least partially admit the reality of her situation. Otherwise, there would not be anything to bargain about. Really, though, bargaining is a form of denial. It says: "I may be sick, but I still have some power to alter the sickness." As in so many of the dying person's responses, the urge to gain a sense of control is paramount.

With What External Forces Do People Most Often Try to Bargain?

There are few studies on the subject. The answer is probably that most bargaining is done with God. As the saying goes, "There are no atheists in foxholes." Although this is not entirely true, either on the battlefield or on the deathbed, it is safe to say that many previously unreligious people call on God for more time, for a remission, for a miracle. In return, pledges are made to improve one's way of life, to donate money to a charity, to behave better toward others, and so forth. How often these promises are kept if the ordeal is survived is known only to the person in question—and to God.

How Does Bargaining for More Time or for a Cure Differ from the Bargaining That We Do in Everyday Life?

It differs only in intensity. Just as we bargain for goods, as we make deals in business, so we bargain with the doctor: "Cure me, and I'll give this hospital a new dialysis machine." With ourselves: "I know that if I can force myself to stay on this vegetable diet, it will help me." With fate: "Let me go back to Peru just one more time, then I'll die without a struggle." Fundamentally, the procedure is no different from the tit-for-tat of the marketplace, except, of course, that the trading is done in the coin of life and death.

Isn't Bargaining a Little Naive?

Not as far as the dying person is concerned. Who are we to say, moreover, that the promises and prayers go unheard? At worst, bargaining is a phase in the dying person's reaction agenda, a very human attempt to come to terms with a new and inscrutable situation. After all, no matter who we are or what we have done, death is always something new. When we die it is always for the first time.

Should Bargaining Be Encouraged or Discouraged?

Neither. Bargaining is going to occur in some form or other no matter what the onlookers do, frequently without the dying person identifying it as such. To belittle such attempts or to point out their lack of logic can be a thoughtless act of cruelty, depriving the person of needed support.

What If the Bargains the Person Is Making Are Utterly Unrealistic or Even Crazy?

Let them be. The more fantastic the bargaining, the more profound the person's terror. Now is obviously not the time to come flinging the ice water of reality in a person's face. From another standpoint, outrageous bargaining can indicate that the bargainer has become particularly regressed in the face of her fear. Children, we know, live in a magical universe where to just say something, to just believe in it, makes it so, even when presented with the most logical proof to the contrary. Under intolerable stress grown men and women will adopt the same posture; they will believe what they wish to believe. This kind of childlike response to pain is really at the heart of bargaining. It is a kind of magical thinking—if I wish for it enough, it will come true.

How Long Does the Period of Bargaining Go On?

Ordinarily, bargaining goes on for a shorter duration than anger or denial. It can also be associated with both these activities; the stages do not necessarily follow each other in orderly succession. Neither is bargaining always easy to identify, especially by the one who is doing the bargaining. The key notion behind it is summed up in the words "but" and "if": "I'm sick, I know, *but* if I do such and such, or *if* you do so and so, everything will be better."

Is Bargaining Always Aimed at Saving or Extending One's Life?

Not always. A person may bargain for a remission of pain, for a chance to leave the hospital on weekends, for more energy, for the opportunity to die at home. Or bargaining may center around the lives of loved ones: "Just let my son get cleared of the charges against him and I'll be able to die in peace."

What Clues to the Dying Person's Thoughts and Fears Can Be Learned from the Kind of Bargains He or She Makes?

Bargains made by a dying person are often associated with his or her foremost guilts and regrets. Perhaps a man feels that he has not paid enough attention to his children. On his sickbed he vows to be a more attentive father if his life is spared. Perhaps a woman has experienced religious impulses all her life but has not had the inclination to talk about them or act on them. Now she assures God that she will become a missionary in His cause if she lives.

It Would Seem That a Person Bargains for Those Things Closest to the Heart.

What dying people bargain for represents not only their deepest fears and guilts but also their dearest treasures. In this sense it is grave and touching to witness the things people request: the child who promised the nurse her stuffed panda if the nurse would make her well; the elderly woman who begged just for time enough to return home from the hospital and water her plants. It is well worth paying attention to these requests, especially if one is counseling the dying person. They are often hints of the deepest points of incompleteness in a person's life.

After the Stage of Bargaining, according to Kübler-Ross, Comes the Stage of Depression. Does Depression Follow Bargaining Because the Dying Person Now Senses the Futility of Trying to Make Deals with Fate?

Not necessarily. Depression does not mechanically "follow" bargaining; it simply tends to come a bit later, after a person has lived through avoidance, fury, and negotiations with fate. Depression appears in earnest when one can no longer hide from an affliction, when one sees that anger feeds frustration rather than eliminates it, and when one perceives that bargaining is not a process to depend on. It is as if all the trump cards have been played out and one is still losing the match. Kübler-Ross describes this condition as having passed through the "Not me!" and "Why me?" and arriving at the "Yes, me!" stage.

Can't Depression Come at Any Time during the Dying Process?

Yes, especially if a person is a depressive type by nature. Such a person is going to respond to bad news with melancholy, just as an angry type is going to respond to it with rage, an optimistic type with hopeful resolve, and so on. Realization of imminent death does not usually change us; it simply makes us more of what we already are.

Does Depression Mean That the Person Has Given Up?

Not necessarily. The feeling comes closer to ordinary depression as many of us know it, but it is more intense. Think of how it feels to be depressed: low on energy and motivation; the world seems hard and barren, ugly and false; what's the use? We have not necessarily given up. We just see the world through a glass darkly and ourselves in the worst of possible lights.

I Thought That by Definition a Person in a State of Depression Was Hopeless.

It is a moot point whether a dying person *ever* really gives up. He is despondent, of course, and understandably so. The facts indicate that his life will soon be over. This, however, does not mean that he cherishes no hopes or that he does not wish for a cure. Do not mistake depression for hopelessness. The first may include a helping of the second, but never to a total degree: "While I breathe I hope."

But There Are People Who Simply Do Not Wish to Live.

It is true, there are people who have given up totally on life. Such people have, however, often given up long before they became sick. There are also those who have lived in such great pain and incapicitation for so long that death is a relief: people in an iron lung or on life-support machines; people suffering from advanced degenerative diseases. Such persons are usually in a state of despondency far more advanced than normal depression and may indeed live only with a hope for oblivion.

What Are Some of the Signs of Depression?

The person may become uncommonly formal and inaccessible, preferring solitude to company and requesting that visits be monitored to a trickle. Normal patterns of outgoingness and extroversion are altered; the person seems distracted, "not really there." Topics of discussion once pursued with animation now elicit leaden disinterest. Nothing seems of value. Nothing seems worth the doing. A person's former enthusiasms are overwritten by apathy and a curious unconcern for familiar pleasures. Tears may follow. Internally, the person is grieving for good times past, for opportunities missed, for friends long dead. "Nothing," wrote Dante, "is more painful than the memory of great happiness in times of great suffering." For many people, moreover, this is a time of conscience and review, their lives now backlit by sensations of remorse rarely experienced during better days. The many sparkling things of this world suddenly seem lackluster and false. The person feels that he has lived in vain. Oh, why have I lived on this earth at all!

In psychological terms, depression classically results from an experience of loss, and death is the greatest of all losses. Everything one treasures will pass away. Nothing abides, nothing endures. Faced with this unalterable reality, a sick person may withdraw into himself, announcing that "Nobody understands how I feel, nobody knows what it's like"—and he's right, not one of us among the living does know what it is like. Depression, with its concomitant recognition of life's impermanence, is a painful coming to grips with the truth.

It Seems That One Could Say There Are Different Kinds of Depression: Depression about Death Itself, and Depression concerning the Loose Ends Remaining Behind in Life.

Kübler-Ross has names for these. The first she called "reactive depression," the second she calls "preparatory depression."

Reactive depression derives both from a general sense of loss and from worry over important unfinished business: "How am I ever going to pay for three operations plus a year of medical care? What will happen to my dog when I die? My husband is in an advanced stage of diabetes: who will attend to his diet? The insurance papers are in the safe-deposit box and I can't find the key. My 6-year-old son has become sullen since I've been in the hospital; he wakes up every night screaming for his mother." The scenario is different for each person, but there always *is* a scenario, one or more incomplete transactions that need immediate loving attention.

Preparatory depression is more inward and silent. It is an "anticipatory grief"—the depression stems from the fact that the patient knows that he is dying and is attempting to prepare for it. While reactive depression is concerned with taking care of the details left behind in life, preparatory depression is concerned with letting go of life. Whereas reactive depression looks to the past, preparatory depression anticipates the future.

How Can One Help a Dying Person Who Is Depressed?

Reactive depression is easier to deal with than preparatory depression because it stems from tangible problems that can be improved with practical solutions.

Approach the depressed person's problems in clearly defined steps. First, learn what the nature of these problems are—whether they are personal, financial, family, or legal. Second, discuss them as thoroughly as possible with the dying person, learning all the details and nuances. Third, see what specific measures can be taken to clear them up. Although this schema may seem to be an oversimplification, sometimes a single sage word of advice, a sincere promise, even a document signed and made official can relieve an enormous burden. When the problems are aired and defined, the solutions are already half-achieved.

What Are Some of the Specific Instances in Which Practical Help Can Be Given to Relieve Reactive Depression? I Suppose, for Example, That Help with Legal Matters Would Be Such a Case?

Calling in a lawyer to help straighten out nagging inheritance problems will often ease a dying person's mind concerning the future welfare of his family. This is especially true if a will has not been drawn up or if it is outdated.

What about Children?

Anything that gives the parent palpable proof—preferably written—that their offspring will be in good hands is beneficial: documented information on how the child's education will be handled, guardianship papers, plans for a trust, pictures of the child's new room, inheritance papers, and so on.

What about Worry concerning the Future of One's Body After Death?

Some people find themselves constantly preoccupied with fantasies of the grave and of decomposition. Others experience the same concern on a subliminal level, in dreams, where the images can be even more compelling. Morbid concern with the future of one's body after death is a more common cause of depression than is supposed, and its importance should not be overlooked.

One method of defusing such considerations is to make sure that the dying person knows where his body will rest. Procuring a picturesque burial plot in a familiar place has a reassuring effect—in one's hometown, in one's place of birth, in a family plot, in a cemetery with a particular religious affiliation. If the person is too weak to visit the location, describe it to him and show him pictures.

If appropriate, assurances should be given that the person will be buried in a well-protected casket or that his body will be placed in a metal vault, in an aboveground mausoleum, or in whatever variety of container he prefers. In other instances people need proof that their bodies will be cremated, placed in a plain pine box, or buried at sea, while for still others donating their remains to medical research provides them with a sense that their death will enrich humankind. And so on. Whatever sets the person's mind at ease is good. For religious people, discussions with clerics on the immortality of the soul and the resurrection of the body can be of aid. So can work with a therapist if a person's morbid concern becomes too all-consuming. Obsession with bodily decay, as we have said, is a particularly overlooked cause of depression, mainly because the person himself may not realize the extent to which it is bothering him.

What Else Can Be Done to Help a Dying Person Deal with Worries concerning His Family?

During crisis times, especially during prolonged terminal sicknesses, the family of a dying person finds itself violently disoriented and torn apart. Children may be ushered off to stay with grandparents, with aunts, even with friends of the family whom they scarcely know. The chambers of a once raucous, happy household now ring cold. The children know that something is wrong, that daddy is sick, that mommy is in the hospital, but what *is* a hospital, anyway? There are muffled phone calls in the night, undiscussed visits by the parent to unidentified places, long absences from home—what does it all really mean? No one is saying.

Roles may be reversed. The father assumes care of a newborn or places a child in a day-care center. The mother may be forced to shoulder breadwinning chores, often with fierce belt tightening at home. Costs of medical treatment for the sick person can literally wipe out a lifetime of savings; and cancer treatment (one of the largest industries in the United States) wears a family's budget down to the bone.

Faced not only with imminent death but with the prospect of the family's ruination, there is little wonder that dying persons become depressed. Yet in such dark hours there is help. Even if monetary problems are not immediately solvable—and often they are, provided that someone versed in money management is consulted—the ruptures within the family can be healed by the intervention of social workers, by community help organizations, by family counselors. Therapists trained in helping families through crisis situations can be contacted via hospital referrals, through the social worker, even through the doctor himself—calls for such help are frequently heard among families of the dying. Doctors, are ordinarily not unreasonable concerning fees and are willing to work out equitable payment plans, especially if the family is impoverished. The same is sometimes true of hospitals. Bringing the subject up directly with the doctors is a wise policy. So is talking the matter over with a financial professional.

Whatever means are taken to improve the family plight, the money situation should be faced head-on. Working out financial terms in advance can be a great comfort, both for the dying patient and for his family. Most important, neither the dying person nor his dependents must remain passive in the face of the problems, nor must they assume that their sociological and material woes are irreversible. Indeed, it is passivity itself, with its concomitant sense of helplessness and futility, that ultimately causes depression in the first place. In the long run the best antidote to depression is action, even if the action is purely along the lines of everyday detail.

Some People Are Depressed for Religious Reasons. They Feel That Although They Have Led Decent Lives, God Has Abandoned Them or Cursed Them with a Terrible Disease. What Do You Say to Such a Person?

Religion is such a highly personal matter that unless we are particularly intimate with a person and share many of his or her beliefs, it is best to turn such discussions over to those better qualified to give meaningful answers: members of your religious group or whomever one is comforted by may be called in.

But What If the Person Insists on Talking to *You* about Their Religious Dilemma?

How else can one respond but according to one's belief? This must be done with tact and compassion. There are, of course, many answers, religiously speaking, that a person can give to "Why me?" One of the most explicit is that pain may not necessarily be a divine punishment but a divine trial. This, the dying person might be reminded, is insisted on time and again by practically every major religion and in practically every major religious text. As it is written in the Islamic scripture, *The Koran* (XXIX, 2): "Do men think that they will be left alone on saying, 'We believe,' and that they will not be tested?"

It can similarly be pointed out that whereas in our society it is a foregone conclusion that death is vulgar, calamitous and unnatural, in many other cultures quite the opposite is assumed, that death is a release from the anguish of this valley of tears, an entranceway into a state incalculably more enrapturing and free than ordinary humanness. "The gods conceal from men the happiness of death," writes the Roman poet, Lucan, "that men may have the power to endure life."

Whatever you say to a person facing a religious crisis, restrain your use of clichés, handy avoidance phrases, and most of all, insincere assurances. If you do not have anything to say, say so. If you wish to be heard, speak your piece simply and plainly, without undue elaboration or self-justification. Remember, a depressed dying person is often in a state of heightened sensitivity. One must choose words with great care if this sensitivity is not to be violated.

After Undergoing Surgery, a Person Will Almost Invariably Be Depressed If the Operation Has Caused Disfigurement. How Can One Help a Person in This Instance?

We are taught from infancy to equate our body image with our value as socially desirable men and women, and any dramatic alteration of appearance may send out psychological shock waves that paralyze and mortify. Certain parts of the body are especially charged with symbolic significance: a woman's breasts, for instance, or a man's penis. Their removal can convince a person that his or her very identity as a man or woman has been destroyed.

How can you help someone who reacts this way to body alteration? First, note that a person whose body has been blemished by the scalpel or by disease thinks of the scarred parts as being far more unsightly than they actually are. This reaction is almost inevitable. A person who overreacts in this manner should be assured that he or she is a good deal more intact than their imagination allows. Timely compliments help. On the doctor's part, frank discussions should take place with the patient *before* the operation occurs, giving a sympathetic ear to the patient's fears and explaining exactly what the patient may expect during and after surgery. Studies of women who have undergone mastectomies show that many feel residual anger at the doctor for not having warned them how deep the cut would be and how much of the surrounding pectoral muscles would be removed along with the breast.

As far as a married couple is concerned, husbands and wives should also be informed beforehand what to expect, both to prepare them psychologically and to prevent overreaction should the surgery be drastic. Children should also be spoken to ahead of time, lest any untimely candor on their part prove devastating.

After the operation when the patient returns home, family

members should welcome her, support her, and pamper her. They should also encourage her to speak freely about her feelings and listen attentively to complaints, rages, anecdotes, and whatever else she wishes to spew. Anything that brings glad tidings is welcome: new clothes, surprise visits from loved ones, vacations, presents. Most of all, the patient should be encouraged to venture out into the world again—if this is possible—and not to languish at home fantasizing about what people will say and think. If this is not possible, if a person is bedridden or incapacitated, it is important that they be discouraged from turning away visitors from fear of being "discovered." (Studies show that unless home care is affectionate and consistent after a disfiguring operation, a person is likely to become radically depressed.)

In the case of amputation, the promise of prosthesis—artificial replacement of a part of the body—can be a great comfort. This is especially true in the instance of mastectomy, where medical advances have provided breast replacements that are quite acceptable. Plastic surgery is also a major support; just the promise of such benefits can help get a person through the rocky initial time period after the operation.

The principal problem that a person faces from disfigurement is loss of self-esteem. Despite positive support from others and despite even a relatively normal image in the mirror, the person comes to think of herself as a scarred misfit, an outsider. In counseling people who are going through such anguish one should address this specific sense of alienation and concentrate on literally reestablishing a person's normal sense of wholeness.

What about Dealing with the Second Type of Depression, Preparatory Depression?

Here there is little that one can actually "do" to help the dying person. Ordinarily, we assume that every situation in life can somehow be improved or changed. We are all members of the "nothing is impossible" generation. When faced with the awesome spectacle of a person mourning for his own death, however, respectful silence somehow seems the only appropriate response. Now nonverbal communication becomes more important than wise words. Stroking the dying person's brow; a massage (if it is medically permissible); smiles; open, sincere looks; hugs; kisses; holding hands; and silence are the finest gifts of sympathy. The dying person will surely appreciate this medicine far more than a barrage of encouragements which both parties know are unrealistic.

Here also more than at any other stage of the dying process, the person must not be pushed or crowded. She is already partly out of this world. She is working silently, gropingly, to sever herself from the past and prepare herself for the coming dive into the great mystery. What's the sense of trying to bring her back with cheerful promises? Why assume that she wants to come back?

Does This Mean That One Should Never Try to Speak Encouragingly to Someone Who Is Close to Death?

It is a question of using right judgment. There are no rules graven on bronze tablets; each person has different requirements. Some, for example, may need verbal assurance when they are dejected. It is therapy for them. Others will enjoy a bit of conversation, perhaps on the light side, and then they will opt for privacy. Still others may wish to maintain the charade that they will soon be getting well. If they insist on it, oblige them. The point is not to force the issue, not to try to joke the person out of his withdrawal or minimize the seriousness of his plight, not to tell him to "cheer up" or that "depression never helped anybody," but not to be too brutal or heavy-handed with the truth, either. If conversation does seem appropriate, why not let the person set the tone and direction himself? If conversation does not seem right, perhaps the person will enjoy simply having you sit quietly by. Ask the person which he prefers. It is too late now for lies, even white ones. Chances are that you will be informed quite directly.

What about the Use of Antidepressants and "Mood Enhancers" for People Who Are Deeply Depressed?

This is a controversial subject, one in which no ready-made answers can be taken from any book. Certainly, if a dying person is mired in inescapable depression and requests a drug to help him cope, an antidepressant would seem appropriate. To force drugs on the depressed patient as a matter of course, however, can be arbitrary and worse perhaps, an act of tampering with processes that are best run by their own clocks. A good analogy exists in medicine. Today it is accepted practice to look at symptoms accompanying sickness—fever, headache, coughs, and so on—as destructive forces that must be obliterated or at least repressed. Among certain alternative and traditional forms of medicine, however, symptoms are viewed not as agents of destruction but as evidence of *the body's own attempt to cure itself*. Fever, for example, is believed to be the body's attempt to burn up invading microorganisms. Coughing is thought to be a way of clearing the lungs of phlegm, and so on. The cure, in other words, is effected by working in cooperation with the symptoms rather than palliating them into oblivion.

The same model can be applied psychologically. The appearance of depression in a dying person, painful as the depression may be for both patient and family, can in many cases be viewed as external evidence that the psyche is processing the problems of death and attempting to come to terms with them, and that the resultant depression is a symptom of this process and not a malevolent and incidental side effect. To anesthetize this process would then seem a slur on nature as well as a slap in the face to the person, as if to say: "We know how to cope with this problem better than you do, sir; just take this little capsule and for God's sake, cheer up!"

Are You Saying That Mood Enhancers Should Never Be Used?

No, only that they should be used in the patient's wisest interests, and that in many cases it is best to let the patient decide whether he wants them or not. Although it may be inconceivable to us, the living, that a dying person would not *want* his mood enhanced, this is sometimes the case.

Isn't a Patient Sometimes Depressed Not Just Because He Is Dying But Because of the *Way* He Is Dying—In a Hospital, Helpless, Away from His Familiar World and from His Loved Ones?

Even in the best of hospitals the everyday needs of patients will be neglected. Some patients remain stoic in the face of this neglect and refuse to communicate their grievances, believing that this is the "brave" way to do it all. Resentments build up and depression results. Others complain too loudly and eventually the staff stops responding. The end result in either case can be alienation and withdrawal.

Patients should be encouraged to talk about their day-to-day irritations and to seek help when social or logistic problems become too hurtful. Depression over hospital conditions can be offset by simple measures, a change of room, say, or a television set that works properly. Little joys and little improvements should not be minimized as therapeutic tools. For example, an elderly single woman, a Jewish Hungarian refugee, was on the ward of a large city hospital with an undiagnosed spinal ailment. As the weeks passed the woman became more and more disconsolate. Her doctors assumed that the depression stemmed from a physiological quirk of the condition—until one day a brief conversation with another patient overheard by a passing nurse revealed the source of her dejection: The hospital was not providing her with kosher food. The fact that the woman had not indicated this dietary preference on her admittance form in no way diminished her silent frustration. When asked why she had failed to indicate her needs, she replied that she did not want to make trouble. As soon as an acceptable menu was provided, the woman's spirits improved.

The point is that a patient's needs must *be* communicated. The patient should be encouraged to air all significant annoyances, and members of the dying person's support system should be attentive to the loved one's everyday requirements as well as to his or her greater spiritual ones.

There is, moreover, for those who find institutional life intolerable, no law which says that a person must die in a hospital or that the hospital has any proprietary rights over the person's comings and goings. If existence on a ward proves intolerable and if the family is willing, a person may return to die in the privacy of his own chambers. If this is not feasible, an alternative solution is the hospice, where facilities are designed to accommodate the specific needs of the dying (see page 264). This choice may prove a particularly acceptable compromise when a person needs the benefits of chronic specialized care but finds the conventional hospital atmosphere incongenial.

Does a Patient Tend to Be More Depressed at Certain Times Than at Others?

Yes. Especially right after the visits of loved ones. Also, at night; following lab tests; on holidays; after a repeated course of treatment has failed; on personal anniversaries and birthdays; when watching happy, healthy people on television shows; when someone in the room dies; when visiting hours are over. In certain ways a hospital is like any other institution, a boarding school, even a prison, where members are encircled by rules, social pressures, and brick walls. Conditions that might depress an inmate in any institution—poor food, impersonal treatment, overbearing authority figures—are also depressing for those in a hospital.

What Do You Do with a Person Who Claims That He Just Wants to Be Left Alone to Die?

Sometimes there simply is not anything that you can do. Be available for the person, make sure that he knows you are there when he wants you, and allow him to work out what he must.

This, of course, assumes that the person is close to death. Patients in early stages of terminal sickness who insist on alienating themselves might profit from therapy sessions, religious counseling, or from group work with other patients.

Can't Depression Be Purely Physiological, Part of the Disease Itself, and Not Necessarily a Result of Any Psychological Imbalance?

Although it is not always easy to separate the physiological from the psychological, it is true that certain ailments, especially nerve diseases, affect the brain directly and may cause constitutional depression. One should consult with the doctor on this question.

Is There Any Proof That Depression Makes Death Come Sooner?

The question is really this: To what degree do our emotions affect our state of health? Certainly, there is evidence that the two are linked, although the intricacies of the relationship are far from satisfactorily understood. There is also an indication from study findings that low morale can directly affect a person's will to live. For example, McMahon and Rhudick (McMahon and Rhudick, 1967) studied 25 elderly subjects in a veterans' home. The average age of the group was 84. A year after the initial interviews were made it was found that (1) three out of four of those found to be depressed had died, (2) four out of five suspected of being depressed had died and, (3) only one out of the sixteen rated as not being depressed had died. A study by Weisman and Hackett (Weisman and Hackett, 1961) suggests that among persons who are already ill, any sudden loss or shock will hasten their death. Another study by Tas (Tas, 1951) indicates that among concentration camp victims at Bergen-Belsen, those who showed overt signs of deep depression during their captivity tended to die quickly, whereas inmates who remained optimistic and resolute had a considerably higher survival rate.

The answer, therefore, is yes; depression probably does hasten death, but not always, not in every case. There are times, as we have seen, when it can represent a very natural phase in the course of self-preparation.

In What Way Does Depression Lead to Acceptance?

It does not always lead to acceptance. It may lead away from acceptance if a patient becomes too identified with his anguish. On the other hand, depression and all the painful realizations that it brings can help cut the strings which, Gulliver-like, keep one bound to this life. Remember, the dying process is a *process*, a series of interrelated changes and recognitions; a private, interior procession. The person comes face to face with the trauma and melancholy which dying evokes. He lives with these feelings, dreams with them, flails out against them, pleads with them, represses them, flees from them, disguises them, distorts them. He goes through every conceivable mental and emotional loop-the-loop, and when he is quite finished he looks up and there is the reality of his death standing once again, just as before, looking at him with the same impassive, impenetrable expression. Day after day of this, week after week, whatever the time span—eventually the person tires. He begins to slow down inside, the angry metabolism of his denial spent. At this point something relaxes. Slowly, instead of frenetic avoidance a kind of inner quiet dawns. In whatever fashion, via whatever route, the person has begun to accept and healing begins to take place.

When Exactly Does Acceptance Begin in a Dying Person?

Frequently in the dying process there comes a time when not only the body believes it is about to die but the heart and mind believe it too. They don't just know it, they believe it. This recognition may be accompanied by a sudden physical turn for the worst, as if a certain point of no return has been passed within the organism itself. It is at this point that a person often slips into peaceful acquiescence where resistance ceases and the pain level often drops, sometimes as if magic. The person is ready to die. "A dying man needs to die," wrote the journalist, Stewart Alsop, as he lay in his hospital bed with leukemia, "as a sleepy man needs to sleep, and there comes a time when it is wrong, as well as useless, to resist."

Does Everybody Ultimately Come to the Stage of Acceptance Before They Die?

No. But many do, even those who fight death bitterly along the way.

Does the Fact That the Patient Has Accepted Death Mean That He Is Happy?

Not necessarily. Willingness to meet one's death seems to be something of an emotionless experience. Not in the sense of heartlessness or apathy, but in the sense of silence. Stillness. When one is in a state of profound peace, he is neither happy nor sad. He is beyond both these conditions. He is at rest. From all we can surmise, real acceptance shares something of this quality.

Does This Mean That a Person Who Has Accepted Her Death Is No Longer Angry, No Longer Susceptible to Avoidance or Despair?

Acceptance is not invariably a permanent state. Attitudes may wax and wane, especially if a person is far from the actual moment of her death. One day she may be angry. Another day she may accept. Another day she may accept for a while and then deny for a while. There are many possibilities. None of these reactions are mutually exclusive and none of them are fixed.

Can Anyone Really Accept Death? It Seems Impossible.

Many have. The problem is that we do not know what it feels like to be dying. Nor do we understand the chemical and psychological changes that take place within a dying person over a period of time. The dying person literally *learns* to accept death, just as we learn to walk or to talk. The activity is both biological and psychological, inspiring changes of a kind that only those who have experienced them can understand. Just as a young person has no idea of what it means to be old, so the living cannot understand the inner state of the dying. Just as nature, working through the mind and heart, prepares the human being for birth, for adolescence, for adulthood, so in ways we do not comprehend it may also prepare men and women for death. This is why health care professionals report that people who die quickly or without adequate preparation usually die in a more distressed way than those who have had time to prepare. The Catholic prayer, "Oh God, protect me from sudden or unexpected death," takes on a clearer meaning when seen in this light.

Does This Mean That the Person Who Accepts No Longer Fears Death?

It means that the person no longer runs from death. It does not necessarily mean that he embraces it, just that he is ready for it should it come. For many people this state is a liberating one, and fear vanishes. For others apprehension may still be present, but it is accompanied by a general sense of quiet concession. For still others there is a strange and not unpleasant feeling of release, even excitement, and for a few, triumph. It is different for different people.

Does This Mean That Accepting Death Means Giving Up Hope?

Accepting death is not the same as wishing for it. This is an important distinction and worth dwelling on. The problem is that while tenacity and a fierce will to live are applauded in our society, they frequently become unrealistic and even turn into a form of denial. Despair is scarcely the proper alternative to either, however, so what, then, is real hope in the face of death? It is knowledge that nothing is certain until it happens, and that willingness to deal with whatever comes one's way is a more productive stance toward affliction than futility. Hope is readiness to accept, but at the same time to wait and see. Hope remains grounded and receptive. It does not tantalize itself with expectations. It says: "I will live as much as possible in the time that remains; and wait; and watch."

Hope, then, is both a suspension of judgment and an appreciation of the present. In its best form it is an affection for time's moment-to-moment offerings, an affirmation of existence. Hope says: "Whatever will be will be, whether it is life or death. I'll leave it at that and live my life as best I can."

In this sense hope and acceptance are the same.

Isn't Hope Just Another Form of Denial?

No, not if it conforms to the qualities we have just described. Right hope knows that there is a danger but it continues to wish for life. Denial avoids knowledge of the situation entirely and fosters a false security. Hope is at once optimistic and practical. "Hope," as Avery Weisman remarks, "means that we have confidence in the *desirability* of survival" (Weisman, 1972, p. 20).

One Should Hope, Then, But Not Become Dependent on That Hope?

Yes.

How Can One Foster Hope in Dying Persons without Lying to Them?

By being frank but not pessimistic. By being honest but positive. No matter how bleak the diagnosis, it is always best to leave a porthole open somewhere, a little "but in the end, who knows?" for the person to remember and contemplate. For in the end, who does know?

How Do You Give Hope to a Dying Patient?

For some, the promise of an afterlife is the best of all hopes. For others a simple statement by the doctor that a chance exists may buoy up a person's spirits. Helping patients realize their most signal accomplishments, helping them discern the patterns of the past and the value of their successes may dispel despair. Many health care professionals have observed that individuals who have the most difficult time dying are those with the poorest self-images.

No one with a terminal ailment wants to think of himself

as waiting helplessly to die. When nurses, doctors, family, and others treat the sick person as a "terminal" case, writing him or her off as dead already, the patient quickly acts accordingly. Families and professionals should make every effort to treat the dying person the same in sickness as in health. The patient should be allowed to participate in daily decisions, especially those he made while at home. He should be encouraged to discuss his malady if he wishes, and should not be made to think that he will alienate others if he speaks frankly or emotionally. Nor should humor be forgotten, especially if the sick person likes to laugh. Although death is a serious affair it does not have to be an entirely humorless one, and indeed, a sense of humor has been the foremost help for some people who, unable to fend off death with medicine or postpone it with tears, have in the end gotten their satisfaction by laughing at it.

Hope can be instilled by keeping a patient interested in what is going on in his environment. Even if one is certain there remains little time to live, an active interest in daily life is a refreshing tonic. Keeping busy is the key. Many patients like to be read to. Or to tinker with hobbies. Those who enjoy newspapers and magazines should be kept well supplied. The worst thing is to let a person feel useless or a burden to others. Anything that can occupy, divert, enliven, or turn one's thoughts to pleasant subjects will be an aid.

Finally, even if a person is seriously ill he should never be told that his situation is hopeless. This is an iron-clad rule. It should not be broken. Let the person come to such a conclusion himself if he must, and deal with it as he will; but never be the one to seal off all paths of hope.

Do Patients Who Have Hope Recover More Frequently Than Those Who Do Not?

An optimistic, life-affirming attitude seems, by all the information that is available, to help patients not only adjust to their pain but to fight back against the disease.

Are There Different Types of Hope? Do These Tend to Appear at Different Stages in the Dying Process?

In a way, yes. The first kind of hope is anticipational. The person lives in expectancy of being cured, of having a remission and living a normal life once more. This kind of expectation usually comes early in the person's illness.

If and when an ailment appears to be irreversible, the hope may then be accordingly modified. Expectations now become more limited and time spans shortened. The hope may no longer be directed toward a cure but toward specific and immediate concerns, hopes for a visit from friends, say, or for improved pain medication. This diminished scope of expectancy does not mean that the person ceases to long for a complete cure, only that this wish becomes subordinate to the hopes of day-to-day living.

In What Ways Does a Person Show That She Has Accepted Death?

In the ways that one might suppose. By demonstrating less concern with daily matters and with current events, with other people, and with her family. The person may become calm concerning her state of health where once she was anxious to learn every detail about the day's diagnosis. She may seem more at rest, more dreamy, more at peace—but at the same time, more distant. Many bridges have been burned. She may show no inclination to resurrect them.

Often the patient needs time alone. She will request that visiting hours be cut short. She may even terminate visits from loved ones, having said what she considers to be her goodbyes and wishing now not to string things out more than she must. The dying person is tired. She wants to sleep. When visited she may share her feelings by means of simple gestures or expressions that sum up the inexpressible. Or she may not communicate at all. Fear, anger, frustration, all seem behind her. Quite consciously she has already begun her journey from this world.

So a Patient's Interest in Life Tends to Diminish After He Has Accepted Death?

To some extent this is true. How could it be otherwise? This does not necessarily mean that the person closes down entirely, or becomes totally inaccessible, only that a kind of distancing process takes place between him and the rest of the world.

Is This Sense of Distance and Separation Inevitable?

Not invariably. Some people accept death and still maintain apparent interest in the details of life. Usually, this is done for a specific reason. The person may wish to keep informed of the day-to-day reports of a new grandchild perhaps, or to learn the outcome of a long-pending legal settlement. She may also maintain the *illusion* of interest to keep the attending professionals, the doctors and nurses, from neglecting her, or to assure her loved ones that she has not given up.

What Should Be Done When Sick Persons Declare That They No Longer Wish to See Any Family Members?

Although it may be a terrible task for loved ones to accept such summary dismissal, it may also be a necessary stage in the letting-go process, especially if the dying person's time seems close at hand. Unless the dying person is reacting out of anger toward family members—and grudges ordinarily tend to disappear in the last days—such a reaction should not be read as a rejection but as a sign that the person is now prepared to die.

Doesn't the Family Often Take the Dying Person's Withdrawal as a Kind of Rejection?

Yes, but usually it is nothing of the sort. The patient is going through a natural and ancient process. He is cutting all bonds with the things of this life. This is a difficult fact for those close to the dying person to accept, not only because they feel rejected but because the dying person's acceptance somehow makes things final—perhaps too final. They themselves may be having difficulty letting go.

During such a period the family must make special efforts not to mistake the patient's withdrawal as a sign that he has ceased caring for them. The dying person is like a man about to embark on a journey. He is preoccupied, he is making ready to depart, and much of this thought and energy is turned in this direction. The best way to help him is to wish him well and let him go.

On this subject Kübler-Ross has an interesting observation, (Kübler-Ross, 1974, pp. 37–38). She claims that although many people do eventually accept dying, many more would do so if those around them, the health care professionals as well as the family and close friends, would *allow* the dying person to let go. If the people surrounding the dying person would support the acceptance process instead of insisting that the patient "fight it out to the end," or that life be prolonged as long as possible despite even the wishes of the patient himself, then, claims Kübler-Ross, acceptance of death might be seen as less of an agony and more of a relief.

Should One Expect a Dying Person to Become More Intimate, Profound, or Philosophical near Death?

Do not anticipate heroic utterances or deep thoughts from those who in better days were not so inclined. On the other hand, the dying can sometimes speak with a simplicity that is both poignant and poetic, and many in their last hours reveal an uncharacteristic lovingness and concern, their better nature allowed to peek out at last from behind the battlements of ancient psychological defenses, the taboos against expressions of deep feeling having now become senseless and the masks of personality having fallen away. Frequently, sick persons will show a wonderful unselfishness toward others. They will go to enormous lengths to protect other persons' feelings, to put them at ease, to help them acknowledge what they themselves have already accepted.

Doesn't This Contradict the Idea That Most People Don't Undergo Major Character Changes When They're Dying?

It is not that a person changes, or that his personality becomes utterly unrecognizable. It is more that the better part of the person's character, the part you always thought was there, the part you saw only for brief moments, is freed and shines forth. For some, dying is a revelation. It gives them the freedom to be themselves once again after lo these many years. Dying is a sacred thing.

Should a Person Be Encouraged to Accept Death?

If the person appears to be working along these lines already, the subject might be approached in a circumspect way. You might let it be known that you are here to help, willing to talk, willing to serve as a sounding board and as a friend. By *no* means should a dying person be lectured to. Under no condition should she be informed that her mode of death must live up to a certain ideal or that she is obliged to die in a prescribed way. Above all things, a person shold not be made to feel that there is a special "style" of death that she must cultivate, whether it be the much vaunted "dying with dignity," whether it be "acceptance" or "peace" or "martyrhood," and that if she does not demonstrate this lofty technique at the last hour she will fail both God and man. Like every other important human truth, the notion of dying as a "growth" experience can be misconstrued and misunderstood. When this takes place what is meant to be a mercy turns into a persecution.

Our purpose, we the living, is to help the dying be as comfortable as possible in the last days, both in their physical person and in their thoughts. That's all. Nothing else. Our task is not to educate the dying, not to save them, not to set them straight, but simply to make it easier for them to find their own way.

Do Most Dying People Ultimately Accept Their Death?

John Hinton in his well-known book *Dying* (Hinton, 1967, p. 104) claims that approximately half of dying people come to openly acknowledge their death and to accept it. Another 25 percent, he claims, speak with undisguised anguish about their death, while the last 25 percent deny it entirely and do not speak about it at all. Hinton mentions another category also, one in which people experience a kind of quasi-acceptance of death. Here death is acknowledged without joy or relief, but without terror or despair either. People who meet their end in this way tend to speak little about it, and seem to be quietly, though not happily resigned. If reference is made to the subject at all, it is spoken of with a submission quite visibly tinged with regret.

The Notion That the Dying Process Entails a Number of Stages Implies a Kind of Order to the Whole Thing. Must a Person Always Pass through a Fixed Repertoire of Stages When Faced with Death? Isn't It Possible That These Reactions May Come All at Once, or One without the Other, or in a Different Pattern, or Not at All?

As Kübler-Ross herself has frequently maintained, her outline of the dying process is a generalized scheme. Its purpose is not to prove that every human being will deal with the crisis of death in the same predictable way, nor that it is proper to die in this manner and wrong to die in any other. All of these stages—denial, anger, bargaining, depression, and acceptance—have been observed among the dying by many people at many times, and in many combinations, and all are common, although not inevitable reactions. They have been, Kübler-Ross suggests, arranged in one particular sequence ony because this is the order that she, and others as well, have observed most often.

Isn't There Danger That Members of the Dying Person's Support Group Will Come to Expect These Stages and Be Angry or Disappointed If They Don't Occur When They're Supposed To?

Kübler-Ross has warned health care professionals against taking the concept of stages too literally and thus forcing particular expectations on the dying. When her ideas first became current it was common for certain doctors and nurses to label patients who did not follow the prescribed steps as "resistant" or "insensitive," or even as abnormal. Those who remained too long in one stage were thought to be "bogged down," and the therapist was called in. Those who failed to exhibit depressive or angry symptoms were said to be "repressing." Those who made no efforts to accept death were admonished to "try harder." The five stages were often handled as a kind of scientifically proven theorem, and worse, as a form of religion, with all the accompanying dogma and liturgy, the representatives of this new cult insisting with messianic righteousness that their ideas be applied to every situation, the wishes and needs of the patient notwithstanding.

"The outline of these five stages," Kübler-Ross wrote in 1974 (Kübler-Ross, 1974, p. 71), "is only the common denominator that we found in most of our terminally ill patients. Many do not flow from stage one to five in a chronological order, and this is totally irrelevant to their well-being. Our goal should be to elicit the patient's needs, to find out where *he* is, and then to see in what form and manner we can help him best."

Are There Other Maps of the Dying Process besides the One That Kübler-Ross Proposes?

There are many, some related to Kübler-Ross's doctrine, some opposed. Avery D. Weisman, one of the earliest and most profound writers on death and dying, concluded that there is no predictable sequence to the way people pass through the final days (Weisman, 1972). According to Weisman, the process is a haphazard one, the individual tossed from one emotion to the next, with little indication that these reactions follow a particular succession or plan. Another professional, Arnold Hutschnecker, in an essay on personality factors in dying patients (Hutschnecker, 1959), suggests that people die in a fashion that most accords with their basic personality: an angry man will die in an angry way, a patient man in a patient way, a repressed man in a repressed way, an accepting man in an accepting way. Moreover, Hutschnecker suggests that the disease one suffers from affects the way one dies. It is, he says, possible to distinguish a cardiac patient from a cancer patient (the cancer patient denies his symptoms, is emotionally passive, hopeless, and dependent, whereas the cardiac victim is aggressive, rebellious against the doctors, insisting on fighting to the end), or a cancer patient from, say, a patient with renal failure.

Still another professional, Edwin Shneidman, proposes that the dying undergo what he terms a "hive of affect" whereby a mixture of emotions, including the familiar anger, denial, depression, and acceptance, come and go in a random manner without any predictable sequence to bind them. Rather than a chronology of steps that moves from point A to point Z, Shneidman, in his own work with patients, has observed a continual seesaw effect, "a waxing and waning of anguish, terror, acquiescence and surrender, rage, and envy, disinterest and ennui, pretense, taunting and daring and even yearning for death— all these in the context of bewilderment and pain." Rather than seeing any order in the process, Shneidman suggests that dying is typified by a "complicated clustering of intellectual and affective states, some fleeting, lasting for a moment or a day or a week, set, not unexpectedly, against the backdrop of that person's total personality" (Shneidman, 1974, p. 6).

If Theories Differ So Widely, Who Is One to Believe?

The point is not to believe or disbelieve any of them, only to see which apply to your particular situation and to make whatever use of them you can.

All that these maps of the dying process are meant to establish are guidelines and signposts to make it easier for the dying and the dying person's associates to identify what is taking place during the mysterious process of death, to know, as well as possible, what is happening when it happens. If these descriptions contradict one another, if they do not match each and every situation, it does not mean that one is necessarily right and the other wrong, only that death is a mountain with many paths to the top, and that each observer will see only those paths—and only that part of the mountain—which his experience allows and his perspective reveals.

3

The Experience
of Dying

In Addition to the Reactions Noted by Kübler-Ross, What Does It Feel Like to Be Dying? What Are Some of the Main Emotions Experienced by a Dying Person?

Grief. An indefinable dread. A sense of injustice. Exhaustion. Embarrassment. Relief. Restlessness. Jealousy of others who seem healthy and high-spirited. Confusion. Euphoria. Alienation.

What Is the Most Predominant Emotion of the Dying Person?

Probably loneliness. As an older man phrased it, "It's as if I'd died already, the way people act towards me, very formal, it makes me feel that I'm by myself all the time, even with my grandchildren and friends here." And another: "It's like they're afraid of you. They don't want to get too involved with you. They'll take care of you and act respectful. They'll fall all over themselves to do things for you, but they also are, like I said, afraid of you, as if you'd contaminate them if you put your arms around them."

The Saying "You Die Alone" Seems to Have Particular Significance Here.

In Tolstoy's masterpiece of short fiction, *The Death of Ivan Ilyich*, Ivan describes the experience of dying as being on the bottom of the sea, or as being continually stuffed into a bag that has no bottom. Wrote Matthew Arnold: "Spare me the whispering crowded room, / The friends who come and gape and go, / The ceremonious air of gloom— / All, which makes death a hideous show."

There are many metaphors in literature and life to describe the vast sense of aloneness that a dying person feels. The nephew of a woman who was dying of lung cancer reported a dream with this kind of poignantly poetic imagery. He pictured his aunt sitting in a formal garden, gazing out into the circle of dark woods that surrounded it. She was a little girl with pigtails now, dressed in a checked dress. Nearby several of the woman's relatives hobnobbed brightly with friends at a cocktail party. No one seemed to notice the dying woman, nor did she notice them. Quietly, hands on lap, with an expression of worried absorption, she stared intently into the deep, mysterious forest and said nothing. When the man later discussed this dream with his aunt, she burst into tears and cried out that this was just how she had been feeling during the past several weeks, like a little child frightened and abandoned. She then launched into a long, melancholy discussion of her loneliness.

If It's True That We All Die Alone, What Can One Do to Help a Sick Person Not Feel So Isolated?

It may be true that we all die alone. But that does not mean that you cannot be next to the person when they are doing it.

Does Sitting Attendance with Dying Persons Really Help to Relieve Their Anxiety?

Perhaps of all the things we can do for the dying, it is this— the gift of companionship and availability—this is the greatest service. Letting the person know that you are present, interested, caring, and available is the alpha and omega of how the living can help the dying.

Sometimes It Is Difficult to Give a Particular Name to the Emotions That Are Happening to One. It Is Simply a General Sense of Overwhelming Oppression.

This can be especially true when persons first realize that they are dying. At first a cacophony of feelings leaves one bewildered and out of control. Some experience themselves as being strangely cut off, the "this-is-not-really-happening-to-me" syndrome. Others feel suffocated by worry and fright. Still others are numb. Eventually, these emotions will change. Dying is a multi-staged affair; psychological states do shift; they do not remain static. In many cases fear and disorientation give way to quieter, more resolute feelings. Do not despair. It is a process of coming to terms with, of learning to live with.

Isn't the Patient Also Frightened of Desertion?

It is one of the greatest fears. Even if one has made her peace with man and God, and has accepted her death, most of us have a crucial need to know that others are still committed and available when the need arises. In many ways the last days of a person's life are like the first. Physically, the person is as dependent on other people as is a newborn baby. And like a newborn, her strongest fears are often of abandonment.

Is the Fear of Desertion Justified? Are Most Dying People Eventually Abandoned?

Death is almost as problematic for the family as for the dying person. Thus many relatives stop coming to the dying person's room because the scene is "too painful" or because they feel that they can no longer be of help, although both reasons speak more of avoidance than of charity. If friends and family do stay in contact, they may do so from a safe distance, in the waiting room, over the telephone, through the medical reports, by letter, thus salving their conscience while they avoid intimate contact.

The fact is that many persons are deserted on their deathbeds because those closest to them are threatened by all that the scene silently implies; it is too vivid a reminder of their own tenuous situation as human beings. Dying people are prophets without a country. They are the modern Cassandras. Ironically, however, in the long run it is not so easy to run from the dying person either, for removing oneself from the scene of death now may later lead to guilt feelings and remorse feelings that will not be easy to shake off.

How Can a Person Ensure That He Will Not Be Deserted When His Time Comes to Die?

There is no sure method. But one good way is to discuss the problem with those you would choose to have near you at the end, and to do it some time before the moment arrives. Communicate your specific wishes to the chosen persons—that you want them to be by the bedside when you are dying, that you want them to fetch a member of the clergy when the time comes, that you want them to be responsible for choosing whether or not to use heroic means to prolong life, and so on—and come to agreement about it all *beforehand*. This way a kind of insurance is purchased ahead of time; few people will go back on their word to a dying person.

Don't Patients Have a Great Deal of Frustration to Deal with Along with Their Loneliness and Fear?

Frustration frequently comes camouflaged as other emotions, especially anger. When this happens one must be alert to the fact that such outbreaks are simply frustration in disguise. Who is most likely to exhibit this behavior? People who have had a particularly hard time dealing with small daily pressures during their lifetimes will be most prone to fits of frustration when dying. They throw scenes easily and quickly alienate staff and family. They are more difficult to administer to as patients and usually less capable of holding together in times of stress.

Nor is frustration limited to the patient. Everyone involved feels the powerlessness of the situation and may react accordingly. The doctor in charge, discouraged by his inability to cure the patient, may take out his frustration on an innocent nurse who misspells the name of the prescription, or on a family member who asks just once too often whether there is a chance that his relative will survive. The same is true for the nurses, the loved ones, everyone involved. All are being pushed to the limit. At certain moments their strain may be converted into irritation and even anger.

It All Seems to Return to the Patient's Sense of Helplessness.

Helplessness is usually at the base of the frustration, for both patient and staff. Whatever can be done to give the dying person a sense of control will help neutralize this demeaning sense of impotence and uselessness.

What Can Be Done to Help a Sick Person Feel Less Helpless?

Little things will help. Sick people hate to be reminded of their handicap. Treat them as if they were normal. Do not jump every time they lift something too heavy, do not make an embarrassing fuss in front of others if they happen to overdo. Even if the persons are handicapped, they may appreciate it more if you stand by patiently and allow them to struggle with the top of the milk carton or straighten their own pillow than if you rush in and handily put things right. At least let the ailing one set his own limits, and give him help only when he asks. It may be difficult, of course, to bite your tongue while he exhausts himself proving to others that he is as good as ever. A raise of the eyebrow or a concerned smile may be sufficient warning in such cases. If it is not, only you can decide whether a well-meant intervention will be worth the frustration it may cause in one who is already quite aware of his ever-growing limitations.

Friends should be encouraged to relate to the sick person without special ceremony and without that sugary solicitousness which is so often read by the sick person as condescension. Dying people want nothing so much as to be treated like ordinary man and woman, not to be rendered "special" via the lugubrious tone of voice and the too kindly look in the eye that promises an understanding which the dying person knows cannot fully be there. The best thing you can do is create an atmosphere of support and naturalness. Include the dying in whatever decisions they were once included in. Consult them on issues they were once consulted about. Let them feel, as much as it is possible, that they are *still alive*, still among the living, that their vote still counts, even if it is voiced in a whisper, that their opinion still matters, even if it concerns events they may never live to see concluded.

Do Dying Persons Generally Behave Differently from Other People?

On the whole, no, they do not. Entering a hospital ward mixed with different cases, a visitor would find it difficult to tell the terminal cases from the nonterminal, even after spending time talking freely with everyone present. This does not mean that many things are not going on inside the sick person, only that on the exterior it is business as usual—the person watches television, combs his hair, discusses the baseball scores with his neighbor in the next bed, laughs or does not laugh, all more or less in accordance with his usual nature.

If a Person Knows That She Will Soon Die, How Can She Carry On Living in Such a Matter-of-Fact Way?

Peer pressure, for one. The patient does not want to make a spectacle of herself in front of others. She also does not want to appear cowardly or overly demanding. Another reason is that the dying are simply involved with other things—they could scarcely think about death all the time or they would stop functioning. And dying persons do function, usually quite well.

Denial also has much to do with it. Even those who are certain that their days are limited spend much of the time in another psychological part of themselves, a part that forgets. More than this, some people appear at ease because they *are* at ease. They are making the most of the time they have left, and not uncommonly are enjoying the ordinary details of life in a way that they never knew before—this rather than pass their final days in fear and dismay. It is an irony of our human situation that it often takes the threat of death to bring out the love of life. It is an irony of fate that we are often never more alive than when we are about to die.

So the Personality of a Dying Person Does Not Necessarily Change Even If a Person Knows That He Is Dying?

It has been remarked many times that kind people become kinder when they are dying, loud people become louder, bland people become blander, mean people become meaner. Dying persons, contrary to popular mythology, rarely undergo profound character changes. Such melodramatic transformations happen more often in movies and novels than they do in real life. Usually, the dying simply become more of what they always have been. Their personality traits, both good and bad, tend to become compounded rather than transformed. Edwin Shneidman sums it up: "My general hypothesis is that a *dying person's flow of behaviors will reflect or parallel that person's previous segments of behaviors, specifically those behaviors relating to threat, stress, or failure.* There are certain deep *consistencies* in human beings. Individuals die more-or-less characteristically as they have lived"(Shneidman, 1980, p. 206).

Is This Always the Case? Don't Significant Changes Sometimes Take Place?

Occasionally there will be a marked change. Usually, the changes are for the better—a cruel person will ask others to forgive him, a fear-ridden person will turn wonderfully calm, an emotionally closed person will become open and vulnerable—but not always. Sometimes the process is reversed, especially for people who have lived extremely repressed lives.

For example, a 96-year-old many-times-over grandmother was much beloved by her devoted family. She had not been known to complain or behave unkindly to anyone as far back as anyone could remember.

The woman, who had been brought up by a stern father in her youth and was later married to a dictatorial husband, had had cancer for some years. It progressed slowly and for a long time seemed to make no difference to her state of health. Eventually, it began to affect her mind, and she was brought to a nursing home.

There, almost immediately, the enchanting old lady became a kind of naughty despot, throwing her dinner tray on the floor, pulling the nurse's hair when the time came to have her temperature taken, stuffing the toilet with newspaper, and generally making a menace of herself with pranks that could only be described as childishly malicious. The superego values that usually kept it in check had now somehow become eroded by the woman's ailment. The repressed little girl in the old woman ran wild and free.

Do Most People Generally Fight against Death, or Do They Go Meekly When the Time Comes?

Again, this depends on a person's personality type. There are no rules. Shneidman describes several different behavioral patterns demonstrated by those suffering from cancer (Shneidman, 1963, p. 201). The first he calls the "postponer." This patient is tenacious and refuses to give up. He will fight literally to his death, and do a great deal of denying along the way. The second he calls the "acceptor." This type goes quietly and philosophically. Third is the "disdainer." He doesn't believe that he is dying and scorns all that is done to help him. Fourth is the "welcomer." He is tired of life and quite ready to let go. Fifth is the "fearer." He demonstrates an unusually intense abhorrence of death and fights it to the end, not out of the will to live but out of the fear of dying.

To Shneidman's categories could be added several more specific portraits:

The unafraid. This person shows little overt fear concerning his own death and may even spend time trying to allay the fears of others.

The uninvolved. This person is unusually aloof from the

process of death and not (apparently) overly concerned with the outcome. He has not necessarily given up. He is simply impassive and strangely uninvolved.

The stoic. This person feels the usual amount of anxiety in the face of death but for whatever reasons refuses to reveal any outward sign of distress.

The "make the the best of a bad situation." This person refuses to let it all get him down, no matter how dire, insisting on entertaining friends at his bedside, on regaling visitors with funny stories about the ineptitude of the hospital staff and the foibles of the doctors, on generally carrying on gaily to the end, as if nothing were amiss.

And so on. The point is that many variations can be played on the theme of dying, all depending on a person's particular type. As a rule of thumb, a person can be expected to die basically in the fashion by which he has lived.

How Do Most Dying People Picture Death?

Some see it as a release. Others see it as an escape from this life into a blissful afterlife—or as a time of coming damnation. Sometimes it is seen as a frightening annihilation, a kind of black hole, or, relatedly, an annihilation of all consciousness that will be pleasant in its oblivion.

Does Everyone Who Is Dying Have a Picture of What Death Will Be Like?

Some withhold judgment or are simply incapable of picturing what a state of nonbeing would entail. When they think about their coming death they do not dwell on what it will be like *there* as much as what it will mean not to be *here*.

Do Attitudes toward Death and the Afterlife Change As a Person Approaches the Final Hours?

If a person is going to have a change of heart concerning this matter, it is usually at this time, when death is imminent.

Perhaps most commonly, unreligious people become religious. Very seldom do we see the opposite.

Do People Who Are Dying Necessarily Want to Be Saved from Death?

Apparently, many of the dying are quite ready to die when the time comes and have no burning wish to be brought back. This is true especially when a person's physical condition has deteriorated, or when her energy level has gone below a certain point of no return.

When a Person Is Terminally Ill, Does She Often Have Dreams Concerning Her Death?

Dreams of death among the dying are not unusual. These dreams (see Herzog, 1966) are not necessarily of the nightmare variety but may tend to deal with more archetypical imagery: riderless horses, the moon, dark forests, descents into the earth, and so on.

Should Dreams That Predict Death or Recovery from Death Be Taken Seriously?

While premonitory-type dreams have often been reported among the dying, interpretations of such dreams can sometimes lead into murky waters. For example, if a dying person dreams of his death and soon passes on, such a dream is no more oracular than the vision of a man who, while falling, imagines that he will shortly hit the ground. As we know, wish fulfillment is one of the main determinants of the dream machinery. People tend to dream about what they want to happen rather than about what will happen. Not always, of course. There are instances of dreams coming true. But usually this is the case.

Thus in most instances dreams reflect a person's desires and expectations more than they predict future events. This may be especially true when dreaming of a miraculous recovery. It can also be the case, moreover, in the opposite instance, when a person in extreme pain dreams of dying. Such dreams may be less an actual prediction of death and more a cry from the subconscious of the sick person for the end of physical suffering.

Does It Help Dying People to Be Aware of Their Dreams? Can't Dreams Sometimes Be the Unconscious's Way of Tying Up the Loose Ends of One's Life?

Sick people are often too fatigued or disinterested to pay much attention to their dreams. Because a person is seriously ill does not necessarily mean that his dreams will be more enriching or profound than usual. Similarly, because a person does not have revealing dreams does not mean that there is anything lacking in his intelligence or sensitivity.

There is no doubt that in some instances dreams can be a helpful index for discovering what is happening in the inner mind; work with them can be especially helpful if a therapist is involved. In general, a review of a terminally ill person's dreams will point toward significant psychological patterns, connections, and incompletenesses in the person's life: proper interpretation may help a person come to peace with much unfinished business.

Are Dying Persons Frequently Prone to Hallucinations?

At a certain point many patients begin to lose touch with reality, although not necessarily all at once nor in a dramatic way. Little indications show up. Persons mistake the nurse for one of their children, but just for a minute. They discuss events of the long ago past as if they were imminent, and so on. Ordinarily, this happens only in the later stages of a fatal ailment.

The patient may fade in and out of delusions, perhaps realizing that she has been victim of such flights of fancy but unable to prevent them when they happen again. At times such fantasies may become prolonged or macabre. The person may see apparitions, receive visits from dead friends, and so on. In the final days hallucinations may become part of a general delirium and ultimately merge into coma.

Is It Not True That Some People Become Very Lucid and Aware in Their Last Moments?

Yes, some do, especially if they are not under heavy sedation. It has often been noticed that shortly before a person dies the person will report feeling particularly placid and clearheaded. It is as if he or she has passed through the needle's eye and come out the other side. Nor is it unusual for people who have suffered much pain and anguish while going through the dying process to pass the actual moments of their dying in relative peace and joy.

What Can One Do When a Person Claims That He Longs to Die?

Perhaps what he is saying is that he no longer can endure the pain. Generally speaking, people do not long for death as much as for a release from the suffering of life.

It is also of value to ask *why*. What is the person really saying when he claims that he wants to die? Ask him. Perhaps it is not death that he longs for as much as it is increased compassion from those around him. It may also be his method of initiating discussion concerning matters which he is afraid to bring up directly. Question the person. Guide him with careful, directive queries. Let him tell you what is at the bottom of his pain. It may have nothing at all to do with death.

What about Sex and the Dying Person? Do Terminally Ill People as a Rule Still Care about Sex? If They Do, How Do They Handle It?

Assuming that a person's ailment has not damaged the sexual centers, and assuming that the person is still vigorous, sex usually maintains its allure. This does *not* guarantee that one's sex life will continue as before. The husband or wife of the dying person may feel, unconsciously perhaps, that their mate should be above such considerations. Or even—it would be difficult for most to admit—that there is something unwholesome about the dying person, especially if this person is suffering from deteriorative physical change. It is almost as if one would "catch" death by being too intimate with its carrier. Furthermore, it somehow just isn't done. A dying person is, well, sick. Not up to such things. Death is a serious matter. Sex is, how to say it—frivolous. And isn't there something wrong with mixing pleasure and death? Oh, if the truth be admitted—isn't the dying person really dead already!

But of course he isn't. While others may well view the dying person as a ghost, he perceives himself as he always has, as a live human being who counts. He sees no reason why his normal functions should be discontinued—just as long as he is able to perform them—and he does not understand why others do not agree.

And, of course, he is right. There is no reason why sex should cease the moment one is officially deemed "terminal." In fact, the dying person needs all the solace he can get, and sex can help, freeing the person if but for a moment from his predicament, offering him a kind of letting go which in its own way is akin to the final letting go. (It is perhaps no accident that in Elizabethan England the term "to die" was slang for having an orgasm.)

But Doesn't Serious Sickness Usually Cause a Decline in Sexual Interest?

It can, but not always. A person may, it is true, become obsessed with his symptomology, and ultimately lose interest in diversions of any kind. From this standpoint the inability to perform sex is more a problem for the therapist than for the physician. Sometimes also, sexual desire will decline sharply in the beginning of an ailment, then return at a later time. There is no universal pattern. Most evidence points to the fact that sex continues for many people long after the incipience of a terminal disease, although its frequency, intensity, and sometimes style of performance may be affected.

Does a Patient Ever Experience an Increase in Sexual Interest?

Yes, particularly as a form of denial. The person may feel *driven* to perform, as if the evidence of intense sexual activity serves as a rebuttal against his diagnosis. If death is the lack of all life, sexuality is life's final evocation. Sex in this sense becomes a symbol of security for the dying person. As long as he can maintain arousal, he believes, and continually demonstrate his potency, death will be kept at bay.

People So Rarely Speak about the Sexual Problems of the Dying Person.

When you put death and sex together you perhaps have the most taboo package ever assembled. Many doctors are embarrassed by this question and rarely have more to offer than ambiguous warnings and canned advice. Mental health professionals will sidestep the issue, and religious counselors are not usually consulted on the matter. The fact remains, however, that sex remains; and common sense tells us that the sick man or woman should be able to consult physician, counselor, mate, or friend on the matter—anybody who is in a position to help.

Can't Drugs and Medication Sometimes Dull a Person's Sexual Desire?

Yes, and the pity of it is that doctors often fail to inform a patient that such side effects may occur. The result is that the person believes her sexual decline stems from the disease itself, not from the drug, and that her sexual life is over forever. Her mate, in turn, must bear the brunt of this synthetic ailment, and the patient must bear the embarrassment and guilt that accompanies her pseudo-impotence. The complications that can follow such a grim comedy of errors are not difficult to envision.

The fact is, clearly, that it should be the responsibility of every physician to tell the patient in advance when a particular medication may interfere with the sexual function; and it should be the responsibility of every concerned patient to ask.

Which Ailments Actually Damage a Person's Sexual Functioning?

Most prominent are certain forms of cancer such as Hodgkin's disease, leukemia, and, of course, any disease that attacks the sexual organs. Endocrine maladies such as diabetes mellitus, nervous system malignancies of the brain and spinal cord, and any kind of radical surgery that severs connections to the genital areas will also be damaging.

If a Person Has in Any Way Become Disfigured by a Disease, Doesn't This Make Sex More Difficult?

Yes, for both parties. The patient feels mortified to be seen, to reveal her body, even to loving eyes. She may feel guilty that she is forcing the other person to perform a distasteful act. She may suppose, accurately or not, that her mate is attending her more out of pity than attraction.

On the mate's side any kind of drastic deformity in the partner's anatomy may in fact cause distaste and even revulsion. There is no getting around it. The mate hates himself for feeling this way, but what can he do except feel guilty? The question then arises as to whether the mate should go through with the love act even if he feels secret distaste at the prospect. The issue is made more complex by the fact that even if the act is consummated under such circumstances, any man or woman sensitive to their bed companion will detect a hesitation and a drawing back.

If One of the Partners Has Been Disfigured through a Disease or Operation, How Can a Couple Make the Best of the Situation?

The problem should be discussed candidly, though tactfully, by the parties involved, and if possible, the aid of a professional third party should be sought. In the end the sad truth may be that the couple's love life *will* be impaired. We cannot do more than we can do, we cannot be more than we can be. In most cases, however, especially where the relationship is firm and caring, couples will reach an accommodation. Such a meeting of minds may take time and may require sacrifices and a shift in expectations. Perhaps too, the lovemaking will be less satisfying than previously, and this for any of a number of reasons.

The fact remains, however, that an intimate contact will have taken place, and this counts for a lot.

How Do You Help a Person Who Has Irrevocably Lost Her Sexual Functions?

You help her mourn for these lost pleasures the way she might mourn for any other profound loss: by speaking about it, crying over it, learning to live with the loss through time; also, by not hesitating to touch her; and by remaining physically intimate with her even though she may no longer be capable of actual intercourse.

Isn't Sex Dangerous for Those with Advanced Heart Disease?

Studies show that less than 1 out of a 100 patients with severe heart troubles die directly from the excitement caused by sexual activity. The energy output for sexual intercourse is comparable to that of many mild exertions such as a brisk walk at the rate of 2 miles per hour or a climb up a flight of stairs. "If the patient can perform exercise at levels of 6 to 8 calories/min (vigorous walking, Master 2-step test, 600 kpm/min on a bicycle ergometer) without symptoms, abnormal pulse rate, or blood pressure or ECG changes," writes a medical expert, "it is generally safe to recommend that he resume sexual activity and undertake most types of industrial employment" (Lief, 1975, pp. 123–126).

Wouldn't You Say That of All the Negative Emotions a Dying Person Experiences, Fear Is the Most Prevalent and Debilitating?

Yes, and this fact is demonstrated clearly at those times when a patient manages, if even for a minute, to get free of it. At such a moment other anxieties seem magically to fall away too—the angers and jealousies and mortifications—as if the very source of negativity had dried up and left a free, open space in its stead. Sometimes, physical pain declines or even goes away entirely when fear is diminished.

Why Is Fear So Fundamental to the Dying Process?

The fear that a dying person undergoes is not *a* fear but many fears. It is a cluster of negative emotions, all variations on a single theme and all parts of a single constellation. Remember, it is not just death itself that is so terrifying but the process of dying, with its threat of pain, disfiguration, loneliness, and loss of control. When someone speaks of fear of death what she is really talking about are dozens of fears, a multitude of different protective reactions, all related and all ultimately united around the same center.

What Are the Most Prominent Fears That a Dying Person Experiences?

Generally speaking, there are four categories.

1. *Religious fear*:   fear of damnation, retribution, punishment in the afterlife
2. *Fear of pain*:   fear of psychological and bodily suffering
3. *Separation-abandonment fear*:   fear of being parted from our loved ones, of being alone, of leaving the familiar things of life
4. *Existential fear*:   fear of what will become of one after death, of what it will be like to not exist

Could You Be More Specific? What Are the Particular Fears Experienced by a Dying Person?

The following list, although not exhaustive, provides a good sample of specific fears commonly reported by the dying:

- What experiences will be denied me by my death? What will I be missing?
- What will become of my body after I die?
- What will it be like not to have a body?
- What will happen to the welfare of my loved ones?
- Will my mind die before my body?

- In what ways will my loved ones mourn me?
- Will all traces of my personality disappear after death?
- What will be the fate of my lifetime plans and projects?
- What alterations must my body undergo before I die?
- How will I react to all the coming pain and stress?
- How will I deal with my loneliness?
- Will I be buried alive?
- Will I become addicted to drugs?
- How much pain must I endure before it is all over?
- Will I become helpless?
- Will the doctor forget me?
- Will my family neglect me? Will they be there when I need them?
- Will I lose control over my body functions? Will I become incontinent? Will people be disgusted by me?
- Will I die alone?
- Will I be punished for my sins after I die?
- Will many people come to my funeral?
- What kind of legacy will I leave behind?
- Will I upset my family greatly by my death?
- Will I die like a coward?
- Will I be quickly forgotten after I die?
- Will my family be able to pay all the medical bills?
- Is the doctor competent?
- Is my life a failure?

To this list of fears might be added:

- Fear of dying in obscurity
- Fear of prolonged illness
- Fear of rotting in the grave

- Fear of not being able to die when one is ready
- Fear of being kept alive on life-support machinery (and hence, of becoming a vegetable)
- Fear of suffocation
- Fear of losing one's mind
- Fear of the devil
- Fear of being a bother to other people
- Fear of the unknown
- Fear of the infinite
- Fear of nonbeing

Do Older People Fear Dying As Much As Younger People?

By the time people reach their sixties and seventies they have completed the cycles that constitute a full life, cycles of profession, family, friendships, personal growth, and so on. For this reason, although they certainly do not look forward to death, most older people fear it less than do the young or middle-aged.

When death arrives for younger people it finds them still in the middle of their life cycles. Naturally they feel cheated. Something in them yearns to finish what is incomplete. The need for wholeness is basic to all human beings, and when it is frustrated—perhaps the most common complaint among younger dying people is, "I never had a chance"—it becomes considerably more difficult to let go. This does not mean that young people, people in their twenties and thirties, do not eventually reach an accommodation with death, only that their anger and disbelief tend to delay the process. The French philosopher Montaigne remarked that "old men go to death, and death comes for the young."

Who Fears Death More, Men or Women?

According to available information, women avoid thinking about death more than men do but they are more willing to discuss the subject. Women are less fascinated with the macabre imagery of death but tend to wish for death more often. Women fear the decomposition of their bodies more than men, and men worry more over how the consequences of their death will affect their dependents. Women envision death in terms of loss and mourning, men in terms of violence and frustration. Women have greater concern with pain and suffering. Men dream about death more often than women do but are less likely to believe in life after death (Vernon, 1970, p. 204).

What Other Social Factors Influence People's Attitude toward Death?

Some interesting findings from surveys on the subject indicate the following:

- People who live in residential housing have less fear of death than do those who live in institutions.

- Elderly people involved with leisure activities or committed to important projects have less death fear than those of their age who are aimless and uninvolved.

- Those in a state of poor health tend to look forward to death more than do those who are healthy.

- Elderly widowed people evade the question of death; single, separated, and married people look toward their death with a more positive attitude. (To this, parenthetically, could be added the fact that, statistically, married people tend to live longer than single people and tend to be hospitalized less often.)

- Uneducated people evade the question of death more than do those with some education; college-educated people tend to accept the inevitability of death more easily than do those with less schooling.

- In general, the middle class fears the pain of dying more than do the lower and upper classes, while members of the lower class have more concern with the consequences of life after death (Vernon, 1970, Chap. 7).

Doesn't Fear of Death Sometimes Take the Form of Seemingly Unrelated Fears?

Some people, such as the Pulitzer-prize-winning scholar Ernest Becker, believe that *all* fears are basically fears of death, that at the bottom of our daily worry, frustration, and stress will inevitably be found the terror of death (Becker, 1973). Others are reluctant to go as far as this, yet still argue that death fear is a profound factor in human behavior and that it can indeed come disguised as neurosis, paranoia, depression, schizophrenia, physiological ailments such as insomnia, and in some cases pathological criminal behavior.

At What Point Does an Ordinary Fear of Death Become Neurosis or Even Psychosis?

It is normal to fear death. It is abnormal when this fear disrupts a person's ordinary daily functioning.

There are many typical examples: If a person insists on walking to a destination rather than taking a taxi because he is afraid of dying in a traffic accident; if a person refuses to ride an elevator because she is afraid the cables will break; if a person is obsessed with feelings of impending disaster and finds himself dwelling on thoughts of catastrophe; if a person pales at the mention of death and abruptly changes the subject; if a person's dreams are populated by morbid symbols of death or by graphic incidents of dying and mayhem; if a person has an overwhelming dread of sickness or disease—any of these somewhat illogically fearful responses to ordinary situations may indicate an unhealthy attitude toward death.

Can Hypochondria Be the Result of Death Fear?

In certain instances. A person worries inordinately about this organ, about that limb, in a manner that only partially disguises the real problem: a terror that *all* of her will soon stop working. In some cases the anxiety can become an extreme form of hypochondria known as death panic, an ailment characterized by a sudden rush of frightening physical symptoms accompanied by a conviction on the part of the sufferer that she is on the veritable razor's edge between life and death. Such a condition can sometimes be quite severe. The person's palms will sweat, her body will tremble, palpitations will run across her entire frame. In extreme cases she may become delirious or even lose consciousness, but when a physician is consulted no ailment can be found. Those who suffer from such seizures are, of course, troubled and may require treatment in the hands of a professional.

Does Fear and Anxiety about Death Remain Constant throughout the Period of Time in Which One Is Dying?

Very few things remain constant during this time. Fear and anxiety especially have their own rhythms. E. Mansell Pattison (Pattison, 1977, pp. 47–59) has divided up the terminal period into three stages which he terms the "acute phase," the "chronic living-dying phase," and the "terminal phase." During each of these periods, he maintains, a person's fear reactions are subject to profound change.

In the *acute phase* the patient finds himself face-to-face with a problem that has no solution. The encounter awakens many unresolved neuroses, neurosis of dependency, say, or of narcissism. These may trigger a period of stress that becomes overwhelming and which mounts day after day until it peaks, usually at a time considerably before the arrival of death.

Next comes the *chronic living-dying phase*. The person now slowly and resolutely faces the specific psychological issues which have produced this terror. This is the time of growth, accommodation, learning and acceptance. The person looks at the various sources of his fear and, perhaps with help from a loved one or a professional, learns to endure the poignant truths of separation, loneliness, and extinction.

Finally, in the *terminal phase* the person ceases to grapple directly with fears of death. Ideally he has put them to rest. He now withdraws into himself as his body functions decline.

Pattison's tri-fold scheme is mirrored in the observations of many professionals, and offers yet another view of the stages in the dying process. Most agree that the initial period of terror usually surrenders to a more composed interval of introspection and psychological confrontation, which in turn gives way to a time of final withdrawal.

Can Sudden, Unaccountable Anxiety Attacks Come from the Fear of Death?

In some cases of free-floating anxiety there is evidence that the problem can be traced to negative experiences with death in childhood or to unconscious fears of bodily destruction. Death implies three frightful threats to human beings: extinction, helplessness, and alienation. Any of these fears by themselves are capable of producing anxiety neurosis. Merged into one looming symbol, they are an irresistible force to stir the unconscious.

Can a Person Die from the Fear of Death?

Only on the rarest occasions, and usually from heart failure due to shock. Over a period of time abnormal fear of death, however, is hard on both body and mind in the way that any excessive worry will be. Too much of it can lead to physical debilitation.

Is It Really Possible for Human Beings to Overcome Their Fear of Death?

Near the end many do. Before this time though, during the course of everyday life, most of us can probably never hope to conquer fear of death entirely. It is too fraught with threats to ego survival and with the primal terror of pain. It *is* within our power, however, to frequently ponder our death while we are quick and healthy, and hence to become familiar with it—friendly even, if friendly is the right word—to make death a part of our consciousness while we are among the living, just as we make love and sleep and hunger a part of our consciousness; all this so that when death finally comes to us, as it must, it comes as less of a shock, less as a surprise, less as an angry stranger, more as an old and honored guest.

This is why during the Middle Ages it was frequent practice to spend several minutes each day quietly contemplating one's death. Perhaps such a thoughtful meditation would not be out of place today and might even embower the charred hole left by modern man's elimination of those reminders, ethical, philosophical, and religious, by which people of the past so willingly put themselves in mind of their mortality. "There's something wonderfully consoling to me," remarked a patient with cancer, "to think that so many human beings have died before me. Billions and trillions, so many people like me. All of us. How could something so natural be bad?

It Is True That Fear of Death May Sometimes Be Exaggerated, and That When the Moment of Death Arrives It Is Often a Peaceful and Painless Event. Nonetheless, the Thing Dying People Fear Most—Physical Pain—Remains Real for Many throughout a Good Deal of the Dying Process.

First of all, is this true? Do most dying people inevitably live through severe pain throughout their life-death interval? The answer is an emphatic no. By some estimates fewer than 30 percent of terminal cases experience pain, and by other estimates fewer than 50 percent. According to the famous turn-of-the-century British physician Sir William Osler, in a ward of 500 dying patients, only 20 percent showed signs of severe distress. In a more recent study (Exton-Smith, 1961) it was found that only 14 percent of the dying patients suffered from pain that could not be relieved. John Hinton reports that two-thirds of patients suffering from fatal illnesses in a general hospital experienced pain that required treatment for relief, and that of those treated, only 12 percent continued to have discomfort (Hinton, 1967).

The suffering of those who do experience great pain can usually be palliated if not entirely relieved by the use of medication. In many cases where pain is present it will manifest only at certain times and may even decrease as the disease progresses. This is not, of course, to minimize pain nor to imply that dying is a bed of roses, only to make it clear that the popular image of death as inevitably synonymous with agony is a misconception.

Why Is It So Difficult to Measure How Much Pain a Person Is Actually Suffering?

Pain is an extremely subjective phenomenon. There are no machines, no scientific standards to determine its degrees. It remains a mystery why a headache will incapacitate one person but be laughed off by another. How, then, are we to decide who is "legitimately" in pain, or what "in pain" really means; and further, how is the person not in pain accurately to judge the person who is? "Pain is always something new for him who suffers," writes A. Daudet (Daudet, 1934, p. 15), "but banal for those around him. They will all get used to it except myself." Also, how are we to judge objectively the precise point at which a person's misery goes from "normal" to "unacceptable," or at what moment discomfort passes into suffering, and suffering into agony.

What, Then, Is the Ultimate Criterion?

If a person says she is in pain, she should be treated for pain. Perhaps it is that simple. Treatment can be chemical, social, psychological, whatever. The important thing is that the person not be ignored. Moreover, in terms of prescription medications, there is one criterion that can always be applied: When pain fails to respond to simple over-the-counter remedies such as aspirin or low-level painkillers, the pain should then be considered serious enough to warrant concentrated medical attention.

What about the Person Who Is in Pain and Is Not Helped by Conventional Pain Reduction Therapy?

It is rare that physical pain cannot be controlled, at least to some degree. Most suffering eventually responds to medication.

It is simply a question of trial and error until the right drug is found. When all conventional methods fail, however, there are still additional measures that can be taken. Make sure that the patient is comfortable. Sometimes a little pain can exacerbate a greater one: Attention to an uncomfortable mattress or a bandage that is too tight will take the edge off. A turn or shift in body position may help. Certain positions, too: Breathing can be made easier if one sits up, abdominal pain may be relieved if the legs are raised, sleep may come more easily if a person is turned onto his right side, and so on.

Check for bedsores. They become a perpetual agony when not tended. Pain usually improves at certain times of the day; or after meals; or on an empty stomach; or when the person is lying down rather than sitting up. Look for these little advantages and make use of them.

If the patient is unable to speak, go down the list of possible things that he might need and tell him to shake his head or blink his eyes whenever the desirable choice comes up. For some people the more forgotten and humble parts of the *materia medica* may be of profit, such as hot compresses, depth massage, plasters, cold towels, herbal teas, warm or cold baths, and the like. Experimentation with alternative methods is a simple matter and, assuming that the technique is medically appropriate (you would not give a massage to a person with spinal damage, for example), these alternative methods can sometimes be surprisingly effective.

Stay by the suffering person. Physical pain is inflamed by psychological distress, and the presence of a loved one can itself be a medication. Diversion also works. Engage the sick person in conversation, dwell on subjects you know he enjoys discussing. It is amazing how talking about things one loves reduces pain.

Pain control should be one of the primary concerns of any health care institute, and in the case of the dying person, whatever works, no matter how unorthodox or even bizarre, is welcome. As in many branches of the medical profession, the treatment of pain can be a qualitative art as well as a quantitative science.

What Other Methods of Pain Relief Exist?

Drugs are, of course, the most common and will be spoken of at length; however, other methods should also be mentioned. It is possible, for instance, to deaden nerve connections by injecting analgesics directly into the nerve connections, a process that gives relief for as long as the medication remains active. More drastically, certain injected chemicals can disable local nerves permanently, numbing the problem area forever but rendering it painless as well. Even more effective, though more problematic, is the deadening of pain centers through brain surgery, an alternative used only in extreme cases. Spinal operations perform a similar function, severing the nerves connected to the problem spot, but they are effective only when the pain is localized and has not spread to different locations in the body, as in a cancer or tubercular metastasis. Fluids can sometimes be drained directly from engorged bowels, or can be removed by tube from the lungs when breathing is labored.

Are There Any Other Methods That Have Proved Effective Against Pain?

In certain cases hypnosis has been used successfully. Some make claims for acupuncture, electrotherapy and biofeedback. Forms of physiotherapy are especially good if carried out under the eye of a well-trained and compassionate physiotherapist. Self-suggestion has helped some patients, especially if used every day. (Yogis have demonstrated remarkable control over their nervous systems along with an accompanying insensibility to pain, thus demonstrating that it is possible—if not easily practicable—to control pain through the mind alone.)

Will Controlling Anxiety Reduce Pain?

Absolutely. This is a very important matter for the patient, his doctor, and his family to understand. It might even be said that in many ways anxiety control *is* pain control. That is, in many ailments the pain seems to come from the ailment. In reality, the pain comes from tensions caused by concern over the ailment. If the anxiety is relieved, the pain will lessen.

So Anxiety Can Increase Pain.

It can increase pain. It can create its own forms of pain as well.

How?

The sick patient is confused and frightened. She is living through probably the most anxious time of her life, and her body responds by becoming tense, just as it might during any highly pressured situation. As a result, her organism responds with tension-anxiety reactions: backache, diarrhea, insomnia, intestinal pains, dizziness, shortness of breath, general malaise—the whole list of tension symptomology, none of which stems from the disease per se but from its resulting anxiety response. It is easy to imagine how one set of symptoms might be mistaken for the other.

Shouldn't the Doctor Know the Difference?

If the doctor has a particular fear of death herself, she may avoid confronting this fear reaction in the patient. Rather than discuss the problem of death fear directly and take the appropriate steps to relieve whatever tension suffering she observes, she opts to address the safer question, that of chemical pain control, prescribing narcotic medications that reduce the patient to quasi-consciousness, increasing the dose each time the patient's tolerance shows signs of increasing. In the end we have one addicted patient, one denial-wrought doctor, and a situation that might have been better handled—and more easily handled—by going to the real source of the pain.

What Should One Expect of the Doctor in This Case?

For one thing, the doctor should be alert to recognizing tension pain and be able to distinguish it from disease symptomology per se. Willingness to slow down, to avoid the notorious rushed bedside manner so prevalent on the hospital floor, to listen carefully to complaints and then read between the lines, all are specifics against tension, as is the courage to speak openly with patients who wish to discuss their fears. Seeing the patient as a waking mind and a living heart as well as a sickly body is a vital necessity. All too easily a physician confines himself to the patient's physical symptomology, leaving questions of emotional need to those "trained" in such things, as if body and soul could be so conveniently separated, as if the process of healing was confined to the behavior of organs alone.

It would not, moreover, hurt any physician to be familiar with the induction of hypnotic relaxation techniques, or to have access to someone who is. If the doctor is too busy to bother with such things, family members might try their hand at it. Many books have been written on relaxation therapy, and regimes for light suggestion and autosuggestion are readily available. In many cases it would also be advisable for a physician to consider prescribing *mild* tranquilizers before instantly dispensing the more powerful narcotic medications, especially if there is any indication that the pain stems from the anxiety-hysteria-depression syndrome rather than from direct somatic causes.

Then Depression Can Also Be Responsible for Causing a Patient Physical Pain?

It can exaggerate pain that is already there, and it can bring its own variety of pain.

Perhaps a further word about depression is in order. In many people's minds depression means "the blues," a feeling of desolation, of being "down." Although desolation is often part of depression, medically speaking many people undergo clinical depression without experiencing any sensation of melancholia or despair. They encounter instead what are called "neurovegetative" symptoms, direct physiological disorders such as early morning awakening, appetite loss, muscular pain, impotency, insomnia, fatigue, lack of energy, and headache. This is depression, too—the point being that depression can cause adverse physical manifestations as well as, and sometimes *in place of*, psychological manifestations.

Many dying patients are thus depressed and do not know it, and their doctors do not know it either, for instead of psychological symptoms the patients exhibit physical ones. These symptoms, in turn, are read as side effects of the disease and are treated as such. In point of fact, they would be better treated as end products of depression.

What Is the Best Method for Relieving Depression-Caused Physical Pain?

The following quote from an article on pain and addiction by Thomas A. Gonda addresses this question thoroughly (Gonda, 1970, pp. 267–268). Gonda refers to bodily distress caused by depression as "substitute pain." He writes: "The establishment of a successful patient-physician relationship, in the presence of covert depression, depends to a large extent upon the appropriateness of the physician's condolences. It is most important for the patient to feel that the ministering physician understands what he has experienced and recognizes his despair. Responses to the patient's questions should be as simple and encouraging as is consistent with honesty. The physician must serve as a guide for the patient's family and friends as well as for others ministering to the patient–either aggravating the patient's feelings of isolation, loneliness, and rejection nor promoting the patient's tendency towards regressive behavior. As the substitute pain complaint subsides and denial shifts to recognition of the painful reality, the depression tends to increase. A firm insistence at this stage that the patient participate in his treatment and be consulted in family decisions often lifts the depression substantially. The greater the involvements in such tasks—in regular work insofar as possible, as well as in diversions (for example, active recreation, hobbies, passive entertainment, occupational therapy)—the less likely is pain complaint to be a prominent symptom."

What about Pain Control for a Person Dying at Home?

If the person chooses to die at home, family and doctor must work together, making sure that the pain medication is correctly chosen and checking that it is modified appropriately as time passes. If the family is not able to hire a nurse, efforts to learn basic nursing techniques would be advisable, techniques such as turning the bed, putting in a catheter, moving a patient from room to room, taking temperatures, changing bed garments, monitoring pulse and blood pressure. Local community colleges teach courses in such methods as do adult education centers and town hospitals. Consult your newspaper or telephone classified section for classes. Moreover, the family or caretaker should learn these skills *before* the sick person is brought home, so that if mistakes are made they are made out of inexperience, not out of ignorance.

It has been noted that patients who suffer much pain in the hospital often obtain immediate relief the moment they return home. The mental-emotional equation cannot be overlooked in the question of pain. Allowing the dying patient to reclaim her familiar room, surrounding her with loving attention, providing a ready ear to problems, letting her become involved in daily household decisions once again, supplying entertainment and pleasant diversions, all have an analgesic quality that is frequently underestimated by those who would reduce the question of human suffering to physiobiology.

Does Pain Always Increase As a Disease Progresses?

Usually it does, especially with chronic degenerative diseases. This is not an absolute law but a general tendency, and as a rule pain control must be increased to offset it. However, as mentioned previously, a considerable number of people experience a *decrease* of pain in the days immediately before death.

What Kind of Pain Causes the Most Concern?

People are most concerned with suffocation and choking, then with nausea and difficulty in swallowing. Biologically, the breathing apparatus and the swallowing mechanism are particularly vulnerable to psychological and physiological distress, and both react quickly to any adverse bodily changes. Patients know this instinctively and respond sensitively to disturbances in these areas.

Is There Any Way of Telling in Advance How Much Pain a Person Will Suffer?

Estimates can be made, but one can never know for certain. Although diseases tend to take similar courses, each person's physiology is different. It should never be assumed that because a person has a particular disease he will inevitably suffer in a particular manner.

What If a Patient Has Pain but for Whatever Reasons Does Not Seek Help?

A group of professionals (Anderson et al., 1973) determined from a study that a surprisingly large number of terminally ill patients refuse to ask for pain relief. Usually, these patients suffer from embarrassing ailments such as an inability to control their bowels, and—so powerful is their fear of social judgment— they opt to lie in agonized silence rather than risk exposure.

If a person suffers an embarrassing ailment, if she seems to be in pain and is unduly reticent to seek relief, the best tactics are to (1) persuade her that the staff is accustomed to dealing with a wide array of unpleasant physical side effects, and that hers are probably no worse than anyone else's; (2) assure her that all attention will be kept private, that the curtains will be pulled, that her case will not be discussed in public, and so on; (3) inform her that it is a patient's *right* to have pain relief; and (4) convince her that pain relief will allow her the freedom to function socially and to live her life in a more normal, relaxed way.

Are Pain Medications Dispensed Automatically to Those Suffering Painful Ailments? Or Must They Be Requested?

Most nurses are trained *not* to give pain medication unless a patient requests it. It is therefore wrong for a patient to assume that his pain will be controlled automatically or even that the attending physician will consider pain an issue until a complaint is raised. Although some doctors foresee such problems and willingly discuss them with the patient beforehand, most do not, so ordinarily, medication must be asked for. This is simply the way the system works.

What If Pain Medication Is Requested and Not Provided?

It is another question entirely if pain relief is requested but is not forthcoming, or if it is supplied in insufficient quantities and no attempt is made to upgrade the dosage. A patient is morally and legally entitled to receive pain relief. If it is requested and the staff, for whatever reasons, refuses to do everything in their power to supply it, basic patient's rights are being violated.

What Can Be Done?

The patient (or the family, if the patient is not able) should speak with those in authority—the doctor, the head nurse, members of the hospital administration. Usually, these situations arise from misunderstandings and are easily corrected. If pain relief is not forthcoming after taking the problem to higher authorities, however, the patient and his family might consider changing physicians or even moving to another hospital. Usually, such drastic measures are not necessary.

Should One Expect Members of Different National, Ethnic, and Racial Groups to Respond Differently to Pain?

In some cultures such as the Japanese or the British, a high premium is placed on the stoic acceptance of pain. In others, the Italian, say, or Spanish, or certain countries in the Middle East, a person is considered peculiar if he does not complain, and loudly. This can make for misunderstandings and hard feelings in health care institutions where persons from many cultural backgrounds are mixed together in various caretaker-patient relationships, each with different values concerning the expression or repression of pain response. When dealing with a person in pain it is well worth noting his national or cultural background and taking clues from this observation as to how best to provide for his needs.

What about People Who Consider It "Unmanly" to Take Pain Medication?

This would again seem a matter of choice. It is not up to us to judge such a person's attitude or to try to reason with him. If a person has strong feelings about this and is indeed able to bear the pain without medication, such is his privilege. We are all due the death we choose.

Certain Religious Groups Do Not Allow Their Members to Take Medication, Especially Narcotic Medications.

It is the same thing. If a person wishes, for whatever reasons, to refuse pain relief, it is that person's choice and should be respected. Forcing patients to take medication, especially when it runs contrary to their religious principles, often causes more suffering than it prevents. The problem does not often come up, however, as members of religious groups opposed to medicine ordinarily provide special care and separate institutions for their sick and dying.

Does the Age at Which People Go through the Dying Process Have Any Bearing on the Amount of Pain They Will Undergo?

Because their bodies are stronger and, as it were, not biologically ready to die, young people often have greater pain than those in their later years. According to observations made in an English hospital by John Hinton, 45 percent of patients under 50 years of age had considerable discomfort; 32 percent of those between 50 and 70 had discomfort; and only 10 percent of those over 70 had much unrelieved physical suffering in their terminal period (Hinton, 1967, p. 75).

Is There Anything a Patient Can Do for Himself to Help Control Pain?

Perhaps the most useful thing is self-induced relaxation. This may seem of negligible value in the face of the pain experienced by the seriously ill, yet just a few minutes of antistress technique will prove its worth, even in severe cases. As mentioned, tension increases pain. This is true. In every case. By using autorelaxation methods, the Jacobson technique, for instance (see Jacobson, 1964), or systems of autosuggestion and meditation, considerable help can be gained against neurotensive disorders.

Many People Are Not Familiar with Methods for Inducing Self-Relaxation. Could You Give Some Examples?

There are numerous methods of self-relaxation, most of them propounded by exercise schools, therapy groups, and mental health professionals. We will list a typical method here which is used as a general relaxant by professionals prior to putting patients under hypnosis.

Begin by finding a quiet place and a quiet hour. Lie on the back with the arms to the side and the legs comfortably spread about 20 inches apart. Take ten deep breaths and relax thoroughly for several minutes. In this preliminary period it will be helpful to visualize pleasant scenes such as a memorable visit with friends or a cool mountain lake on a sunny day—any mental picture that brings peaceful associations. After letting this positive imagery flow for several moments, begin active relaxation by concentrating attention on the head. First, tense the scalp tightly and hold the tension for about 10 seconds, paying attention to the area being tensed, studying it. Tighten vigorously, then release. Feel the looseness that instantly follows.

Next tense the forehead. Hold. Study it. Release, relax. Now the eyes and nose (flare the nostrils and tighten the tip of the nose). And the mouth. The lips. The ears. The back of the head. The chin. The tongue and muscles of the mouth. Puff out the cheeks for several moments, study them, relax them.

Feel the increased relaxation that follows each tightening. This relaxation is a guaranteed result. Now go back and do it again.

Proceed in this fashion down the length of the entire body. Tighten the front of the neck for 10 seconds, study it, release, and relax. Treat similarly the shoulders, the chest, the upper arms, the lower arms, the wrists, the hands, and the fingers. Tighten, study, and after 10 seconds relax. Then the rib cage, the stomach, the abdomen, the back (upper, middle, and lower). Now the hips and the buttocks (a great deal more tension is stored here than we realize). The groin. The thighs (front and back). Tense, study, relax. Then the calves and the ankles and the feet (keeping the legs flat to the floor, point the toes slowly in the direction of the head, hold, then slowly point them in the opposite direction). Do this several times. Tense and relax.

When tensing and detensing, make sure that the mind is as inactive as possible. It is imperative that all distressing imagery be excluded. Any negativity tends to increase anxiety and to cancel out whatever relaxation is gained.

When the entire exercise is finished—it should last from 5 to 10 minutes—take ten more deep breaths (deep breathing is a sound antidote to tension by itself, even when unaccompanied by exercise). By now a deep, warm relaxation will be felt all over the body, the kind that is rarely experienced in daily life. Remain in this state as long as it is comfortable. It is an excellent way to fall asleep at night.

I've Heard That Certain Hospitals Allow Dying Patients to Administer Strong Antipain Medications to Themselves. Is This True?

It is true, but to answer the question fully a bit of background is necessary.

This method of self-prescribed pain medication is commonly used in organizations known as *hospices*, both in the United States and in Europe. The hospice, or Hospice Movement as it is sometimes called, was started in 1948 at St. Christopher's Hospice in London. A hospice can be either a separate institution or a section of a hospital where special care is provided for dying patients, ensuring that they spend their last days quietly, productively, painlessly, and lovingly attended to. A friendly, noninstitutional atmosphere is encouraged here, and nurses and doctors are dedicated to providing patient-oriented services. In some hospices patients live in private rooms decorated to their tastes and furnished with their own belongings. In others patients spend much of their time commuting back and forth between hospice and home. In any hospice, visiting hours are open, friends and family are encouraged to come at any time and are included in hospice activities, and visits from children, whatever their age, are heartily welcomed. No pretense is made concerning the fact that patients in a hospice are dying, and honest, open dialogue between staff and patient is a pivotal point of the program. The hospice, in other words, is an institution dedicated to making the experience of dying as serene, dignified, natural, and supportive as possible.

Although this movement is, of course, unconventional in light of existing facilities for the dying, and although it has not been accepted with much enthusiasm by the orthodox medical community, it is gradually catching on, and more and more hospitals in America and Europe boast of a well-maintained hospice ward on their premises.

One of the concepts that hospice philosophy is famous for (and in some circles infamous for) is drug prescription. Terminal pain, it is believed, must be looked on as a separate illness and must be treated according to the requirements of each person. Hospice doctors believe that a good portion of pain results from the *fear of pain itself*. If this concern can be eliminated, pain will be eliminated. Narcotic medications are therefore given freely to dying persons in the hospice environment, although in carefully balanced dosages to ensure that the patient remains alert and active. Once the narcotic has broken the pain-fear cycle, dosage is stabilized and even reduced to a nonaddictive level, with the patient still experiencing the same degree of freedom from pain she felt with heavier doses.

A method some hospices have employed to facilitate this process is to encourage patients to supervise their own mixture of drug medication. In British hospices, for instance, patients are allowed to prepare themselves a drink called a Brompton's Cocktail. Typically, this drink might include morphine, liquor, phenothiazine, chloroform, cocaine, and other powerful stimulants or sedatives, as the case demands, all made palatable with a cola or syrup base. The patient adjusts the dosage according to his tolerance and taste—he is, after all, the best judge of his own comfortability level—and increases or decreases proportions as he chooses. Each person, believes the hospice movement, has unique chemical requirements for pain relief; to be most effective a pain remedy must be personally tailor-made by the patient.

Doesn't the Patient Become Addicted?

Although addiction is often the result, hospice philosophy maintains that if a patient is soon to die, why deprive him of the comfort and relief that a well-balanced drug program can provide. In fact, claim hospice doctors, by providing relief with narcotic drugs *before* the pain becomes too serious and administering it as often and as freely as the patient requests, the terror of pain, with all its accompanying tensions, will be eliminated and with it, automatically, much of the angst of dying.

Are All Painkilling Drugs Addictive?

All are not, but many are. Most of the powerful ones contain codeine, morphine, or other habit-forming substances. One should consult one's physician on the question of narcotic drug potency.

When a Person Is First Placed on Heavy Pain Medication, How Does He Generally Feel?

For the first few days the patient may expect to feel somewhat drowsy and foggy-headed. His body is adjusting. After this he may become more clearheaded, especially if the physician monitors the dosage carefully and adjusts it so that the dosage is properly balanced between relief and sedation.

If the Patient Feels Dulled or Heavily Drugged after Taking a Painkiller, What Can She Do?

She can request that the dosage be changed or that a different type of medication be applied. Sometimes, of course, the heavily drugged feeling will be inevitable and certain side effects unavoidable if the pain is to be eased successfully. Just as commonly it may simply be a question of altering the dosage or changing the prescription schedule.

The doctor, moreover, is by no means clairvoyant and will not necessarily know what the patient is experiencing until the patient tells her. What is essential here is that the patient make his needs known directly, and that he not remain passive or polite when the question of pain comes up.

Must Painkillers Make a Person Feel Drugged?

By no means. Again, it is a question of making sure that the right balance of medication is applied (as practiced especially by hospice physicians), at least in most cases. One of the problems often encountered by both patients and family in a terminal situation is that the doctor, reacting to his own uneasiness with death, dispenses powerful narcotic drugs too liberally, stupefying the patient into nonthreatening oblivion. This may be an unconscious act, as it no doubt is also unconscious on the part of the nurses, who may find a heavily drugged patient not only more tractable but less of an advertisement for death in general. Nonetheless, the practice is insidious, not infrequent, and perhaps worst of all, unnecessary in many cases. If members of the ailing person's family feel that the drug therapy is too extreme, they should discuss the problem with the doctor, request that the medication be reviewed, that alternative prescriptions be tried, that an attempt be made to find a balance between the relief of pain and the inducement of insensibility.

What Kinds of Side Effects besides Drowsiness Can Result from Pain Medication?

Barbiturates will sometimes cause confusion, disorientation, and malaise. The amphetamines, given for depression, may cause undue restlessness and disorientation. The phenothiazines, given for extreme mental reactions such as paranoia, can cause headaches and personality change. Many drugs produce annoying side effects such as itching, headache, diarrhea, dry mouth, nausea, or dizziness. Sometimes a second drug is required to relieve the symptoms caused by the first.

Each drug, even the gentlest (including aspirin), has its own set of counterindications. An open dialogue between patient and physician will ensure that the patient is forewarned whenever side effects are likely. If the doctor or nurse is not willing to reveal this information—some doctors avoid mentioning side effects beforehand from fear of planting the suggestion in the patient's mind—there are several books on the market which give detailed descriptions of prescription drugs and their side effects. These include:

Berkow, Robert (ed.), *The Merck Manual.* Rahway, New Jersey: Merck, Sharp and Dohme Research Laboratories, 1977.

Davies, D. M. (ed.), *Textbook of Adverse Drug Reactions.* New York: Oxford University Press, 1972.

Graedon, Joe, *The Peoples' Pharmacy.* New York: Avon Books, 1976.

Lingeman, Richard, *Drugs from A to Z.* New York: McGraw-Hill, 1974.

Long, James W., *The Essential Guide to Prescription Drugs.* New York: Harper and Row, 1982.

What If the Patient Prefers to Take Weaker Pain Medication, Have Some Pain, and Remain Alert?

Some people opt to live with a low level of discomfort and remain as alert as possible, up to the end. The important support for them is the knowledge that a pain remedy *is* available should they change their minds. This knowledge alone can give a person the freedom to say yes or no to drugs.

What about Alcohol as a Pain Killer?

The analgesic power of alcohol is often underestimated or neglected in the case of the terminally ill patient, especially in hospitals, and for obvious reasons: It would not do to have a ward populated with patients who are inebriated one hour and hung over the next.

Nonetheless, even small amounts of alcohol have a wonderful ability to reduce physical pain and, as a kind of million-dollar bonus, to ease psychological tensions in the bargain. If taken in moderation at home or in a permitted institutional environment, alcohol will generate a state as tranquilizing as that produced by certain narcotics. Because the sensations are more familiar, moreover, it works in a way that is less disorienting than drugs.

In the hospice environment, regular cocktail hours are kept, and visitors are encouraged to bring bottles of wine or liquor rather than the conventional plant or basket of fruit. Interestingly, alcohol as a sedative and painkiller, for some unknown reason, works better for men than for women (Saunders, 1972, p. 254).

How Does a Patient Behave When He Is Entering the Last Phase of a Terminal Illness? How Can One Recognize When the End Is Near?

Withdrawal is the key to recognizing the last stages. The dying person closes into herself physically and psychologically. She may become unusually quiet, stop eating, sleep a good deal, and exhibit a marked decline in energy and vitality. She may look especially pale, hollow-eyed, pasty-skinned, and emaciated; whatever deterioration the affliction has brought seems increased by several degrees. Psychologically, her behavior mirrors her physical decline. She loses interest in reading, visits, and television. She prefers silence, quiet, and rest. She may complain of being lightheaded. She may become irrational and regressed. Part of her seems as if it has already departed.

Patients approaching the end are often surrounded by an atmosphere of fatigue, gentleness, disorientation, and resignation. It is difficult to define this atmosphere in any scientific way, but those trained in caring for the terminally ill intuitively know the signs, often predicting quite accurately the day or even the hour when a patient will die.

Is Panic a Common Reaction among the Dying?

Only if there is a good deal of pain, or if the patient cannot catch his breath (nothing causes panic more than a sensation of suffocation). Otherwise, the level of agitation remains generally subdued, the patient's social caution over "making a scene" keeping displays of emotion in check. Most patients in Western countries endure their death with silent suffering rather than frenzy. In lands where the verbal expression of pain is not so regulated and the taboo against shows of negative feelings not so prominent, the picture can be quite different.

Do People Usually Know When They Are About to Die?

Yes, most people who are awake toward the end know when the time is close at hand. Sometimes they will make remarks to this fact, often in a matter-of-fact or even lighthearted manner, and it is wise to heed them when they do.

Are Most People Awake When They Are Dying?

No, most people are either in a coma or in a drug-induced half-sleep.

Do Hospitals Allow Visitors to Be with the Dying Person While He Is Actually Dying?

Usually, friends and close family are allowed to stand by the bedside. Often, the patient will ask for a particular person or call out the name of a loved one to whom he wishes to speak.

Do Most People Pronounce Dying Words?

Most people have "last" words, although not necessarily dying words, if by dying words we mean profoundly significant remarks voiced at the point of death. The reasons for this are many. A majority of persons die in a coma or quasi-conscious state. Some are too weak, or unwilling to talk. Some do not know the fatal moment is upon them and make no attempt at communication.

"Last" words, on the other hand, are simply the final utterances we or any one else happens to overhear the dying patient speak. They may be meaningful words or poignant reminiscences. More often they are lacking in any special significance, uttered, perhaps, without the person's knowledge that he is speaking for the last time.

Should the Family Expect Last-Minute Instructions or Revelations from the Dying Person?

If there are instructions or revelations, they will usually be issued long before the hour of death. The scene of the dying person gasping out his final requests—or revealing that terrible family secret to his astonished heirs—is mostly the stuff of melodrama.

Physiologically, in What Manner Do Most People Die? Do They Go into Convulsions? Do They Writhe and Scream?

Generally, most people die in a coma or in a state of quasi-consciousness. Usually, the actual moment of their passing is gentle and often detectable only by the hospital machinery that monitors their functions. In a large percentage of cases a person simply closes his eyes.

Does It Hurt to Die?

Apparently not. From all that we can tell, the actual moment is painless and has been described as everything from a sublime flight out of the body to a quiet, uneventful slide into oblivion. A particularly interesting description was left us by the famous American author Stephen Crane as he lay dying at the age of 29. He wrote: "When you come to the hedge that we all must go over—it isn't so bad. You feel sleepy—and you don't care. Just a little dreamy—some anxiety about which world you're really in—that's all."

Is There Any Way to Predict in Advance How a Person Will React to the Dying Process?

There are several criteria. None of them are foolproof, of course, but together they provide a relatively accurate picture.

First, how emotionally mature is the person? Those who live sensible and reasonable lives usually die sensible and reasonable deaths. It is a flagrant generalization, but probably a true one, to say that people of good character usually die with more dignity and peace than do those of bad character.

Second, how religious is the person? People with profound faith (not just habitual churchgoers or those who pay lip service to religion) tend to die in a peaceful way.

Third, what is the person's ethnic background? People from certain countries react differently to stress situations. Some let it all out. Others keep it all in.

Fourth, from what kind of ailment is the person dying? Some sicknesses are brief and relatively painless, others are slow and excruciating. The amount of pain, disfiguration, and disintegration that one experiences will naturally influence the ability to cope and adjust.

Fifth, what kind of support does the person have available? A concerned family, a sympathetic physician, a good therapist, a compassionate cleric, an involved social worker, a supportive hospital, and so on, will all be determinants in how well the patient adjusts to the terminal phase. Their attitudes will affect his attitudes. Sometimes they will *create* his attitudes.

Are Semiconscious Patients or Patients in a Coma Really Unreachable?

It is easy to suppose that patients who are unconscious or heavily sedated are non compis mentis as well, but this is not necessarily the case. Interestingly, it has been found that patients under hypnosis are sometimes able to recall entire conversations that were held over their anesthetized bodies during a hospital operation. Occasionally patients will even have *conscious* recall of what took place. The point is that though the person may *seem* utterly insensible part of his or her mind may be taking in everything that is said and done quite clearly. It is best when standing by the bedside of a nonresponsive patient to choose your words wisely, and not to discuss the person as if he or she was already in the past tense.

It Is Said that Some People Die in a State of Ecstasy. Is This So?

Yes, people occasionally seem to pass from this world in a state of euphoria that has no name. Usually, these are persons who, for whatever reason, are not under the influence of heavy narcotic medications and are no longer affected by physical pain. Some writers, such as Severin Icard, have even spoken of an *ivresse agonique*—a rapture at the point of death—suggesting that the dying person, freed now from the weight of ordinary matters, suddenly becomes privy to insights denied him or her in everyday life. The last words of Schiller ("Calmer and calmer . . . many things are growing plain and clear to me") are interesting in this respect. Hear Shakespeare's description of this experience from *Romeo and Juliet*:

> *How oft when men are at the point of death*
> *Have they been merry! which their keepers call*
> *A lightening before death.*

> (ROMEO AND JULIET, ACT V, SCENE 3)

The dying words of many well-known people attest to the fact that for some the last moment is a beatific one. A sampling might include: "Oh, relief has come" (Robert Owen); "Had I a pen and were able to write, I would describe how easy and pleasant a thing it is to die" (William Hunter); "Yes, yes, all is well" (George Crabbe); "I hope with all my heart that there will be painting in heaven" (Corot); "It's so good to get home" (William James); "Joy!" (Hannah More); "Beautiful! (Elisabeth Barrett Browning, when asked how she was feeling); "It's very beautiful over there" (Thomas A. Edison); "I'm so happy, so happy" (Gerard Manley Hopkins); "See in what peace a Christian may die" (Joseph Addison); "Happy" (Raphael); *"C'est bien"* (Andre Gide).

4

Caring for
the Dying

In What Other Useful Ways Can We Help Care for the Dying?

Family and friends should plan to spend plenty of time by the person's bedside, just being there. Encourage acquaintances to drop by for a quiet talk or a friendly drink, and if this is not possible, to phone now and then, just to check in. Be sensitive to the person's needs, and schedule your comings and goings to accommodate his best hours. Do not overtire the person, of course, and do not feel that you have to be present every moment of the day and night. Do, however, try to keep visits regular. They are about the most heartening tonic that a dying person can have.

Encourage the patient to continue doing whatever it is that gives him enjoyment. If he has hobbies, if he enjoys fine food or movies or Monday Night Football or building model airplanes, see that he is encouraged to pursue his interests. If he loses interest in them, which he very well may, do not push him, make sure they are available should he have a yen.

As much as possible, treat the dying person like a living person. Do not be overly solicitous. Let him continue to make business decisions and household decisions, to laugh and argue and kiss and feel silly and act important and cry and do all the human things that make a person feel like a person. Do not baby him too much or make him feel helpless. On the other hand, do not encourage him to overextend just so that he can prove to himself that he is as strong as he ever was—because he isn't. There is often an urge among the family of the dying person to keep things as natural and normal as possible, and this is quite right. Yet it should not be forgotten that the situation is *not* normal, not really, and that at times normalcy must be surrendered up to nature's implacable demands.

Be there when the person wants to talk. Don't force him to talk when he would rather be still. If you and the patient are having personal problems, now may be the best time to clear the air. Perhaps the help of a professional third party would be useful in this direction. Be caring, loving, and demonstrative—but *only* to the degree that the patient is comfortable with these demonstrations. The sickness of a loved one naturally brings out great emotions in others, but even such a good thing can become excessive, especially if the patient finds lavish displays of feeling embarrassing. The patient's family or support group should feed him love and compassion only at the rate at which he is able to accept it.

Some dying people spend a part of their last days in prayer and meditation. If they are so inclined, make sure that they have adequate quiet for these practices, that a member of the clergy of whatever denomination is available when wanted, that religious services can be attended if possible, and that any religious dietary or ritual customs can be practiced without impediment or embarrassment. For some people the last days are the most sacred moments of life, and impressive spiritual efforts are made at these times. In such instances it is incumbent on the person's family to offer as much support and encouragement as possible.

Dying People Do Not Have the Luxury of a Future. What Can Be Substituted?

They do have a future; it is just a shorter future. This future can be enriched, first, by substituting *short-term goals* for long-term goals, that is, day-to-day goals or week-to-week goals, such as quilting a blanket, going home for the weekend, visiting a grandchild, writing a short story, planting a garden. Most people want to leave some legacy behind them, something to be remembered by. So you might encourage them to write their autobiographies, or to amass a scrapbook of old photographs which traces the history of their family back several generations. These and other personally oriented projects have both content and meaning. Interestingly, some believe that the compelling need that dying people feel to complete such projects can sometimes literally "trick" them into living longer.

Second, the dying person can be introduced to *new goals*. For example, many chronically ill people have taken up painting or gardening or electronics or sewing or a musical instrument or the study of philosophy. They have interested themselves in community projects or in philanthropic pursuits, taken courses and started home correspondence study programs, and studied languages. Now is the time to pursue those interests which were always put off until tomorrow. The very fact that time is limited gives these interests an urgency and excitement which is normally missing from the lives of those of us who believe we will live forever.

A Person Suffering from a Chronic Disease May Be in Bed for Long Periods of Time and Suffer Extreme Boredom. What Can Be Done to Relieve the Tedium?

Keeping the person's mind occupied is the best thing, through conversation, reading, games, visits, tape-recorded books, listening to music. Television is a standby, of course, although it can eventually become as tedious as the spaces it is designed to fill. Of all the amusements and pleasures yet invented, human contact is by far the most satisfying.

If a person is at home, her regular schedule can at times be pleasantly varied by visits from friends, the pursuit of hobbies, keeping up correspondence, finishing undone tasks. Telephone conversations are a welcome relief from monotony, as is a change of scene, a daily walk (if possible), or the sight of something beautiful such as a painting or a work of nature. Children are a wonderful diversion as well, and parents should not be shy about having their little ones visit the chronically ill. The present generations, which in our time have become such strangers to death and dying, were largely made this way by their own parents, who sheltered them not only from contact with the dead but from knowledge of mortality itself. For children, visiting dying relatives is a good education as well as an excellent introduction to the concept of death. For the dying it is a wonderful diversion and a bittersweet reminiscence.

Sometimes When Family Members Take Care of a Dying Person Day In and Day Out, They Experience a Kind of Burnout.

This is something that the dying person's family must watch for carefully. Relatives and friends can work with a dying person for only so long before reaching the limits of their endurance. Just as the body becomes fatigued, so the spirit can be overexposed to the strain, worry, and anguish that nursing care demands.

In order for a person to be at her best when administering to the dying, she should learn to pace herself and to gauge her limits. If after long periods of taking care of a sick person she observes a tendency toward increasing irritation, or chronic fatigue, or depression, it means that a pause is in order. She must go one step back in order to take two steps forward. The sick person will understand; and even if he doesn't, a day off, a quick vacation to clear the head, a change of scene may still be necessary—for both your sakes.

Sometimes the Patient Will Make Others Feel Guilty If They Are Not by His Side Every Hour of the Day.

Family and friends must balance their own needs against the needs of the patient. A person cannot be everywhere at all times, and cannot be everything to everyone, no matter how hard she may try. If there are others in the picture, especially children, the family of the loved one must avoid giving in to the temptation to lose themselves entirely in the patient. Something must be held back for oneself and for one's dependents.

Sometimes it is simply a matter of telling a demanding patient that you have such-and-such a responsibility to take care of and that you cannot be at the hospital until so-and-so a time. Be direct about your reasons, spell out your time schedule as clearly as you can, and inform the person as precisely as possible when you will be returning. Sometimes all that a demanding patient really needs is reassurance that you *will* be coming back and that he will not be left alone. Very often, behind his guilt-provoking cries, there is a simple childlike terror of being abandoned.

What Are the Most Important Emotional Supports We Can Bring to a Dying Person?

They are more or less the same supports as those the living thrive on: compassion, nonjudgmentalness, patience, and an honest interest in the person's welfare, thoughts, feelings, and opinions. A willingness to listen closely to what the person says, to consider it, and to give it the credit it is due. Perseverance. Faithfulness. Sincerity. The promise that you will not run out, that you will be there to the end. In fact, it is often a helpful practice somewhere along the line to tell the patient this quite directly: that you are there for him, that you won't desert him, that he can always depend on you.

Basically, there are only two ways we can make a dying person comfortable: by assuring her physical comfort; and by assuring her psychological comfort. The first requirement is met through all those great and small things that family and medical staff do to ensure the person's organic well-being. The second is a more subtle process. It is met only by constantly recalling the fact that someday the dying person in the bed will be *you*, and that every kindness you would wish for and need then, the patient wishes for and needs now.

If a Person Is Hospitalized, Is There Any Way Her Environment Can Be Made More Comfortable?

In hospices, rooms are often furnished with the patient's own furniture and belongings. Although this is usually not possible in a standard ward hospital, it does not mean that the ambiance cannot be spruced up a bit with books, pleasant wall hangings, and pictures by the bed. A person's favorite keepsakes can be brought to the hospital to brighten the area: beloved photographs, treasured objects, even pictures for the wall. And although it has become something of a cliché, flowers and plants are a perennial brightener of spirits.

Poor menu is a common source of unhappiness among the hospitalized. So, diet permitting, the patient's support group can supply her with home-cooked food, tasty desserts, and favorite snacks. Good food will frequently do a surprisingly efficient job of picking up a person's spirits. Some people on a ward also crave privacy. Make sure that the curtain is kept drawn for such people, when they desire it, and that visitors announce themselves before barging in.

If You Are Spending Much Time with a Dying Person and He Seems Gloomy and Preoccupied, What Is the Best Method of Making Him Feel Better?

It depends. Sometimes the person does not want to be cheered up. He may be attempting to face his death squarely and to make sense of it. Cheerfulness would be inappropriate and unnecessary.

Or he may just be scared. Once more, trying to force levity is ridiculous for everyone involved.

Rather than attempting to cheer up the person, it is better to let him set the tone, and go from there. If he prefers silence, you prefer silence. If he wants to talk, to reminisce, accommodate him. Remember, too, that the dying person is the same being he was before a doctor announced that he was dying. What entertained and diverted him before will usually do so now.

Sometimes We Want to Reach Out and Physically Touch the Dying Person, but the Gesture Seems Forced and Artificial. It Feels As If by Doing This One Is Somehow Violating the Sick Person's Private Space.

You never know until you try. Do not judge this matter of physical contact on the grounds of a patient's prior behavior. When an elderly glass manufacturer was dying of lung cancer in a New York City hospital, his foremost wish was to hold the hand of anyone who happened to be near him—anyone: the nurse, his daughter, the aid, a stranger. For most of his life this man, a stiff, self-important executive type, had assiduously discouraged all physical display of feelings, especially with his family and close ones. Now at the eleventh hour, as he reached out indiscriminately to passersby, physical contact became his last link between the world of life and the world of pain. At the point of death, only the most essential things in a person survive.

Sometimes the Family and Friends of the Dying Person Don't Want to Show How They Really Feel Out of Fear of Upsetting the Person. Will It Harm the Sick Person If He Sees Others Crying or Mourning?

In the past death was always viewed as a communal event. In our time it has become an affair of division and isolation. The family, we are told, has their own special problems that must be separately treated. The patient has his difficulties, too, of course, and the doctor his, and the scholars theirs. Books are written addressing these individual participants with their individual dilemmas, as if each was an island apart. In this age of "individuality," even dying has become a field for specialization.

In fact, shared grief has always been recognized both as a method of therapy and as a means of promoting interpersonal union. To repress feelings in front of the dying person for fear that it will "upset" her is to deny everyone involved the cathartic communion that mutual grieving brings. The fact is that sometimes a person must experience the pain of a loved person to know that she herself is loved. Do not be afraid to grieve in front of others. Do not be afraid to show the person that you love her, and that you will miss her, and that her passing hurts. It may make her cry. But what's wrong with that? How much better the world might be if we all cried together. How much better is the poignant pain of tears than the estrangement of cold formality?

But Sometimes the Family's Grief Can Become Excessive. Can't This Hurt the Patient?

It is always a matter of degrees in such encounters. As in most situations, the happy medium is best. Excessive grief is a drain on others, there is no doubt, especially if the patient is feeble or in a distressed psychological condition. It therefore behooves the family and friends to keep on the good side of that fragile line dividing wholesome displays of loving emotions from intemperate overindulgence.

After a Long Period of Nursing a Patient and Expecting the Patient to Die at a Certain Time, It Sometimes Happens That the Person Gets Well Again. Then a Peculiar Thing Happens. Instead of Being Overjoyed, Those Close to the Sick Person Feel a Letdown and Even Anger That the Person Has Not Died on Schedule. Is This Common?

Yes, it is common. In fact, it is to be expected. If you have worked through your anticipatory grief, if you have lived with the supposition that the sick person will die according to a certain schedule—and if you have made great sacrifices along the way—a kind of aftershock may follow the announcement of a remission or cure. In place of happiness there is irritation and pique.

For one thing, you may be reacting to the fear that the remission is only temporary, and that soon you will have to go through it all again. You may also be timid about reestablishing the emotional relationship you had with the patient before he was sick for fear that he will become sick again and you will be hurt once more.

These are real concerns and should be taken seriously. One must realize that these negative reactions are normal and even predictable, and that in time, after the new adjustments are made, they will eventually fade.

A Dying Person Often Has Many Visitors and Becomes Easily Fatigued. How Can the Flow of Visits Best Be Monitored?

Determine times of day that are best for the patient. Also determine what is the maximum number of visitors a patient can deal with comfortably. Then inform others of these facts. It is best for the family or the patient to be direct about these matters to visitors. Polite but obvious signals can be devised. The announcement that the patient is tired is a cue that is obvious but gracious; as is an announcement that the doctor will be coming soon. Friends and visitors will certainly understand.

What Is the Best Way to Care for and Communicate with Patients Who Can No Longer Talk?

Speak directly to the patient, verbally listing the items or services that she might require: to be turned over, to eat, to use the toilet, and so on. Instruct her either to nod her head, roll her eyes, blink, or make whatever motions she is capable of making when the needed items are mentioned. Although a person's ability to communicate verbally may be destroyed, her mind is often clear. Talk with this person as you would to anyone else, and treat her as much as possible like a whole human being.

What Is the Best Way for People to Prepare Themselves to Care for Dying Patients?

If one is fortunate enough to have time to prepare in advance, there are two levels on which to proceed, the practical and the psychological. The practical entails gaining basic knowledge of nursing techniques. The psychological means preparing oneself to deal with those wrenching emotional stabs which death alone brings. Practical preparation involves a cut-and-dried program of acquiring health care training. One can get this information from books, from persons proficient in nursing skills, from courses and study, and from direct experience as a volunteer at a hospital or nursing home.

Psychological preparation is more difficult, but there are ways. In a study done by Raymond G. Carey on terminally ill patients and the factors that predict which persons will cope best with the dying (Carey, 1975, p. 84), it was determined that one of the most significant steps a person can take to prepare for death work is to deal with someone who is presently dying. "Talking frankly about death and dying may not only help the patient sort out his own feelings," writes Carey, "but also assist the other person to adjust emotionally if he in turn contracts an incurable illness."

5

The Rights
of the Patient

How Far Can a Hospital Go in Controlling a Patient's Life? What Rights, Legal and Human, Does a Patient Have in a Hospital?

It seems to many patients as though they have no rights. There is often a kind of tacit assumption on the part of the medical profession that since "the doctor knows best," the doctor has total control over every aspect of a patient's fate. Next step, by association, is that so does the nurse, orderly, lab technician, pharmacist, menu planner, and just about everyone else who happens to be associated with the hospital.

In fact, the patient does have rights, many of them. It is her body that is being attended to. It is her revenues that are paying for the service. Certainly, this entitles her to very specific considerations, some of them practical and material, some of them psychological and spiritual.

What are they? First, the patient has the right to choose her doctor. If the doctor does not meet with her satisfaction, she has the right to leave him and find another.

Second, while the doctor is ordinarily associated with a certain hospital (and thus determines to which hospital a patient will be sent), the patient has a right to leave that hospital at any time if it proves, for whatever reasons, unacceptable. (Contrary to the impression that many medical establishments impose on the patient, neither hospital nor physician has any legal mandate to keep a person resident at a particular hospital should that person wish to leave.) There are some very fine hospitals in this country and some very mediocre ones. There are also some very poor ones. It is the patient's right to pick and choose.

Third, a patient has the right to comfortable, considerate care at the hands of the hospital staff. She has the right to be advised of what is being done to her, and for her; what the purpose is of the tests that she is undergoing; the name, nature, and seriousness of the disease she is suffering from; how long she will be confined to the hospital; and what medical procedures are being used to make her better.

Simple requirements. Yet there has been so much conflict over this question of patients' rights that in the early 1970s the American Hospital Association published a pamphlet called *A Patient's Bill of Rights*. This articulate document is worth reproducing. It reads as follows:

1. "The patient has the right to considerate and respectful care."

2. "The patient has the right to obtain from his physician complete current information concerning his diagnosis, treatment, and prognosis in terms the patient can be reasonably expected to understand. When it is not medically advisable to give such information to the patient, the information should be made available to an appropriate person in his behalf. He has the right to know, by name, the physician responsible for coordinating his care."

3. "The patient has the right to obtain from his physician information necessary to give informed consent prior to the state of any procedure and/or treatment. Except in emergencies, such information for informed consent should include but not necessarily be limited to the specific pro-

cedure and/or treatment, the medically significant risks involved, and the probable duration of incapacitation. Where medically significant alternatives for care or treatment exist, or when the patient requests information concerning medical alternatives, the patient has the right to such information. The patient also has the right to know the name of the person responsible for the procedures and/or treatment. The patient has the right to refuse treatment to the extent permitted by law and to be informed of the medical consequences of his action."

4. "The patient has the right to every consideration of his privacy concerning his own medical care program. Case discussion, consultation, examination, and treatment are confidential and should be conducted discreetly. Those not directly involved in his care must have the permission of the patient to be present."

5. "The patient has the right to expect that all communications and records pertaining to his care should be treated as confidential."

6. "The patient has the right to expect that within its capacity a hospital must make reasonable response to the request of a patient for services. The hospital must provide evaluation, service, and/or referral as indicated by the urgency of the case. When medically permissible, a patient may be transferred to another facility only after he has received complete information and explanation concerning the needs for and alternatives to such a transfer. The institution to which the patient is to be transferred must first have accepted the patient for transfer."

7. "The patient has the right to obtain information as to any relationship of his hospital to other health care and educational institutions insofar as his care is concerned. The patient has the right to obtain information as to the existence of any professional relationships among individuals, by name, who are treating him."

8. "The patient has the right to be advised if the hospital

proposes to engage in or perform human experimentation affecting his care or treatment. The patient has the right to refuse to participate in such research projects."

9. "The patient has the right to expect reasonable continuity of care. He has the right to know in advance what appointment times and physicians are available and where. The patient has the right to expect that the hospital will provide a mechanism whereby he is informed by his physician or a delegate of the physician of the patient's continuing health care requirements following discharge."

10. "The patient has the right to examine and receive an explanation of his bill regardless of course of payment."

11. "The patient has the right to know what hospital rules and regulations apply to his conduct as a patient."

While this bill of patients' rights is more or less comprehensive, it should be pointed out that it represents an ideal, not a newly passed bit of legislation nor even a widely acknowledged norm, and that only the most conscientious hospitals fulfill all its stipulations.

Nonetheless, the patients' bill of rights is an excellent guideline for both doctors and patients, and can serve as a touchstone for patients to refer to—and to invoke—should they feel that their rights are being violated.

What Can a Dying Person Do If He or She Cannot Afford Proper Medical Treatment and Adequate Hospitalization?

What is often recommended when a person without adequate medical insurance is suffering from a long-term chronic disease is a technique called "spending down." What this means essentially is that the sick person slowly divests himself of all financial assets, putting them in his children's name or in the name of other close relatives. Eventually, he liquidates all his financial holdings this way and has them legally transferred to other accounts, presumably those belonging to people he knows and trusts. When divested of all assets a person then automatically becomes eligible to apply for Medicaid. Once accepted,

Medicaid will take care of those bills which the person cannot afford himself.

The government, it should be noted, has long looked at this practice of spending down with a somewhat suspicious eye and the laws establishing the time period in which the funds must be divested have frequently been changed. It is best to consult a lawyer or a tax expert on the legal requirements concerning bankruptcy laws within particular states before attempting to put this method into practice.

What If the Dying Person Is Young and Can't Qualify?

The procedure is the same for everyone. People in all age groups qualify for Medicaid.

Are Adult Children Responsible for the Medical Debts of Their Parents?

No, legally they have no financial liability. A person is responsible for medical debts when incurred by a *spouse* or a *child*, not by a parent. This is true even if all the parents' money was given to their offspring before the bill was generated.

Will a Hospital Ask for Advance Proof from a Patient That He Can Afford Treatment?

When a patient is being admitted, private hospitals will ordinarily inquire about medical insurance and about the method of payment a person plans to use.

What If a Person Has No Medical Insurance, Has No One to Sign for Him, and Can Furnish No Proof That He Will Be Able to Afford the Hospital's Fees?

If a person enters a hospital in an emergency situation, whether the hospital is city or private, he *must* be admitted no matter what his financial standing, and he must receive medical treatment. Otherwise, a person can be rejected from a private hospital if it appears that he has no means of paying the bills.

What Does the Person Do, Then, If He Cannot Qualify for Admission to a Certain Hospital?

The hospital that rejects him will usually refer him to the nearest city hospital. Here treatment is scaled to what a person can pay.

What If a Person Is Taken In by a Hospital for Emergency Treatment and the Person Cannot Pay the Bill?

As soon as the patient is out of danger, a member of the hospital staff will interview the patient concerning how she intends to pay the bill. If the patient has no plan and it appears that she has no intention of paying, the hospital will have her transferred to a city hospital.

How Will the Hospital Then Collect for the Services That Have Already Been Rendered the Patient?

Many hospitals treat the situation of nonpayment as any other business situation. They may try to put a lien on the person's income or to take him to court. In actual fact, however, in many instances hospitals do not go this far and often simply end up absorbing the costs.

Moreover, the Hill-Burton Act requires the hospital to treat a certain number of indigent patients and to assume the costs themselves. The government then reimburses them. This allowance is not very large, however, and most hospitals usually have their quotas filled by March or April.

Does a Doctor Operate in the Same Way? What If a Patient Cannot Afford a Doctor's Bills?

This is a more individual matter. There is no standard business practice here; each doctor handles the matter in his or her own way. The same thing is true regarding a patient's financial ability to pay before treatment. Some doctors ask for payment in advance, as soon as the patient enters the office or even on the phone before the visit. Others allow greater latitude during

the course of treatment. There is no set operating procedure
in this matter.

What Are Some of the Important Things a Person Should Look for When Choosing a Hospital?

As mentioned, it is often the doctor who chooses the hospital.
If this is not the case, there are a number of important factors
a person should check into before picking one particular hospital over another. Some of these factors include:

- Is the hospital a private or a city or government hospital,
  profit or nonprofit? If it is a government hospital, who qual-
  ifies for admission?

- What kinds of facilities does the hospital have? Does it have
  a blood bank? Enough operating rooms? A number of board-
  certified specialists? A staff with a good reputation? Nursing
  services with registered nurses? Adequate night nursing? Good
  dietary care? Adequate emergency services? Up-to-date
  medical equipment? An intensive care unit? Lab facilities?
  Is it clean?

- How does the hospital treat insurance claims? Does it have
  a separate office especially equipped to handle these claims?

- Is the hospital affiliated with a particular university? Is it a
  teaching hospital?

- Is it accredited by the Joint Commission on Accreditation of
  Hospitals? (This organization accredits only worthy hospitals. Its seal of approval is a strong point in any hospital's
  favor.)

- What are the fees? How are they payable? These factors
  should be researched before entering a hospital. Comparison
  shopping can and should also be practiced—hospital prices
  are by no means all the same.

- Check the size of the hospital. Big is not necessarily bad in
  this instance. A larger hospital, one with say over 150 beds,
  is often more likely than a smaller hospital to have a wide
  range of specialists and medical equipment.

What Is the Best Way to Learn This Information about a Hospital in Advance?

Talk to others who have been hospitalized in various local hospitals. You can also inspect the premises yourself. As to the technical information, a visit to the administration office or a call to the hospital administrator will be sufficient. Many hospitals are profit-making institutions. They want your business. Make sure that they deserve it.

Is a Teaching Hospital Necessarily Better?

Since doctors on the staff of a teaching hospital are teachers as well as physicians, they are normally expected to be well read and up to date on current medical practice. Nonteaching hospitals have no way of gauging whether members of their staff are continuing their education or whether they are working to remain up to date in medical developments, and in this sense teaching hospitals have the advantage.

Does Every City Have a City Hospital?

Every big city in the United States is supposed to maintain a municipal hospital. The public health setup in this country is designed so that technically, no one who needs it will go without medical treatment.

How Big a Disparity Is There between City Hospitals and Private Hospitals?

Perhaps not as big as some people think. As a rule city hospitals are large, impersonal places frequented by the poor and near-poor. Private hospitals are for those who have medical coverage at their jobs, who can afford the ever-increasing premiums on medical insurance, or who qualify for government aid. State hospitals, if they are well funded, often have much advanced technical machinery and a bigger staff than the smaller, less-well-endowed private establishments. State hospitals, as well, may have many dedicated professionals on staff who have passed up the enticements of private practice for work on a *pro bono* level. At the same time, city hospitals can be catchalls for failed physicians and for disgruntled professionals who have been unable to make it in the higher echelons. These institutions can be overcrowded and understaffed, all according to local subsidization; as a rule younger, less experienced physicians will be in charge of them. A city hospital is often a combination of the best and the worst in patient care.

At What Stage in a Dying Person's Ailment Will She Be Admitted to a Hospital?

One important thing about hospitals to bear in mind is that they are obliged to keep a patient only as long as the patient is in an *acute condition of sickness or distress*. The moment the patient's condition is stabilized, he or she will be sent home. Such is the case even if the person is suffering from a terminal disease.

One must not, therefore, assume that because a person is chronically ill he or she is automatically a candidate for hospitalization. Current bed utilization laws define a hospital as an acute care facility, not a chronic facility. In some states, whenever a patient stays hospitalized beyond a certain number of days, the doctor must fill out a form explaining why the patient is still there. If a good reason is not forthcoming the patient will be asked to leave. Nor are these laws totally arbitrary. In theory, at least, they work for the protection of the patient as much as for the efficiency of the hospital. What the laws really say, in effect, is that the hospital has no right to detain a patient for an extended period of time, charging him or her royally in the process, unless the person is in active need of the kind of specific help which the hospital can afford.

If a Person Is Labeled as Chronic and Sent Home, at Which Point Can He Return to the Hospital?

Only when his condition again becomes acute.

If a Person Who Is Chronically Ill Is at Home, Will His Insurance Cover Medical Costs?

Only with the most expensive policies. The fact is that sick persons receive the best coverage when they are in institutions. Our government and insurance systems are both acute-care-oriented and institution-oriented. Policies that cover a person in a hospital usually do not cover him at home. This is why such a large percentage of people today choose to die in hospitals.

The Problem Seems to Be That Some Patients Come to Feel That the Hospital Was Created Not for the Good of the Patients But for the Good of the Medical Staff—That in a Hospital Patients Are Expected to Accommodate Themselves to the Existing Medical Technology Rather Than Vice Versa and to Die in a Style That Is Most Efficient and Handy for the Staff.

Hospitals are here to stay, of this there is no doubt; as David Dempsey remarks in his book *The Way We Die*: "In a highly developed country, people are expected to die at a level that is appropriate to the prevailing technology" (Dempsey, 1977, p. 69). While the critics rail and the patients languish, however, most hospitals continue to make administrative efficiency their first priority, even though most medical professionals would openly admit that the emphasis on expediency in hospitals has already caused facilities for the dying to become woefully impersonal. The cost is felt on all levels, and we are all the losers. (No doubt the quality of treatment for the dying would instantly improve if the professionals responsible for terminal care could see in the faces of their patients the image of their own faces tomorrow.) All that can be done at this point is to continue to call attention to the deficient state of terminal care in most hospitals, attempt to upgrade it, and concentrate on the development of high-quality alternatives such as the hospice movement or home-care programs.

We might add, however, that in many situations, the emotional gap between doctor and patient that exists in the hospital is not directly the fault of the doctor but of the system itself. Hospitals are overcrowded. Administrative personnel often, and quite unabashedly, view the institution they work for as a money-making operation only, like a supermarket or department store, and pressures can be brought to bear on members of the medical staff who do not agree. The staff works long hours and is continually in demand by a never-ending overflow of ailing patients. "From the patient's point of view," remarks a doctor at a New York City hospital, "it looks as if the doctors don't care. From our standpoint we have to run here, then run there, take care of one sick person after the next, each one of whom thinks he is the *only* patient in the world and who requires human administering which we simply do not have the time or resources to take care of. I wish we did. I feel badly that I can't hold each of my patient's hands. But I can't, I just can't. The patients don't understand and think I'm a bad guy. If they only saw things from our side and saw how hard we worked they might reconsider their position."

Both patient and doctor are caught up in a system which, like Topsy, "just growed." No one is quite sure how it all got this way, how the hospital system became so unkind, how the rift between the curers and the cured became so profound. Yet here it is. And this is what we have to work with.

When an Individual Is Thought to Be Dying, Do the Health Care Personnel in Charge Have Any Specific Method of Projecting How Long the Dying Process Will Take?

Yes. They often devise what is called a "dying trajectory."

How Does It Work?

When a terminal patient is admitted to a hospital, the staff gathers all medical data available on that patient—how old he is, how long he has been sick, what disease he suffers from, his past medical history, and so on—and maps out a life-expectancy projection. This projection plots out, in the estimation of the professional, not only how long that person has to live, but the various stages of remission and temporary recovery the person may be likely to undergo.

Do All Doctors Working with Terminal Cases Use This Method?

Not all, but many.

What Is the Purpose of These Trajectories?

To give the health care personnel a perspective on the patient's particular situation. It can, for instance, help the professional assess:

- Approximately how many days, weeks, or months a patient will remain in the hospital

- What information must be passed on to relatives concerning the patient's chances of recovery; the various stages the patient will likely pass through during his disease; what to expect in terms of physical changes in the patient; and so on

- Whether hospital care is best in this particular case or whether a patient should be released to die at home

- What kind of specific care the patient should receive from the staff and how the requirements for this care should change as the patient's condition alters

Is the Trajectory Fixed or Does It Change As the Situation Changes?

To have any real value a dying trajectory must be flexible, which means that it must continually be updated as new changes occur in the patient's condition. There are periods during a patient's incapacitation, moreover, where it is simply impossible to assess any kind of trajectory at all, and where predictions of life expectancy or, for that matter, recovery, must be postponed.

Can the Patient See the Trajectory upon Request?

Not usually. Assuming that the patient knows that he or she is a terminal case, and assuming the patient would want to see it—many do not—such information is usually classified and obtainable only means of a prodigious struggle with both hospital and administrative staff. Moreover, the trajectory is commonly not an official document at all but a kind of verbal assessment made by the professionals in charge.

Does a Patient Have the Legal Right to Refuse Lifesaving Medical Treatment?

This question enters a truly murky area of the law. For many years suicide was a crime technically punishable by trial and imprisonment. In some states this is no longer the case, and a person may attempt to take his life without worrying about prosecution should he fail. Again, though, the law is garbled on this point, perhaps understandably, and so it is when the same question is brought before the dock of medical ethics. Can a person commit technical suicide by refusing life-sustaining help? Can a medical professional be a legal partner to such an act?

Usually yes, but only sometimes. Not always. It depends. For one thing, what of the doctor? Is he willing to take the chance? What means will he use to carry out the patient's request? What repercussions might occur should he be discovered? How will he feel about acquiescing to a patient's death when he has sworn an oath to preserve life? What if the patient wants to die but her family objects? What if she changes her mind just at the point when turning back is impossible? What if, what if? Also, the staff: Health professionals are notoriously concerned with lawsuits, if not from the patient, then from the family. Conservative behavior is the name of the game. A lot will depend on local and state laws covering such matters.

Nonetheless, many physicians will acquiesce to a suffering patient's demands when that patient begs for the relief of death or when the patient makes it clear that an ONTR (order not to resuscitate) should be put into effect should she go into a coma. The doctor may give glucose in the place of medication; he may withhold medication when medication is needed; he may rule against life-support machinery. It depends on many variables. It is, and never can be, a cut-and-dried question.

Can't a Terminally Ill Person Make It Known Ahead of Time That She Does Not Wish to Be Kept Alive after a Certain Point? Isn't This One of the Patient's Basic Rights?

Many think so although again the matter is not always impeccably clear, and in some states there are now laws allowing what is known as a "living will." This is a legal document in which it is stated by the patient that should her condition be judged "irreversible" or "hopeless" by a competent physician (or by an optimal-care committee of a hospital), and should she no longer be mentally capable of making the decision herself, "heroic" means should *not* be used to prolong her life. Such a document protects both the hospital and the physician if life support is withheld. As of 1983, forty-two states had laws authorizing the living will.

You Say This Issue Is Not Always Clear? Why Not?

Because of many contingent possibilities. For instance, a patient may have drawn up her living will when in a state of deep depression. Later, when the depression passes, it is possible that she may view the situation in a different light, although it may now be too late to request heroic methods. Another patient may reject lifesaving means out of fear that these methods will be painful, which as a rule they are not, or from fear that costs will be too burdensome on her family. Indeed, some patients view their living will as a kind of voluntary self-sacrifice. They opt to die quickly rather than impose on their families the kind of monetary responsibilities that prolonged medical care requires.

If a Person Does Not Make Out a Living Will or If That Person Does Not Request That Life-Sustaining Technology Be Omitted, Will Hospitals Invariably Keep the Person Alive?

The primary job of the medical profession is to save lives. Whether or not this attitude is always appropriate—especially in the instance where a patient's cognitive apparatus has been damaged and machine resuscitation does nothing but maintain life signs—the fact is that the medical staff of most hospitals will, in the case of a terminal patient who is failing, energetically marshal all their technological wherewithal and knowledge to keep the patient breathing. This technique, called "coding" in hospitals, requires that the most advanced technology be put at the disposal of the staff to maintain a heartbeat. The methods of resuscitation differ for different conditions, of course. Machines that literally breathe for the dying patient are called into action when respiration has ceased; the failed heart may be stimulated with electric shocks; intravenous injections feed the patient who can no longer feed herself; continuous blood transfusions maintain the electrolyte balance throughout the body; and so on.

The point is that, yes, in most cases the medical staff will take all possible measures to keep a patient alive. As far as the staff is concerned, it is their duty to do so. However, as mentioned, if the patient requests ahead of time that such means be withheld, or if the patient has a heart-to-heart discussion with the physician, and spells out his wishes, these wishes will usually be honored.

What If the Patient Is Mentally Retarded or for Some Reason Is Not Capable of Making the Decision to Withhold Heroic Means?

Then the patient's family or guardian makes the decision for him. In the event that family members are not available, the decision is sometimes made by a committee of hospital personnel.

What Conditions Must Be Met in Order for Those in Charge to Rule against Heroic Life-Sustaining Procedures?

At one time a person was considered legally dead when his heart stopped beating and his lungs ceased breathing. Today, both heart and lung functions can be maintained indefinitely by means of medical machinery, and thus the definition of legal death has shifted. The standard is now "brain death," whereby the cerebral cortex stops functioning and a person's consciousness ceases, together with all ability to think, feel, reason, and otherwise behave in a sentient human manner. If the brain continues to operate, it does so only on the most primitive somatic level.

Does a Patient Have the Right to Die at Home If He Wishes?

Of course, provided that his family or caretakers are willing to take on the job of caring for him there.

Must a Patient Submit to Being Part of Medical Research or Experiment If Asked?

By no means. This point is made in the Patient's Bill of Rights and should be stressed. The fact is that under no circumstances does a patient have an *obligation*, either moral or legal, to participate in research testing, teaching programs, or medical experimentation. Participation in such activities should be done on a purely voluntary basis.

In Some University Hospitals Research Is Practiced on the Patient as a Matter of Course. The Patient Is Either Not Informed of the Fact That He Is Being Used in an Experiment, or He Is Made to Think That He Has No Choice in the Matter.

It is the patient's right both to be informed that he is part of a research activity and to insist that such means not be practiced upon him if he so desires.

What about a Patient Who Is Asked to Participate in Teaching Demonstrations for Medical Students and Interns? Can a Patient Decline in This Instance Also?

It is the same thing. The patient can refuse to be part of a hospital's teaching program if he so chooses.

Can't the Medical Staff Bring Pressures to Bear If the Person Refuses?

This is unethical practice and should not be tolerated. Occasionally, a physician will imply (if not state) that a patient is being selfish by not participating in a particular research program, that he is hindering the progress of science, denying others a chance for a cure, and so on. This may be true and it may not. In either case it is beside the point. The dying person is at liberty to accept or reject any kind of medical treatment, and he has the right to do this without being judged.

On the other hand, many patients do feel that participating in teaching programs or serving as a voluntary subject for a new medical technique is both a hopeful opportunity and an interesting one. If the person chooses to be part of such a program, he has the following rights:

1. To be informed of the risks involved

2. To have the precise nature of the treatment described to him beforehand

3. To drop out of the program should he feel that either his physical or emotional health is being violated

---

What If a Doctor Recommends Surgery for a Dying Person? What Is the Best Way of Knowing If It Is the Wisest Choice?

First, get a second opinion and if necessary, a third. Many health care insurance policies will fully cover the costs of second opinions, as it may save them from the more expensive costs of an operation. Look into it. Find out if there are any alternative means of treatment and if so, what they entail.

Equally important, find out just what such an operation will do for you. Will it prolong life? By how long? What percentage of others have been helped by similar operations? Has their life been extended, and if it has, what side effects have they had to live with as a result of the operation? What is the expected recovery time from the operation?

Where will the operation take place? How often has the surgeon performed this particular surgery? How much success has he personally had with this operation? What kind of coverage will your insurance provide? What will happen to you if you decide not to have the operation?

Some other points to note: Doctors who are part of prepaid health groups generally recommend surgery less frequently than doctors in private practice. Local medical societies will often recommend qualified doctors who specialize in giving opinions on whether operations are necessary. By some estimates 60 percent of surgery in this country is unnecessary.

Sometimes It Seems That Doctors Maintain a Brusque, Off-handed Attitude in Situations That Call for a More Sensitive Response.

A cold, rushed, preoccupied bedside manner is thought by many doctors to be synonymous with medical efficiency. The doctor is, after all, a busy person. The dictates of the clinical method demand that the doctor not allow personal feelings to mix with professional judgments. Besides, he has weighty thoughts on his mind, a heavy schedule. Certainly he cannot be expected to waste precious minutes passing the time of day. This, at least, is the way that many doctors view the situation.

The patient, at the same time, becomes a willing partner to this game and condones the doctor's behavior on the grounds that it is part of the doctor's professional "rights." "As long as he cures me," one woman remarked, "it doesn't matter whether or not he's nice to me."

The reality is that a patient's life *is* to a large degree in the hands of the doctor, and most of us know better than to bite the hand that cures us. Couple this concern with the fact that the profession of medicine is highly glamorized in our society; that many people, albeit on an entirely unconscious level, attribute paranormal powers of skill and perception to physicians; and as if all this were not enough, that doctors are awarded a lofty rank in society's money-status pecking order. Consider all this and it becomes little wonder that the physician is given more benefit of the doubt in his relationship with the patient than is given by any other employer to any other employee in any other adult interaction we know of.

What Can a Patient Do in This Situation, When a Doctor Acts in a Cold, Uninterested Manner?

Either the patient, or the patient's family if the patient is not able, can discuss the matter directly with the physician. It should never be forgotten that the physician is *hired*. He is on salary to you, the patient. As a result he has certain mandatory obligations to you, the patient—among these, plain, ordinary politeness.

Sometimes It Is Very Difficult to Confront a Doctor Directly.

In some cases patients have written letters to their doctors, putting down on paper what they could not bring themselves to say face to face. In extreme cases, written complaints can be addressed to the hospital administration, spelling out in plain terms the violations the patient feels she has been subjected to.

Who Else Can Hospitalized Patients Turn to When They Need Help, or When They Are Having Difficulties with the Doctors or the Staff?

Hospital social workers are useful in this instance, both as sympathetic listeners and as trained go-betweens. In some hospitals special employees known as "patient advocates" are kept on staff to take care of a patient's special interests, and if necessary to represent their patients' needs to doctors and staff. Sympathetic nurses can be asked to transfer messages of complaint tactfully to doctors, although this can sometimes backfire in the face of all parties involved. Indeed, if a relationship with a doctor is problematic, it may be best simply to bite the bullet and face the doctor directly. Most doctors are harried, overburdened individuals and often they are inattentive to their patients' needs through fatigue rather than unconcern. Most will lend a sympathetic ear to a patient's complaints, and many will make an earnest attempt to mend their ways.

Could You Say More about the Social Worker and about the Role She Plays with the Dying Person?

The social worker deals with both the patient and the patient's family. Her role is to lighten the emotional and logistical burden of each. A social worker may, for example, counsel a family in how best to speak to the patient concerning his sickness, or how to deal with their grief in the face of the situation. She may give advice on practical issues such as a family's financial situation, discharge planning, or the practicalities of nursing the patient at home.

For the patient, the social worker is there to help with the social, emotional, and psychological problems that arise. Sometimes the social worker will act as interface between the medical staff and the patient, explaining to the patient in plain, understandable terms what the doctor has said. She may help the patient thread her way through the bureaucratic and administrative snarls that arise in large hospitals. She can also serve as a kind of central clearinghouse for useful information, providing referral services to both the patient and his family.

If a Patient Does Not Get Along with a Particular Nurse or Health Professional, Does He Have the Right to Request That the Nurse Be Transferred?

Ordinarily not. As a rule, the nurse is assigned to a floor on a regular basis, and it would cause too much administrative trouble to have her reassigned, especially on the grounds of a single complaint (and assuming that the complaint is legitimate). Usually, in the case of personality conflicts between patient and staff, the patient is reassigned to another room or to a different ward.

What Can Be Done If the Medical Staff Ignores a Patient?

Nothing can be done to force a doctor or a nurse to become personally involved with a patient. The family or guardian of the patient can, however, make certain that the patient's physical needs are administered to. If there are indications that these have been neglected—in the last days, when patients are unconscious or helpless, the staff will sometimes become lax in this department—the problem should be discussed with those in charge. If no improvements are forthcoming, the matter should immediately be referred to administration personnel.

Is It Helpful for a Dying Patient to Be Moved to a Quiet, Isolated Part of the Hospital? Isn't the Silence Helpful?

Not always. Statistically, patients in isolation die sooner. This is a fact that has often been noted and frequently remarked on by many professional observers.

Although patients may be paying high prices for private quarters, rooms located in remote areas of the hospital away from the rank and file often tend to be neglected by the staff and in some cases receive poorer service as well. If the patient desires isolation, this is, of course, another matter. Otherwise, keeping dying persons near other patients generally assures them of more attention.

Don't Noisy, Overly Active Hospital Environments Tend to Shorten a Patient's Life?

Not necessarily. Studies have indicated that hospitals which are active, loud, heavily visited, and which are filled with many patients, noisy carts in the hall, blaring television sets in the rooms, and so on, have lower mortality rates than those of extremely quiet hospitals with thick carpeting on the floor and a hush-hush atmosphere in the private rooms (Brantner, 1971, p. 23). Although in some ways a boisterous environment may prove obnoxious to a patient, the very activity and energy of it all may also serve as a tonic, a tie to the activity of life.

Do Members of the Medical Staff Go through Any Personal Reactions of Their Own When a Patient Dies?

Although it may not be apparent, both doctors and nurses frequently suffer negative reactions to the deaths of patients, sometimes quite serious ones. In fact, it is often the very experience of going through such encounters time and again that makes professionals reluctant to spend time with the dying.

Mostly this reaction takes the form of depression. Those who have just lost a favored patient may, for example, become lethargic on the job and go through anguished periods of self-doubt concerning their competency as professionals. During these difficult times professionals need all the help they can get—but often help is far from hand. Because there are always more patients dying out there, more buzzers ringing in the night, a professional has no time to disengage from the process for a while, no time to stake out a moment of psychic breathing room. The rate of breakdown among health care professionals is high.

This is why to many people it seems that doctors are eternally on vacation, ever off playing tennis or golf when they are most in demand. Among doctors, however, especially those who work in fields such as cardiology, oncology, and neurology, where most efforts are spent prolonging life rather than curing disease, it is recognized that without such relief they would soon become candidates for their own medicines.

What Is the Best Way to Choose a Doctor?

First, do you like him or her personally? This is important. Second, ask around. Others' experience in this matter counts for a lot. Third, once you have several possible candidates in mind learn the particulars. With what hospitals are they affiliated? (Remember, this is the hospital that you will probably be entering whenever hospitalization is necessary.) What are their comparative fees? Their office hours? Their medical credentials? Will they make house calls in an emergency? How easily can they be reached in times of crisis? Are they located near enough to your home to make visits practical? Are they set up to do basic lab tests in their offices? Are their waiting rooms pleasant and uncrowded? Do you enjoy dealing with their staff?

When visiting the doctor in person, decide how much you like the person's bedside manner? Is he rushed and preoccupied? Does he seem concerned? Does he answer your questions directly and without too much technical jargon? Do you feel that he is competent?

You Mentioned Previously That Dying People Go through Certain Stages Before They Die, Whatever These Stages Happen to Be. Does the Staff Also Go through Stages When a Patient Is Dying?

Sometimes, but of course on a much less intense level. Denial, as we have seen, is common. So is depression, especially immediately after a patient has died. When a staff member becomes attached to a particular person, he or she may indulge in forms of bargaining, sometimes with the patient herself. (A nurse who had become particularly fond of a young mother dying of abdominal cancer would, only half jokingly, inform the woman every day that if she recovered from this one she, the nurse, would personally see to it that the young mother was driven home in a chauffeur-driven Cadillac. This bit of business became a running joke between the nurse and patient for several months.)

What Is an Iatrogenic Disease?

This is a disease caused in some way by the hospital staff or by the attending physician. It is a "medically induced disease." Iatrogenic ailments can result for a number of different reasons. A patient may be treated for the wrong disease, with disastrous consequences. He or she may be given an incorrect and sometimes harmful drug. The scalpel may slip during an operation. A person may become addicted to morphine. A patient may be contaminated with a contagious disease.

Are Iatrogenic Diseases Common?

More common than most people know, but less common than avid critics of the medical community would have us believe.

What Services Should a Dying Patient Reasonably Expect from His Doctor?

He can expect the doctor to be honest, concerned, confident but not smug, composed but not indifferent, available when needed and sometimes when not, medically competent, and personally sympathetic. A good doctor should attempt to cause as little pain to her patient as possible—on all levels. She should encourage the patient to speak frankly of his hesitations and concerns, and should help him adjust psychologically as well as physically to his disease. A good doctor should pay attention to a patient's small problems as well as his large ones and should never allow small complaints to turn into major ones.

A good doctor should view her profession as both a fixed science and an exercise in compassionate intuition; as Florence Nightingale once noted, medicine "is a work which makes either angels of men or devils." Although a patient has no right to assume that money is of no concern to the doctor, the patient *does* have the right to assume that monetary profit is less important to the doctor than commitment to service.

A good doctor, in the words of the famous British physician, William Osler, should possess "presence of mind, clearness of judgment in moments of grave peril. . . . The physician who has the misfortune to be without it [imperturbability], who betrays indecision and worry and who shows that he is flustered and flurried . . . loses rapidly the confidence of his patients." "As I understand it," remarked Sir Hugh Cairns, "a good doctor is one who is shrewd in diagnosis and wise in treatment; but, more than that, he is a person who never spares himself in the interest of his patients; and in addition he is a man who studies the patient not ony as a case but also as an individual . . . who studies the patient's personality as well as his disease."

What, in Turn, Should a Doctor Expect from His Patient?

First, the doctor deserves cooperation and a patient's willingness to follow directions. Generally speaking, he also deserves the benefit of the doubt—until experience dictates otherwise.

A patient should make every attempt to refrain from thinking of his doctor as infallible or magical. Although it is true that medicine affords the physician a chance to study human behavior from inside and out, and that the patient's weaknesses and strengths are usually laid bare before their examiner, not every physician makes use of these opportunities as a learning experience, and lofty powers of sensitivity should not be assumed on the part of the doctor until they become apparent.

Challenging a doctor or quarreling with his methods, especially if one's quarrel is based on supposition rather than medical knowledge, is a practice that is more likely to bring alienation than improvement. ("A foolish patient," says the proverb, "will be treated like a fool.") As well, the patient should never lie concerning symptoms or changes in a physical condition, even if the changes are frightening or embarrassing. The patient owes the doctor honesty, as much as the doctor owes it to the patient in return.

Further, it is the patient's obligation to be punctual for visits, to call well in advance if appointments must be canceled, and to pay bills as regularly as possible. Just as cheerfulness, humor, thoughtfulness, and sympathetic concern are qualities that patients appreciate in a doctor, so a doctor values the same back. Finally, it is best to remember that the doctor is just another human being, often a harried, overworked one, and that nine times out of ten he is trying to do his best in the way he best knows how.

6
How Children
View Death

Most of What Has Been Said So Far concerning Care for the Dying Pertains to Patients of Any Age. What, in Particular, Can Be Done to Provide Comfort and Care for Dying *Children*?

The question of death and children is a broad one and must be broken down into several categories:

1. How does a physically healthy child perceive death? When and how are the child's attitudes toward death formed?

2. How does a child deal with the death of other people, especially of loved ones?

3. How does a fatally ill child perceive his own imminent death? How can other people help him to cope with it?

4. How do family members deal with this most difficult of human trials? How can they be helped?

Michael Simpson (Simpson, 1979, p. 170) talks about the special time when as a child each of us "loses our immortality."

Perhaps it happens when we first learn that there is no Santa Claus. Or when a much loved pet is suddenly annihilated on the highway. "Generally, we don't recall when we lost our immortality (unlike the loss of our virginity, although that's a less significant change)," Simpson writes. "It is a more profound loss of innocence, though more commonly it occurs gradually. Often, it's related to the death of another, when one perceives oneself as in line for the same mortal inheritance."

In the following sections we delve into this multifaceted question of the child's perception of death. Its significance is not only of interest to parents and children but to everyone, for the lessons about life and death impressed upon each of us while young influence the values we live by when middle-aged and old.

The first matter of concern is the way in which normal, unthreatened children visualize their own mortality.

What Do Most Healthy Children Imagine Death to Be Like?

The way a child sees death is determined largely by his or her age in the childhood cycle. Those in infancy, early childhood, middle childhood, and late childhood all have a profoundly different view of what death means and how it works. Over the past fifty years a great deal of research has been done on this subject by child psychologists, and while there are no unimpeachable certainties, the outlines are gradually becoming understood.

Perhaps the most significant study done on children's death awareness was carried out in 1948 by a Hungarian psychologist, Maria Nagy (Nagy, 1948). Working with nearly 400 children from the ages of 4 to 10 in postwar Budapest, Nagy armed her young subjects with paints, paper, and pen, and encouraged them to draw pictures of death and to make up stories about their creations.

One of the results of these tests, and perhaps the most important contribution made by Nagy, was to demonstrate that children are by no means blissfully unaware of death, as is often supposed, and that death is very much a part of their waking and sleeping consciousness. The way in which it is *integrated* into the consciousness of children at different ages is where the differences lie.

Very young children, claims Nagy, between the years of 3 and 5, perceive death as a transition or a journey, although what kind of journey they are not sure. The dead are in some sense "less alive" than ordinary people, but they are not entirely vanished either. Speaking to a child concerning a body in the grave, Nagy records the following conversation (Nagy, "The Child's View of Death," in Feifel, 1959, p. 82):

ADULT: What happens there under the earth?

CHILD: He cries because he is dead.

ADULT: Because he is afraid for himself.

CHILD: A dead person is just as if he were asleep. Sleeps in the ground too.

ADULT: How do you know whether someone is asleep or dead?

CHILD: I know if they go to bed at night and don't open their eyes. If somebody goes to bed and doesn't get up, he's dead or ill.

ADULT: Will he ever wake up?

CHILD: Never. A dead person only knows if somebody goes out to a grave or something. He feels that somebody is there, or is talking.

ADULT: Are you certain? You're not mistaken?

CHILD: I don't think so. At funerals you're not allowed to sing, just talk, because otherwise the dead person couldn't sleep peacefully. A dead person feels it if you put something on the grave.

ADULT: What is it he feels then?

CHILD: He feels that the flowers are put on his grave. The water touches the sand. Slowly, slowly, he hears everything.

When a person dies, in the mind of a very young child, the person simply goes away. The child makes little distinction between his father leaving the room or his father leaving this world—departure is death, and vice versa. Contradictorily, this death-absence equation, no matter how feelingly experienced

(one has only to watch a small child on the playground screaming for a missing mother to know how intense this reaction can
be) is perceived not so much as termination but as interruption.
Death as an irresistible finality is not yet fathomed.

Thus, in the mind of a small child, the dead return without
contradiction, perishing and resurrecting in the manner of plastic cowboys or demons in an arcade game. Death is real, but it
is also impermanent, really a kind of sleep, and in fact the two
are viewed by very young children as being almost identical:
You die for a while, then you wake for a while. Then you die
again. For a while.

From ages 5 to 9 the child's view of death matures considerably. Now death is understood to be final, but final for others,
not for oneself. The child alone among all human beings will
escape this fate.

It is not unusual to overhear 7- or 8-year-olds bragging about
their plans to live for a hundred years—which from a child's
perspective is forever—or declaring that by the time they have
grown up, science will have "conquered" old age. The child
starts to recognize beginnings and ends, but it is a conditional
recognition, one that the child believes does not pertain to his
own destiny. "Everybody else will probably die," he says to himself, "but I'll be the one to make it through somehow."

Another fascinating aspect of the older child's view is that
death is now thought of as a kind of quasi-mythological *being*,
not so much an experience as an animistic presence. Ghost
stories become especially popular, as do horror movies and all
the media titillations that portray extermination in personified
terms. Death may be envisioned as a space invader, or a ghoul,
a kidnapper, a crook, any sinister shadow figure that hints at
personal destruction. This figure is neither infallible nor omniscient, and only the stupid child allows himself to be snared.
For as in fairy stories and myth, death can be bargained with
by a clever wayfarer, or outwitted, bribed, even run away from,
and at times even killed. Death himself is mortal.

Finally, there is the last stage, from the ninth year upward
to that uncertain cutoff age around 12 or 13 when the older
child becomes the early adolescent. At this stage an accom-

modation is reached with the inevitable. Death is perceived as universal—everyone dies, including myself; irreversible—time moves ever onward, and only in one direction; and internal—death is not done to me from the outside by some external force but happens within me through a biological process.

It Seems That Certain of the Primitive Ways in Which Children View Death, Such as Personifying Death or Bargaining with It, Can Be Observed in Adult Behavior As Well.

And also among native tribesmen, in remote traditional cultures, and in religion itself (death as an entity that "calls" for a person at the appointed time is a theme found in all religions; "bargaining" with God through prayer is an accepted spiritual practice). Indeed, the relationship between mythology, dreams, and a child's view of the world has often been noted, and ironically, much of what comes organically to children concerning the facts of life and death must later be interpreted via the less natural efforts of psychology and literature. Death is a great mystery, and no one knows whose vision of it is ultimately correct. The child is father to the man.

Is There Any Evidence That Very Young Children, Say Those 6 Months to a Year Old, Are Aware of Death?

Not of death per se but of disappearance. The infant game of peekaboo is an education as well as a game (the name itself is derived from an old English word meaning "dead or alive"). It introduces the concept that things change, that they come, and more important, that they go. The child understands this principle and enjoys it, along with games of a similar kind.

What Are Some of the Other Ways in Which Children View Death?

In a study carried out half a century ago on seventy-six children ranging in age from 5 to 15 (Schilder and Wechsler, 1934), a list of basic childhood attitudes toward death was established. Although certain of Schilder and Wechsler's conclusions have been debated and others seem a bit culturally dated, the list is more or less a representative one:

1. "Children deal with death in an utterly matter-of-fact and realistic way."

2. "They exhibit skepticism concerning the unobservables."

3. "They often accept conventional definitions."

4. "They often remain insensitive to contradiction between convention and observation."

5. "They exhibit naiveté in solving problems."

6. "They regard death as a deprivation."

7. "They believe that the devil punishes orally by withdrawing food or devouring the dead."

8. "They do not believe in their own death."

9. "To very young children, death seems to be a reversible fact."

10. "They believe that death may result from disease."

11. "They have a tendency toward undue generalization of limited knowledge."

12. "They believe in death by overeating, death resulting from violence, death resulting from violence of God."

13. "Fear of death is rare."

14. "They often fail to understand the meaning of death but base their attitudes on the actions of adults."

15. "They may exhibit suicidal ideas."

16. "They are always ready to believe in the death of others."

17. "They are ready to kill."

18. "The tendency to kill may come out only in play."

19. "The degree of preoccupation of children with violence and death can be seen by the way in which they react to ghost pictures."

20. "God appears as a stage magician, controlling ghosts and death."

21. "Appearance and reality are not sharply differentiated."

22. "They exhibit the urge to pass moral judgments on every person and picture."

23. "Their professed morality is utilitarian, since children fear punishment."

24. "Religious morality enters relatively rarely into their attitude toward death."

Do Children Fear Death As Profoundly As Adults Do?

Children fear death *differently* from adults, more obliquely and in a metaphoric way. Since, for example, it is difficult for most children to accept the fact that they, this particular ego, will one day disappear, they project their death fears onto other persons or things. Fear of mommy dying or of a favorite dog getting hit by a car is more real to a child than fear of her own death.

Death is experienced primarily through figurative perception. A child fears a mask on the wall or a villain in a movie. Symbolically—and, of course, unconsciously—the mask and villain are a reminder of mortality. The child is struggling to understand death and in the process may come up with the most irrational notions, believing, for example, that because grandmother's dead body was put into a station wagon for transfer to the funeral home, station wagons kill people.

Death fear can be transferred to unrelated objects and may remain embedded there, sometimes even into adulthood. Rarely, however, does fear manifest directly in a child's conversation; that is, rarely does a child speak openly about being afraid to die. Whatever reference he may make to the subject is narrative, elliptic, and cast in the third-person singular.

Do Children Think Much about Death?

The answer is more or less the same as above. They do, but in indirect rather than literal terms. Note how common the theme of death is in children's games. Space beings, war, cars, even amusements like house and school are filled with urgent imagery leading to slaughter. Always, though, there is the mercy of resurrection running parallel to the carnage: soldiers are blown to bits, then pop up to fight the next round; dolls die of tragic diseases, then rise from their deathbeds.

Death thoughts come up for children in songs, in nursery rhymes, in prayers. "Now I Lay Me Down to Sleep" has been both a solace and a terror to children for generations. Fairy stories are filled with death-dealing imagery, and, as any parent knows, it is the menace more than the happy ending that keeps the child's attention.

Death is therefore very much on the minds of children. They know that it is something serious and disturbing. But since they do not, and perhaps cannot, comprehend fully that it is *they* who will die, their relationship with this mysterious something is impersonal and symbolic.

But Many Children Today See Death All the Time in Movies and on Television.

Modern children are literally bombarded with death, on television especially, and in the movies, in disaster stories on the news and in the newspapers, on billboards, even among the more death-oriented of the rock singing groups, and especially in the ever-present threat of collective annihilation via nuclear, military, or ecological apocalypse. In fact, next to sex, there is probably no subject to which children, and for that matter, *everyone*, is exposed more frequently.

But exposed, strangely enough, in a vicarious way. Unlike children of say, a hundred years ago who frequently experienced the early demise of a sibling or who witnessed a grandparent dying at home, almost no modern child has ever actually seen a dead body and few have known anyone who has passed away. This overexposure to the imagery of death and underexposure to the palpable reality of it—coupled, it might be added, with a kind of glorification of the morbid side of dying—produces a picture of death in the modern child's eye that is bizarre and fictitious. To this already contorted image then add the modern phobia against discussing dying with children or even admitting its existence, and the matter becomes ludicrous out of all proportion.

The modern child has, therefore, not only to struggle with the very difficult concept of death itself but with the peculiar overlay of contradictions and lies fostered by the modern phobia of growing old. In the end one of the most profound double-bind messages of our time emerges for the child: (1) Death is a terrible thing that threatens you everywhere, all the time; (2) death does not exist, don't talk about it, don't even bring it up.

So a Child's Outlook on Death Is Largely Conditioned by the Attitudes of the Parents and by the Attitudes of the Adult World at Large?

The outlook that children have toward death is formed in the way *all* their outlooks are formed, by imitation and assimilation of parental values. In our civilization death is a taboo. So children, along with the ordinary developmental phases they would normally pass through concerning death, have our culture's own peculiar blend of terror, denial, and glorification grafted onto the process. This process then perpetuates itself down the generations and ends up becoming a norm.

Statistically Speaking, Is It True That Most Parents in Our Society Avoid Speaking Directly about Death to Their Children?

To varying extents it is, yes. In a survey taken of high school seniors (Wass, 1976), it was asked: "When you were a child how was death handled in your family?" Thirty-nine percent of subjects told the researchers that no one *ever* mentioned death in their house. Twenty-six percent said that death was mentioned only upon occasion, and then in a cursory way.

Assuming That a Parent Wants to Educate Children Properly concerning Death, What Is the Best Way of Going about it?

There are general guidelines which may be followed when speaking to children about death and which provide a kind of base of operations in this delicate matter.

1. The first, and in a way perhaps the most important of these guidelines is not to set oneself up as the omniscient last word on the subject. The child should be made to understand that death is a great mystery, the greatest of all mysteries really, and that you as parent are simply sharing the understanding of it you have formed through the years. If the child asks you questions which no one can solve, or which you in particular cannot satisfy, admit that the answer is not known. The child will respect this attitude, and by hearing it expressed, may come to sense a bit of the great mystery too. "When I was a child," a retired mathematician remarked, "I used to ask my father a lot of questions about a lot of things. He was a smart man and taught me all the time. But the one answer that stayed with me more than any other, I think, was when I'd quiz him on some imponderable, like, where does infinity end, or what will happen to me after I die." He'd smile, and shake his head, and simply answer: 'Nobody knows.' "

2. Second, avoid overly technical explanations. Children abhor being lectured to. They are constitutionally incapable of prolonged listening to the kind of scientific theorizations which many adults thrive on. Best to give the child clear explanations with simple examples to illustrate your point. Try putting explanations into story form: Grandmother got sick, she went to the hospital where we all visited her, she became so sick there that she felt she didn't want to live anymore; and so she died. Children love stories and hate lectures. If possible, spare them the detailed report.

3. Do not dwell on the lurid details. Vivid descriptions about how the body decomposes in the grave and is eaten by worms and maggots, and so on, may fascinate children but can also give them neurotic fixations. It may, in fact, be your job to put such gratuitously ghastly imagery into perspective by assuring the child that dead bodies do not feel what is happening to them, that it is all part of a natural process, that what comes from nature returns to nature, and so on.

4. Address the child's particular concerns. That is, one child may ask about death out of fear, another out of curiosity, or intellectual wonder, or bewilderment, or morbid fascination, or religious impulse.

It is true, of course, that a child's wish to know will often be motivated by all of these considerations, or at least by more than one. Still, there is a principal question hiding behind all the others. Find out what it is, whether it is fear, fright, or fascination, address it squarely, and satisfy it as best you can.

5. Discuss the matter of death with sensitivity and feeling. This does not mean sentimentalizing or overemotionalizing the matter. At the same time, by reducing death to cold, logical terms, without emphasizing the personal feelings that go with it, something in the child's developing consciousness will go unsatisfied. Try to hit a happy medium between fact and emotion.

6. Read between the lines of the child's questions. Children are oblique. They do not say what they mean or mean what they say. This behavior is not motivated by trickery exactly. Children simply do not have the articulateness or awareness to verbalize what is troubling them; therefore, many of their most heartfelt attempts at communication are expressed in a kind of code, in jokes or in nonsequiturs. Note that when a child asks why the Russian soldiers are always "shooting at America," the real question may be: "Am I going to be killed in a war?" When a child tells his mother he's hiding in the closet so that "God won't find me," he may be reacting to having been told that we die because God calls us back to heaven.

A case in point concerns a hospital technician who dealt with death on a daily basis. Returning home from work one afternoon, he was informed that his 6-year-old son was waiting to speak with him in the study. He found the boy seated in a large easy chair with an uncharacteristically serious expression on his face. It turned out that earlier in the afternoon the child had quasi-intentionally killed a baby mole by dropping a heavy rock on it. Try as he might, the boy said, he could not revive the mole. Would his father help? The boy then produced the crushed animal from his pocket, placed it on his father's desk, and looked up expectantly.

The father launched into a long, patronizing discourse about the physiological processes of death and why it was impossible to revive any creature once the life had gone out of it. The more he talked, the more restless the boy became, until he finally jumped up, ran to the window, and started talking of other things.

The father thought the matter was settled until suddenly the boy broke into tears. "Will death come and drop rocks on me?" he blurted out between sobs.

The fact was that the boy had absolutely no desire to know about death in objective, textbook terms. He did not care about biology. His real question was whether *he* would die, and whether he would be punished for killing the mole, and whether he would receive the same treatment he had meted out. His real question in short, hidden behind childish inarticulateness, was a plea for assurance: "Am I Safe?" It related not to theory or philosophy but to distinct needs, fears, and feelings.

7. Do not entertain preconceived notions of how a child should react. Like preparing the birds-and-bees speech, parents sometimes worry too much about saying the proper thing to a child concerning death. If, for example, after speaking frankly to a child about grandfather's impending death, the child seems unaffected, this does not necessarily mean that she has not heard what was said or is unmoved by the situation—just that children show their feelings differently from adults.

8. Speak to children about death on their own level. Avoid talking down to them. They sense when you are doing this and turn off. However, be careful of making your explanations too complicated as well, especially for younger children (below the age of 7 most children have difficulty handling involved abstract concepts). The following conversation is an example of how to keep a discussion simple and at the same time supportive and informative:

DAUGHTER: Is the bird dead, Daddy?

FATHER: Yes. It died.

DAUGHTER: Died who? Where did it go?

FATHER: It probably died cause it got very, very old. Now it's going back to the earth.

DAUGHTER: Can't you make it well again?

FATHER: No. No one can.

DAUGHTER: Am I going to get dead?

FATHER: Someday you will, but probably not for such a long time that you don't have to worry about it. And when you do you will probably be ready for it too. It's not a bad thing at all. I hope you'll find that out as you get older.

DAUGHTER: Why does the bird look so funny?

FATHER: When something dies it gets very quiet and still and very peaceful. Since it's dead it's starting to go back into nature, into the trees and grass, so it can become part of the earth. That's what it's doing now, and that's why it looks so strange. It doesn't feel any pain or unhappiness at all though.

DAUGHTER: Will you die? And Mommy?

FATHER: Probably that won't be for a long time either and then you'll be a grown-up yourself. You'll be able to take care of yourself. Mommy and I will do everything we can to be sure you'll be fine.

DAUGHTER: Why do things get dead?

FATHER: I don't know the answer to that question. Some people spend their lives trying to find out. They're called philosophers and religious people. They try very hard to understand why we're born and why we die.

DAUGHTER: Daddy, I can't stop thinking about that dead bird.

FATHER: Maybe you're feeling afraid that what happened to the bird will happen to you. But it won't. Death doesn't usually happen to children. It's something that comes later on. And remember, Your mother and I and your grandparents and all your friends love you very much. We'll always be right here with you and we will all help protect you as best we can.

9.   Encourage the child's feedback. Do not make your conver-

sations a one-way street. Children may not only have questions about death but comments from their own viewpoint. Just having the chance to air these impressions and enter into a dialogue about them may be a kind of therapy for a child, a kind of release.

What Can One Do When a Child Has Grotesque Misconceptions about Death?

What can you do if a child's notions of death are gruesomely off the mark and the child insists on sticking to these notions, even when corrected? If, for example, a child stubbornly maintains that people die by going to a funeral, or that death lives in a tree and waits to grab passersby, how should such misconceptions be corrected?

It depends, first, on the child's age. What is neurotic in an older child may be developmentally normal in a younger one. Assuming that the child is old enough to know better, if direct correction does not work, and if insisting on the matter makes the child feel attacked, it may be best to avoid "you" messages entirely, speaking instead about "a little boy I once knew who thought death lived in trees," or about a "child who learned what funerals really are." Telling stories in the third person is a nonthreatening corrective technique designed to slip smoothly around the child's defense system. Almost despite himself the child assimilates the messages, and does it without feeling shamed or put on the spot. During the younger ages it is natural for children to have misconceptions concerning death, just as it is natural for them to have false ideas concerning practically everything having to do with adult life. Such ideas are usually nothing to worry about. In most cases it is best to let time and age be the teacher.

Should Parents Initiate Conversations about Death with Their Children, or Should They Wait Until the Child Brings the Subject Up?

Most children initiate the subject at one time or other, and it is best to let this happen organically, in the course of events.

Do not force the issue or make too big a deal out of it. Children feel put on the spot when coerced and may clam up. Best to let these matters unfold as they will.

But What If the Child Never Brings Up the Subject and Seems to Shy Away When It Is Mentioned? Should Discussions about Death Be Urged on Children?

Perhaps the young person has brought the matter up many times already but in the circuitous manner of a child, and the parent has not picked up on the question. This possibility should be considered. If, however, the question is never raised—and this is rare—or if the child seems to have an insistent reluctance to discuss it, it would be foolish to ram explanations down his throat. Better to feel the situation out for a while and discover the sources of resistance. Sometimes it is something as obvious as fear of ghosts or the belief that mentioning death will "upset mommy." Occasionally a child may have developed a true pathology concerning fear of death, and when this is the case professional help is in order.

How Does One Discuss Death with a Child Without Being Too Gloomy?

Parents sometimes believe that they must sugarcoat all the bad news. Rose-coloring unhappy issues, however, is ridiculously transparent to the child, who is as sensitive to false explanations about death—"Grandfather's been carried off by the angels"—as she is concerning nonsense explanations about babies being brought by storks. The fact is that some things *are* serious. To pretend they are not is itself a form of denial.

On the other hand, parents need not be lugubrious with a child about death. Quite the contrary. Keep the tone on an even, sympathetic level, and avoid oversentimentalizing. Let the talk be thoughtful and weighty but not necessarily solemn. Serious does not mean gloomy. It can mean reflective, earnest, even meditative.

If a young child does not ask the really heavy questions— "Will I die?" "Will you die?" "Where will I go when I die?"—

do not feel obliged to bring them up, especially if the child is very young. The time will come soon enough, and older children will be better equipped to understand your answers.

So One Should Say Only What Is Essential on the Subject and Not Volunteer More Than the Child Requests or Requires?

Yes, but remember, lessons are communicated to a child through nonverbal messages as much as through words. The child will be taking in your gestures and your voice tone as much as the explanations you choose when you discuss these loaded subjects. So be careful, to the extent that you are able, not to contradict what you say by the way you say it.

What You're Maintaining, Then, Is That a Parent Can Unwittingly Give Contradictory Messages to a Child about Death, Even If He or She Sincerely Means to Be Honest?

On the one hand, the mother or father is declaring to the child that death is a natural process, common to all life, not something to be abhorred or feared. At the same time, the gestures used to explain all this, the facial expressions, and especially the tone of voice, may subliminally signal the parent's ambiguity, reluctance, and terror. These will be duly noted by the child.

There is not always a great deal we can do about such habits of expression, of course, for habits of expression are what they are. We can, however, make the effort to be aware of them and to watch ourselves in the process, for in the exchange interesting things may be learned about our *own* attitudes toward death. As the saying goes: "The teacher is the taught."

Does This Mean That We Should Try to Disguise Our Own Fears from a Child When We Talk about Death? Is *That* Honest?

Fear of death is native to all of us and it is difficult to discuss it without subverbally tipping our mixed feelings. But this may be all right too. Especially for older children, there is no reason to pretend that death is a picnic or to disguise the fact that we are afraid to die. Surely it is better to be frank on the subject than never to discuss it at all, allowing our terrors to dribble nervously out through the silent game of denial, through the embarrassed pause in the room when dying is mentioned, through the cover-up language of the tea party.

Is the Death of an Animal a Good Occasion to Introduce the Subject of Death to a Child?

The short life span of domestic animals and the fact that children readily form attachments to them makes the occasion of a pet's death an ideal way to introduce notions of loss and disappearance. The demise of a favorite animal is a kind of gentle rehearsal for things to come, and it plants seeds of awareness. The earlier in life this planting is done, the better. In fact, lessons in death education derived from nature—how the leaves fall from the trees, how the insects die, how the grass withers each year, how the sun sets each night—should begin not long after the child learns to talk. Three-years-old is not too soon.

What about the Use of Fairy Stories and Myth to Introduce the Concepts of Death to Children?

Some people object to fairy stories on the grounds that they paint an unreal picture of life and death—they are after all just that: fairy stories. To use them as teaching devices is believed to feed the misapprehensions and fantasies that are already legion in most children's minds.

Others believe that for children symbolism is a more effective tool of education than rote fact, and that the best means of introducing the child to reality is by reaching the child's unconscious directly, via the semantic of figurative idiom. Some even believe that fairy stories themselves were originally meant not simply as entertainment but as teaching tools specifically designed to educate the emotions of a child (the mind would come later) and to prepare the child for life by introducing him to concepts of good and evil, of effort, suffering, trial, death, rebirth, and transcendence, in as gentle yet as direct and gripping a means as possible—through the ancient joy of story.

The choice of using fairy stories as a means of introducing death to a child is a personal decision on the part of parents. If the child seems to profit by hearing them, fine. If the dark parts of these tales bother the child or seem to warp his notions of what's real, perhaps it is time to switch to the more progressive, meaningful, and sincere modern entertainments, such as Super Heros or Donald Duck.

Is It Right for Children to Visit the Dying?

Visits are an excellent way to combine an act of compassion for the dying person with a lesson in death education for a child. Both parties have something to give at this meeting, and both have something to receive. Remember, the dying person is not a relic to be hidden away from either young or old. He or she has much to communicate to the young person, just as the young one brings life and joy to the room of the dying. A visit to the deathbed of an aunt or grandfather or even another child can be an experience children will remember all their lives. At the least, it will allow the child to say a last hello to the dying person, and the dying person to say a last goodbye.

Some Children Seem Morbidly Fascinated with Death.

This is very typical of children from the age of 5 up to adolescence and is usually no cause for alarm. According to Nagy's theories concerning the development of children's death awareness (see pp. 152–153), it is around this time that young ones personify death and delight in putrescent imagery: masks of rotting faces, jokes about decaying bodies ("Leprosy, I've got leprosy," goes a perennial grade school song, sung to the tune of "Jealousy." "There goes my eyeball, into my highball," and so on). This stage will pass.

Something to watch more closely is a child's ungrounded conviction that he or she—or one of the parents—is about to die. Such fears may have an irrational quality to them which cannot be reasoned with easily. No matter how many assurances are offered, the child still believes that disaster is imminent.

A reasonable portion of such fear is common to all children. Feelings of physical insecurity or fright of abandonment are part of every child's growing up. If such worries become abnormally strong, interfering with normal functioning (sometimes in the form of phobias), and if they go on for long periods of time without change, these are danger signals. A counselor or psychiatrist may be able to help.

Should Explanations of Death Include Religious Views?

If a parent has religious convictions and if she wishes to pass these onto a child, it is certainly in order to speak about such things as the afterlife, the soul, and so on. If, on the other hand, a parent has no religious conviction, it would be a mistake to pretend. Faking it out of a faint belief in a greater hope rarely works—more atheists are made from lukewarm religious exhortations than from bodies on a battlefield. What is important is to tell a child what you honestly believe and to keep the door of inquiry open.

How Should a Child Be Informed That Someone Close to Him—Mother or Father, Sister or Grandfather—Is Dying or Has Died?

This is a time for mercy and honesty. Do not beat around the bush, but do not think that bluntness is necessarily a virtue either. The child will be full of questions, many of which he cannot formulate articulately. Have patience and try to decipher what he is really asking you.

Usually, the child's greatest concerns will be over who will support him now that X is gone, where will he live, how will he survive. In their heart of hearts all children know that they are very small and helpless. To suddenly have this reality emblazoned before them in the fiery imagery of a loved one's death can cause a lasting terror. Bear this fact in mind if the child acts strangely during the months after the death, or if he continually misbehaves.

If it is the child's mother or father that has died, he will feel unimaginably alone and cut adrift. It is hard to fathom how lonely he really feels. The most important of all things now is to assure him that although mommy or daddy may die, or has already died, that so-and-so will take care of him, that his room will still belong to him, that his friends and family will still love him. Do not intimate, of course, that uncle or stepmother is going to *replace* the lost parent or be his "new mommy." This is an affront to both the deceased and the child. But do assure him that someone is here to look out for his welfare and that *under no conditions will he be abandoned*. To repeat: Fear of abandonment is the first matter that must be addressed in a child who has lost a parent. *Fear of being forsaken is more of a concern for most children than grief itself*.

Truth is the best course when talking to the child. Avoid telling any tall tales (mommy's left on a long trip for a while; sister's gone to sleep and she'll soon be waking up in heaven). However, you do not have to recount all the details. No need for physiological explanations or medical terminology. What's the point? Keep it simple and above all keep it kind. If possible, break the news to the child when the child is in familiar surroundings, at home preferably. Keep him close to this familiar locale during the time of the ordeal and for a while after. Sudden trips, travel, or disruptions of schedules will often make a painful situation many times more confusing.

Who Should Break the News of Death to the Child?

The person closest to the child, as a rule, although there are certainly no hard-and-fast rules on this matter. In some cases it may be appropriate to have a beloved uncle deliver the sad facts, or even a family religious counselor. It depends on the child and the situation.

Whoever does it should be prepared for the unexpected when the moment comes: reactions to such information can vary wildly among children, ranging from instant hysteria to (seemingly) utter indifference.

What Words Might One Choose to Tell the Child about a Parent's or Loved One's Death?

If the child has seen that the person is sick and has watched her deterioration over time, you might simply tell him or her that this morning mom did not wake up, that she finally did die. She did not have any pain. She died quietly and in peace. Now we will not have her with us any more.

You can go on to explain things about the funeral, how it works; if possible let the child participate, let him pick out clothes, address notes, whatever. Keep the child involved and stay with him.

Should Children See Adults Crying over Death?

Public tears, although taboo in sectors of our society, are healthy. They are not a sign of weakness, or of hysteria, or even of unmanliness, but are simply the most therapeutic and ancient way the human species has of venting grief. For a child to see someone crying whom she values and respects gives the message that it is okay for her to be sad too, that it is okay at certain times to show what's inside you. Surrounding a grieving child with people who solemnly repress their own deepest sorrow can only cause the child to repress too, and to grow up as emotionally stifled as the ones who have stifled her.

What Are Some of the Things That a Parent Should Say or *Do* with a Child If a Close Relative Has Died?

1. Do not tell the child anything that you yourself do not believe. The child will sense it and trust you the less for it.

2. Do not tell the child that the deceased has gone away on a long journey. First, it is a lie. Second, if the deceased is a parent, this will support the child's already overextended abandonment fantasies: "Mommy left and she didn't even say goodbye! She isn't even coming back. She doesn't love me anymore."

3. Do not discuss personal issues concerning the deceased in front of the grieving child, even if the child seems not to be listening. Children are wondrously adept at eavesdropping, even when they seem otherwise occupied, and what is heard is often misinterpreted.

4. Be careful of telling the child too much about the dead person's disease. Some parents think that being honest with children means providing them with every bloody detail, but this is a fallacy. Especially in the case of medical matters, the child may harbor neurotic fantasies concerning hospitals, sickness, operations, organ donation, and so on. She may come to believe that every time she or anyone else becomes sick, death will be the inevitable result.

5. Do not force a child to see or touch a dead body. Many is the tale of children who have been psychologically lacerated by parents who forced them, age 5, to kiss grandma's dead lips. Although some maintain that making a child confront death directly is a sound form of death education, most disagree. It is too much, too fast, too strong. It can often do harm.

Sometimes for religious reasons children are obliged to kiss or otherwise contact the body of a deceased friend or relative. If this is the case, and if such an act is deemed absolutely necessary, it is a good policy to speak with the child beforehand, prepare him, explain what will be involved, what he will have to do, that he is coming to say goodbye to the person and that the person would have wanted it this way, and so on.

6. Be careful about comparing death with sleep. They may, in fact, be brothers, as the saying goes, but telling a child that so-and-so is sleeping their final sleep or that so-and-so is sleeping with the angels can set up an equation in the child's mind between sleep and death. From then on morbid fear of going to bed at night or terror of the dark can follow.

7. Do not reprimand a child for being angry with the deceased. Children may blame the dead parent for aban-

doning them or for not loving them. Much as this stabs at the heart of the grown-ups, who know how deeply the dead parent loved the child, it is a perfectly normal and even healthy reaction on the child's part to be angry at the parent who, by a child's line of reason, has left him in the lurch. If the anger is thwarted now, if it is scolded or lectured into retreat, it may come out later in neurotic and even destructive forms.

8.   Never discourage a child from expressing sadness about a loved one's death. Although to bystanders it may seem remarkably insensitive, children are often exhorted not to cry at the death of a close relative, to be brave, to act "grown up." In many cases such insistence is really a kind of laziness. It is, after all, easier to coerce a child into being quiet and "good" than it is to deal with his or her emotional wounds.

9.   Be careful about what you say concerning God's role in the loved person's death. This is a warning often sounded, and it is a wise one. To inform a child that "God came and got grandfather" is translated by the young person's formative understanding into the message: "God killed grandfather and took him away." God hence appears as a malicious assassin, someone to be appeased at best but certainly not loved or trusted. The intention to give a child the gift of faith thus ends up producing the opposite results.

When providing religious explanations about death to children, parents must choose their words carefully. "Grandfather thought it was time to leave this earth and return to his place with God" is a lot less threatening than "God came and took grandpa." Young ones, remember, hear everything that is said to them *literally*, without giving the benefit of the doubt to poetic license or metaphor. Parents cannot assume that their children will understand celestial symbolism or fill in the blanks of abstract language the way adults do.

10.   Do not delay telling the child. Although the tendency is

to postpone giving young ones news of death, especially if the child is very small and easily decoyed, informed opinion maintains that the sooner the child is told, the better. Learning about a loved one's death long after the last bell has been tolled can make the child feel left out, neglected, and in some cases deceived as well—"Why wasn't I told when it was happening?" the child asks himself, and when no legitimate answer is forthcoming he concludes that he is unworthy or that he cannot trust his guardians. The longer the adult waits to break the news, the more difficult it will be for the child when the time comes. So one must grit one's teeth and perform the terrible task quickly.

What Are the Typical Ways a Child May React to the Death of Someone Close, Especially the Death of a Parent?

According to Earl Grollman in his excellent prologue to the excellent book *Explaining Death to Children* (Grollman, 1967), the most common of these reactions include:

1. Denial
2. Bodily distress
3. Hostile reactions to the deceased
4. Hostile reactions to others
5. Replacement
6. Idealization
7. Anxiety
8. Panic

To this list we might add:

9. Fear of one's own death or the death of a parent

To review this list in sequence:

Denial is the emotional blocking out of the fact that so-and-so is dead. Bystanders at a funeral often observe children of the deceased blithely playing about among the visitors, and are stung by the cold-bloodedness of these heartless orphans. It is not heartlessness at work here but avoidance.

A danger inherent in childish denial, of course, is that a surviving parent, observing the child's lack of emotional response, starts to believe that the child never loved the deceased mother or father, and thus does not really love *her* or *him* either. Or again, the parent believes that the child's denial means that the child has recovered quickly from the shock of the parent's death, when in truth it signifies that the child is unable to accept the death at all. If a child continually speaks of the dead parent as if he or she is still alive, this can be a warning sign.

Bodily distress, the psychological angst experienced by the child may act itself out directly in the body, sometimes in the form of a metaphor: A child who feels that she cannot speak about the dead parent may have feelings of constriction in her throat; a child who feels utterly helpless in the face of the event may suffer paralysis of the limbs, and so on.

Grief, it should be noted, is often spoken of as a disease. If a child develops unusual physical symptoms during the bereavement period, such as shortness of breath, tendency to hyperventilate, asthma, skin eruptions, lethargy, headaches, insomnia (or the need to sleep much of the time), tightness in the chest, allergies, inability to concentrate, or altered eating habits—these may be the body's form of mourning.

Hostile reactions toward the deceased have already been mentioned. The child feels betrayed. One of the parents—or even a grandparent or sibling—has deserted. If this person had *really* loved me, the child reasons, she would never have gone. Therefore, the dead person is bad.

Children may also exhibit personality changes from the trauma of parent loss, and for a time *behave in an uncharacteristically wild and undisciplined manner.* The child acts out toward teachers and friends. He may turn on the doctor who worked with the dying parent, or blame the mother for not taking good enough care of the father while he was sick. Anyone can become fair game for a bereaved child's malice. Some believe that it is an attempt on the child's part to escape from guilt, to find a scapegoat for the death, which he unconsciously blames on himself.

Replacement happens when a child literally tries to substitute a living person for a dead one. We have all known children of divorce who attempt to make every man or woman who comes to the house into a second parent. The same principle is at work with bereaved children. In most cases it is a normal response to loss.

Idealization is a related reaction, whereby the child remembers only the good things about the dead person and turns these lopsided memories into a kind of icon or idol. This can get unpleasant when a stepfather is told by an angry child that, "My real father would never have talked to me like that," or when a surviving grandfather is informed that "My other grandfather never made me go to bed this early." A bereaved child may resort to the device of idealization, not only because she genuinely does miss the departed but because the process itself is an excellent tool with which to gain power, exploiting as it does that most excellent of all children's weapons against grown-ups: guilt.

Next there is *panic and anxiety*, both classic psychological reactions to death. These can accompany a constellation of physical symptomology, or they can come alone, in isolated forms. Usually, they will pass with time.

There also may be *unreasonable fears concerning one's own death or the death of other close relatives*. The child, of course, has just suffered a great loss and is now educated in the true meaning of finality. It is understandable that having sustained one loss she fears another, her own or that of someone close to her. Mourning children are sometimes overheard making covert and overt references to their own death, and they may cling especially tightly to the surviving relative, not only out of love but from fear of losing him or her as well.

What If a Child Refuses to Admit That the Deceased Is Dead?

This is not an unusual condition, especially in the first few months after death. It puts the parent into a peculiar dilemma, however. Should she prick the child's bubble by insisting that the loved one is gone? Or should she leave the child alone?

As it turns out, insisting that a loved one is dead to a child will not necessarily change the child's mind. The child may pretend to go along with it all, but in his private dreams the dead person lives on. Perhaps the best course is to allow the child his fantasy *until* he seeks confirmation from you. If he remarks one day that daddy will soon be coming home—won't he?—and we'll meet him at the bus stop—can't we?—this is a kind of probing on the child's part, and it offers a chance to remind him, carefully but directly, that daddy is gone for good. The ball is then placed in the child's court. He can do with it what he will. In the end, time usually solves this problem on its own.

How Is One to Know When a Child Needs Help?

It depends primarily on the length of time that the abnormal reactions last. As mentioned, many of the behavior patterns discussed above are to be expected. If none are present, that in itself would be reason for concern. If the reactions drag on for a long period, however, several years, say, and if they seem to be getting worse over time rather than better, professional help should be sought.

If a Child's Brother or Sister Dies, Is the Reaction the Same As When a Parent Dies?

Ordinarily, it is not as intense. Seeing one's parents absorbed in grief, however, causes the surviving child much anxiety and insecurity, and can provoke feelings of abandonment and displacement. Occasionally, the child may even feel jealous of the departed sibling for receiving all the attention. The child may shout, "I wish it had been me who died," and entertain childish fantasies of suicide. Or she may identify with the child, taking on aspects of his personality, speaking like the dead child, participating in the same activities, all to prove to the parents that she is as "worthy" as the departed sibling. The main difference between the death of a parent and of a brother or sister, though, is this: "When a parent dies the child thinks, "Why has mommy or daddy abandoned me?" When a sibling dies the child says to herself, "Perhaps I'm next!"

What Can Be Done for a Child to Make the Death of a Sibling Easier to Bear?

When dealing with a child who has just lost a brother or sister, it is important to repeatedly assure the child that the dead sibling was a separate human being with a separate life, and that what happened to him happened for a particular reason, and that it will not happen to you, the living child. It is important that the child not be neglected during the sibling's sickness, that he be included as much as possible in the process. For example, the child should be brought on visits to the hospital. He should be given honest updates of the sick child's condition.

The surviving child is apt to indulge in his own brand of contagious magic, believing that because death happened to brother, and because he and brother shared the same room, the same toys, the same drinking glass, death will happen to him too. The child may avoid using the deceased's possessions or he may take a kind of ritualistic attitude toward them, keeping them hidden in secret places or taking them out on special occasions and playing only certain kinds of games with them. Usually, all this is a common part of the child's mourning process. It may even take on bizarre proportions, but generally speaking it is the child's way of formalizing his own bewilderment and giving meaning to what seems a random act.

Of importance also is the issue of guilt. Sibling jealousy is, of course, natural within any family. The problem is that if a brother or sister dies, the young survivors believe that the bad thoughts they inevitably harbored about their familial rivals somehow contributed to their death.

This notion sometimes continues in disguised forms for a

lifetime. For example, a man in his fifties, after suffering a string of ailments related to hysteria for more than five years, went to a psychiatrist for help. There it was rather quickly uncovered that when the man was 7 years old he had experienced a secret confrontation with his 17-year-old brother that would mark him for life. It so happened, the man recalled, that one night his brother and his brother's girlfriend had parked on a dirt road near his house and that the man had secretly sneaked up and watched the couple petting. The girl, it turned out, was particularly attractive and friendly, and had often been kind to him whenever they met. The man quite naturally developed a crush on her, and now here she was, being pawed by his own brother.

The man concocted a scheme, borrowed from a recently viewed television program, whereby he would plant a bomb in his brother's car one morning and blow him up when he set out to school. This was a childish fantasy, of course, but it so happened that two days after the event, his brother's car was hit by a speeding motorcycle. The car broke into flames and exploded, and his brother was burned to death.

In the midst of his horror and grief over the event, the man began to believe that his scheme of destruction had actually come to pass, and that he was somehow responsible for it all. For many months this thought ate at his soul. Several times he tried to speak with his parents about the matter, but both were so absorbed in their grief that they found it difficult to pay the right kind of heed to his rather unpleasant confession.

Gradually, he internalized this guilt and for years afterward forgot about the supposed link between his fantasy and his brother's death. But his unconscious did not forget. When the bouts of anxiety persisted, the therapy finally brought it all back to the surface, and the man began the process of coming to direct terms with his brother's ghost.

Don't Children Who Have Lost Their Parents Also Have Irrational Feelings of Guilt?

Guilt is one of the most common reactions to watch for in a child who has suffered a close personal loss. Because it is impossible for a child not to feel hostility toward parents at one time or other, there will always be the memory of these thoughts after the parent is dead. Eventually, the child may come to believe that these bad thoughts caused the parent's death.

As a result, the child feels that he is going to be punished for this "murder," either by authority figures or by God. The child's mourning turns into an unconscious mea culpa, and for the rest of his life he may carry the burden.

Again, it is necessary to assure a child that she had nothing to do with the loved one's death, that indeed, she was one of the prime reasons that the loved one was happy and enjoyed her life. Guilt is a hydra-headed monster which grows two reasons for blame with every one lopped off. It is best to reach the child in the early stages of her bereavement and stem irrational guilts or self-blamings before they get out of hand. The longer they go undiscussed, the more powerfully they will insinuate themselves into the child's being.

What Exactly Can You Say to Children to Help Them Avoid Feelings of Guilt?

You might say: "Listen. There are times when maybe you thought you'd be better off if dad were dead. Cause he wouldn't let you go out for pizza with your friends. Or he made you miss The Muppets. *But these are not the kinds of things that make people sick; and they're not the kinds of things that make people die.*" This is the message that must be said over and over again, in as many different ways as possible.

If a Child's Parent Is Dying, How Much Time Should the Child Spend with the Parent?

As much as possible. In a certain way parents who suffer from prolonged diseases have an advantage. They have time: time to arrange for their child's care, time to put their affairs in order, and, most important of all, time to spend with the child. In the last days much can be communicated on both sides, and part of the mourning process can be worked through before the parent dies. To separate a son or daughter from a

dying parent—and for that matter, from a grandparent or sibling—or to allow only occasional visits to the dying relative robs
everyone involved of an opportunity to bring their relationship
to peace and completion.

What Can One Do to Help the Child Adjust to a Parent's Imminent Death?

In time of crisis children feel helpless and out of control.
No one consults them, no one explains anything to them. They
become manipulated pawns, and they know it. One important
step that can be taken to counter this potential problem is to
include children in the nursing process. A child can be allowed
to help with the feeding of the patient, with the afternoon walk
around the ward, with the bathing and serving. There are plenty
of jobs, both necessary and invented, which children can be
"put in charge of." In this way they become part of the helping
inner circle and come to think of themselves as more than just
a nuisance to the grown-ups. Children love to feel needed. They
must be given a chance.

Another thing that can be done for the child, this time by
the patient, is to work closely with the parent's successor, helping him or her prepare for guardianship responsibilities. This
can also include work with the parent who will survive, especially
if the surviving parent is a father who is not accustomed to child
care.

If the parent is not hospitalized when she first becomes sick,
this process of familiarizing the guardian with the child can be
aided by making sure that the child is in regular contact with
the successor via visits, meetings, trips, and play. When the
dying parent is then hospitalized, the child, if appropriate, may
begin staying with the guardian for longer periods of time,
perhaps even spending nights at the new guardian's house if
this house is someday to become his home.

The dying parent, all the while, continues to communicate
to her successor information on how best to care for the child;
what the child likes to eat; what he likes to play with and wear;
his habits, foibles, loves, and hates. As the parent becomes in-

creasingly incapacitated, more and more of the helping chores pass naturally to the new guardian. By the time the parent dies the child is to some extent accustomed to this parental substitute, and—hopefully—has less difficulty looking on him or her as the primary support figure.

Although this sad weaning is painful for the dying parent to a degree we cannot imagine, there is a blessing in it, too; for now the parent knows that she is leaving her child in good hands, hands that have been specially trained and prepared by the best possible teacher for the job.

How Does One Deal with a Child Who Has Witnessed a Terrible Accident or Scene of Death?

Explaining is best—that this was a chance event, that these incidents do happen, and here is a good example of a horrible thing that everyone tries to avoid. But it did take place, and, yes, there was a lot of blood, and yes, that was an eyeball you saw rolling across the street. Yes, yes, yes. But now it is over and done, and we are both still here, and everything will be okay.

Talk about each ugly and horrendous detail, but only as the child demands. The first child may say "yech!" and change the subject. If after several attempts to bring it up he still wishes to keep mum, then by all means allow him his options. Perhaps he is the kind of child who does best by blotting the matter and putting it out of his mind.

A second child may wish to talk about the accident but is afraid, and then it is your responsibility to help her get the words out. If this proves difficult, try talking about the event in front of other people while she is nearby—with a neighbor, or another child, or your spouse, so that the trauma is exposed and always available to the child for discussion. The fact is that children who hear things talked about around their homes assume that talking is the appropriate mode, and they talk; and that kids who do not hear things talked about come to the opposite conclusion, and they keep it all in.

Finally, a third child may insist on talking about what she

has seen, ad nauseum, describing each gory detail. Let her, but make it clear that dwelling on these details will not necessarily make things better. What the child is really concerned with, through all her talk of blood and guts, is that the same accident *might happen to her*. The best thing a child can be given at a time like this is assurance that she is safe from such an accident, and that just because it happened to another person does not mean that it will happen to her.

Should a Bereaved Child Attend the Funeral of a Loved One?

Studies have often shown that if a child's mourning cycle is repressed, the child may later react by internalizing these emotions in unhealthy ways, sometimes with the loss of the capacity for personal intimacy to show for it. "My parent abandoned me," reasons the child. "I'd better not get close to anyone else again or that person will do the same thing."

Funerals are an ancient ritual designed to counteract such reactions. A funeral formalizes death into a collective event, showing all involved the universality of death and making the survivors feel part of a natural process. The child, who naturally enjoys rituals of any kind (watch them at play), is as much in need of these psychological comforts as the grown-ups, and probably more. At the funeral the child is given anchor in the storm of postdeath heartache. He feels included, remembered. He learns that not just he but *everyone* has been touched by this loss, and feels a sense of abandonment. And like everyone else, he is now a participant in the grief, sharing along in the collective sorrow and catharsis of his whole community.

What If the Child Does Not Want to Go to the Funeral?

Then she should by no means be forced. After you have explained to a bereaved child what happens at a funeral and after you have made it clear how very welcome she is to attend, if the child maintains a strong wish to stay home, this should certainly be heeded. It is, no doubt, her way of coping with the situation. It should be honored.

How Does One Prepare a Child for a Funeral?

By describing, point by point, what a funeral is about and what will happen there:

- Why we have funerals
- What takes place at a funeral
- Why people at the funeral act very sad
- Why people go to funerals
- Where the funeral will be held and which people the child knows will be there
- How long it will last
- What will and will not be expected of the child at the funeral

How Best to Explain to a Child *Why* We Have Funerals?

As usual, the straightforward answer is best. A typical non-threatening explanation might be: "Since Uncle Michael has died and won't be coming back, we're going to his funeral. We'll have a chance to see him there for the last time and to say goodbye to him in our hearts."

What about Very Young Children? Should They Go to Funerals?

There is no point if the child is too young. He or she may disturb the other mourners by wandering around, talking loudly, and so on, and at the same time may be too immature to absorb anything of significance. Better to leave children under 3 years at home.

Should a Child Go to a Funeral If the Casket Will Be Open?

It depends a good deal on how sensitive the child is and what the child's emotional state is at the time. Discussing it with the child beforehand can help, of course, but all the talk in the world will not prepare a young person for the awesome stillness of a cadaver. Perhaps it is best to opt for the conservative approach: If the child seems eager to see the body, even after your discussion, go ahead. If the child is impressionable and upset, it may be best to keep away.

What about the Notion That Forcing Children to Look at a Body Will Give Them a Better Understanding of Death?

This theory, popular a few years ago, has few supporters today. The chance one takes of traumatizing children, especially very young children, by exposing them to the sight of a corpse outweighs any possible educational value that such an experience might provide.

Should Children Visit the Grave of a Loved One?

One is tempted to say that regular visits by a child to the grave site should be *mandatory*. Such visits aid the mourning process through its stages of unfoldment. They help the child come to terms with the permanence of the situation. They provide the child with an act that can be performed in the face of so much passive acceptance, a kind of ritual pilgrimage that can be reenacted over and over again and which will hopefully help offset the feelings of helplessness brought by the hammer blow of death.

In this vein, it might be wise to introduce young children to the concept of death itself by occasional visits to a local cemetery. This is a tranquil and natural way to broach the topic, and most children respond to these strangely meditative places with curiosity and pertinent questions.

What Is the Best Way to Help the Child of a Suicide?

The major question, of course, is whether or not to tell the child what really happened. There are many opinions, pro and con. Certainly, one wonders whether a truth that damages the heart is still really a truth; whether honesty does not have its limits; and at what point candor becomes cruelty. The inescapable catch to it all is that no matter how much one may wish to protect the child, sooner or later she is apt to discover the truth anyway, and then, woe to those who have kept the secret so long!

Probably—this is said with all the humility that such a looming question brings forth—*probably* it is best to tell the child what really happened—but only an older child, only one who is mature enough to deal with the notion of suicide and who is not likely to garble this concept into an impossibly tortured version of the truth, a version in which the child probably casts himself in the role of major protagonist, believing that his own actions somehow caused the parent's self-destruction.

The key factor in dealing with children and sensitive issues is to never tell the child more than he wants to know. Answer all questions. There will probably be a lot of these. But do not give the child unnecessary information or extraneous descriptions, especially if he does not ask for them. Further, while you answer the child's question, make it clear that you are available to speak about the matter at any time, not just now when the event has just happened but *anytime* in the future. The child must not be lead to think that the topic will soon be closed.

What Can You Tell Such a Child to Make Him Feel Better?

That *he had nothing, absolutely nothing, to do with his parent's suicide.* Children of suicides remember all the negative thoughts they ever had about a parent and all the naughty things they ever did to annoy the parent. They add these transgressions up on their mental scorecard and come to the unshakable conclusion that *they* were the ones who caused mommy or daddy to blow out their brains.

The world of the child is egocentric—self-centered; a child sees everything in his social world, good and bad, as somehow stemming from his own actions. Especially if the deceased parent resented the child and was given to such phrases as "You'll be the death of me" or "You drive me crazy," the child is likely to take all of this in a literal way and make herself into a kind of cosmic culprit. There is an extremely high rate of schizophrenia and antisocial behavior among children of suicides, especially those who never received proper guidance after it took place.

When working with the child of a suicide, the issue of guilt must be tackled head-on. Children must be allowed to express freely any irrational notions about why mommy or daddy did what they did. They must be guided through the Scylla of anger and the Charybdis of self-hate. In many cases this is a job for the cleric, the therapist, the social worker, or others specially gifted in working with children.

What Exact Words Might One Choose to Explain a Parent's Suicide to a Child?

To a child of, say, 5, you might say that dad felt real bad, that there were some problems that he could not handle, and he thought that the best thing that could happen would be to die. So he made that happen for himself, and it makes me feel incredibly sad. It makes us all feel incredibly sad.

To a 10-year-old you would say essentially the same thing, but with more information and specifics. The older child will ask how he did it, why he did it, and so on. He will want the details.

What Can Be Done to Help a Child Adjust to the Death of Someone Close?

Keep the deceased alive in the young person's memory. Do not speak of her in a tragic tone, and do not overidealize her. Simply recall her as she was, as a lovable, fallible, *interesting* human being, one worth having alive in the heart.

Children enjoy keeping pictures of the deceased and owning objects that once belonged to a dear friend or relative. This child wears a locket bearing a photograph of her dead grandmother inside. That child cherishes a box full of his father's war letters from Vietnam.

Something that is also important, especially in light of the fact that children may be depressed after the death and hence apathetic, is to urge them to become involved in activities, *any* activities. Sports are especially good because they are both physically invigorating and socially involving. But so also are memberships in local Scouting organizations, 4-H clubs, and after-school activities. Help the child cultivate a hobby such as horseback riding, drawing, model railroading, electronics, or cooking. Reading is good, too—anything that keeps a child's mind and/or body occupied and brings in fresh, wholesome impressions to counteract the melancholy ones.

Encourage memory of the deceased but do not let it stop a child from forming intimate relationships or from giving his affections, say, to a new guardian or stepparent. Some relatives feel that they must prevent other parent figures from infiltrating their children's lives, for fear that the interloper will make the child forget the deceased. But the heart has many pockets, and it is a cruel testament to the deceased to discourage his or her offspring from developing new attachments. True, the child should keep the memory of his parent alive. But life goes on and we must go with it.

Close relatives such as aunts and uncles, and older brothers and sisters, can help take up the slack left by the parent's demise. It is amazing how therapeutic a once-a-week visit by a beloved older relative can be for the bereaved child. The child himself will select role models from among his teachers and friends and figures of authority. It behooves those now in charge to make sure that he chooses wisely and well.

Earl Grollman adds several important items to this important list (Grollman, 1967, pp. 26ff.): "A parent should encourage what Sigmund Freud calls the 'ties of dissolution,' " he writes. "That is, reviewing with the youngster pleasant and unpleasant memories of the deceased. As each event is reviewed, a pang of pain is felt at the thought that the experience will never be repeated. As pain is experienced, the youngster is able to dissolve himself of his emotional ties with the dead person. A gradual working over of such old thoughts and feelings is a necessary part of the mourning at any age, and a prelude to acceptance of the death as a real fact.

"Assist the child to unburden his feelings through catharsis, confession, remembrance, and release. The child needs to talk, not just to be talked to. He should be given every opportunity to discuss the person who has died and be permitted to feel that, if he wishes to do so, he may even express antipathy as well as affection for the deceased.

"Demonstrate in word and touch how much he is truly loved. A stable and emotionally mature adult who accepts the fact of death with courage and wisdom will bring the truth to the youngster that the business of life is life. Emotional energy formerly directed towards the absent person must now be directed towards the living. This does not mean wiping out the memories of the deceased. Even in death, the absent member can and should remain a constructive force in family life and be remembered in life without constant bitterness or morbidity.

"The necessity for carrying on day-to-day routines will aid the process of adjustment, and, in time, special interests and pleasures will again assume their normal place in the scheme of things—for both parent and child. The relationship between parent and child will be essentially the same as before death. When parents accept the reality of death and the need for life to go on, they and their children can maintain their own healthy relationships and find new ones to give meaning and purpose to life, permitting young personalities to develop and mature."

7

Caring for
the Dying Child

What about the Dying Child? Does He or She View the Reality of Death Differently from a Dying Adult?

According to the work of at least one pioneer researcher, Myra Bluebond-Langner (see Bluebond-Langner, "Meanings of Death to Children," in Feifel, 1977), the dying child is more acutely aware of her condition than people long supposed. Children tend to fight the notion of death less intensely than adults and to speak about it less directly. Adults, therefore, concluded that children are not overly concerned with their condition.

But they are. Inside. According to Bluebond-Langner, ailing children perceive death in many of the same ways as adults. Forms of bargaining and denial are common, as is a reluctance to discuss long-range plans. Anger is a frequent reaction. So is depression and withdrawal.

There is also a very real concern with not wasting time, with taking advantage of the days and weeks that remain. The illusion of timelessness that healthy young ones play under is a luxury not afforded the sickly. "Children are concerned about the time they have left," writes Bluebond-Langner. "They will often push themselves to get things done. They will also get angry when people take too long to remember things, to answer questions, to bring things to them. The parents and staff often commented on such behavior. 'They demand because they know time is short.' 'It's as if they know that if they wait too long, they might be dead by then. They're not being difficult. . . . That child knows everything.' "

The world of the dying child is filled with images of disease and intuition of death. The theme of annihilation comes up constantly in games, drawings, and conversations, although often in a detached way; and alongside these, next to the usual magical fantasies, comes quite sophisticated factual knowledge on the part of the dying child of the disease itself. Even very young children sometimes show an amazing awareness of how medicines work, how they help, what their limitations are—and what it means when they stop working.

Denial is part of the process, and vacillation is frequent. One day a child will speak of never going back to school. The next he will be making plans for a back-to-school wardrobe. Adults do not have a corner on this market. Children are less concerned with what will happen to them after death than with what they are leaving behind on earth. They are loath to part with their dollhouse furniture or their bicycle. They may demand a careful inventory of what will happen to these items after they die. "Grave imagery is far more prevalent than heaven imagery," writes Bluebond-Langner. "The child's view of death was expressed in terms of what he would miss on earth (for example, birthdays, TV programs, school), rather than what would be waiting for him in an afterlife. The child was concerned with leaving this world, people, and things he knew, not with going to another world."

In short, the dying child is far more sophisticated concerning perceptions of the human condition than his healthy brother or sister. The concept of terminality, which as a rule does not become clear to children until they are in late childhood, is evidently apparent to dying children, even the very, very young ones.

If a Parent Has Just Learned That a Child Is Suffering from a Fatal Disease and That the Child Must Go to the Hospital, What Is the Best Way to Prepare the Child for the Trials Ahead?

The hospital experience can be unimaginably intimidating for a child. Even the more enlightened health care institutions operate via a revolving-door policy, with dozens—hundreds—of patients coming in each day and dozens—hundreds—going out. This rush of human traffic makes it ever more difficult for staff members to treat each new case with the tenderness it deserves, even if this happens to be their goal.

According to the *American Journal of Nursing*, a child will be in contact with as many as fifty-four different staff members during his first day and night of admission to a hospital. Many of these hospital workers will jab the child with needles, strap him to revolving platforms, take blood, push buttons that bring pain. Sometimes the child will be isolated from his parents and kept in a separate room, away even from the doctor or nurses. The no-nonsense high-tech environment, the white-uniformed personnel scurrying about their busy rounds, the institutional smells in the dark halls at midnight, the attitude of authorized omniscience which those in charge wear like sheriff's badges, all these authoritarian devices serve efficiently to keep the adult population in docile submission. It is, after all, for the patient's "own good." But the child reacts quite differently to this juggernaut. Notions of his own good do not mean a great deal when he is being abandoned. To him this institution seems a house of pain and torture; without a nod to its redeeming value as a place of healing, all he wants is out.

Thus the first thing a parent can do for a dying child is to consider the possibility of bypassing the hospital completely and caring for the child at home (see Chapter 8). If this is feasible, if one of the parents is available, if there is enough room at home to carry it off, there is absolutely *no question* that a sick child thrives far better in his own territory than in the barren exile of a hospital ward.

Is This Better for the Parents, Too?

It is harder work to keep a child at home, and it requires more of an hour-to-hour commitment on the part of the parent. But in the long run it is better for the child's happiness and for the parent's sense of participation. Since separation anxiety—fear of being parted from the parents—is the deepest fear that children experience (it is, as a rule, more profound than their fear of death), it becomes especially necessary for a chronically ill child to be kept at home and to be continually warmed and reassured by the members of his or her immediate family.

But It Is Not Always Possible to Care for a Dying Child at Home.

Home care is not always possible. This is true. Also, in the acute stages of an ailment it may be necessary for a child to spend periods of time in the hospital for tests, operations, and observation. When this is the case, a parent can take several tangible steps to make life more tolerable for the child.

What Are the Steps That a Parent Can Take to Make the Child's Time in a Hospital More Bearable?

First, pick a hospital that allows the parents to stay with the child overnight or at least during most of the day, and which lets parents accompany the child during tests and examinations. Ten years ago such hospitals were scarce. Today, although many hospitals still take a hard line, things are changing. Some offer open-door policies where the parent remains with the child day and night throughout the length of the visit. Although many European hospitals have practiced this enlightened system for years, American hospitals are just beginning to catch on to the fact that a happier child makes a better patient. Whatever the policy of the hospital happens to be, take full advantage of the visiting hours. Stay with the youngster as much as possible. *This is the single most important thing that you can do to help the child.* Almost anything is bearable if mommy or daddy is in the vicinity. "It is crucial to the child's morale that parents spend as much time as possible with him," writes John E. Schowalter (in Schoenberg, et al., 1970, p. 54). "It has been shown that even the non-fatally ill child reacts strikingly to the absence of the mother during the experience of hospitalization. Severely ill children may show severe signs of regression, such as prolonged periods of anger or withdrawal. Bowlby describes three phases of response to separation. These are protest, followed by despair, and then detachment. Once the latter stage is reached, the child may begin to ignore the parents even if they do begin to spend more time with him, and a vicious cycle of mutual withdrawal often takes place."

Make certain that the child is visited regularly by other members of the family and that he or she is kept well supplied with toys, books, and diversions. If you must leave for the night, tell the child in no uncertain terms what time you'll be returning the next day, and call if you are going to be the slightest bit late.

When you visit the child, be prepared to hear frequent tears over trifles, or to see a fit when it is time for you to leave, or to witness rude displays toward the nurses and doctor, or to listen to complaints of nonexistent aches and pains. The child is sick, and she is a stranger in a strange land. It is all very confusing and disorienting. Do not judge her as you would under normal conditions. On the other hand, do draw the line somewhere, and stick to it. This is a sensitive time, when too little loving attention can make the child feel deserted, but too much indulgence can turn her into an unmanageable monster.

Before bringing the child to the hospital, tell her in general terms what will be in store for her there. Talk about the sleeping accommodations, the doctors and nurses. Describe the funny way the food will be served, the examinations that will be performed, the new kinds of people she will meet, the medicines, the fact that the children's ward will (sometimes) be stocked with toys and plenty of other children. One of the first things the child will want to know is whether she will be getting shots. If this is the case, tell her the truth. There is, however, no rule against a little benevolent bribery either. For every shot she gets you will give her a treat, a small toy, whatever. Accentuate the positive but do not give the child a false impression. It is important to be honest now. If you are not, she may not trust you later when lines of communication must be kept wide open.

The child can be given little responsibilities so that she feels some modicum of power over her predicament. You might design a chart for her that she carries around the hospital, a checklist of the rooms she must visit and the different tests she will undergo. At each station she pencils an item off the list and perhaps writes a few lines describing what happened there. This way she has a kind of map to tell her what is coming next, and what has happened already, and thus some modicum of control over the situation is provided.

A compassionate doctor will cooperate in this innocent game. He may, as an example, tell the child that he has a special job for her, that he wants her to keep a list of every place she visits today and give it to him when she is finished, with her notes on it, and that this will be a big help for him in his medical work. The child now feels some sense of purpose in it all. Meanwhile, on the way to the hospital (assuming that the child is just visiting) you can promise that after the tests you will make a special trip together to the toy store, or to the roller skating rink, to the movies, whatever the child loves. This gives the child something wonderful to look forward to at the end of her stay at the hospital, and it helps the time pass.

Hospitals will sometimes provide you with data in advance concerning the tests and procedures your child will undergo. Your doctor can fill you in on the rest. If he will not, there are several books on the market which provide explanations of common medical tests, describing how these tests feel and how they work (see Nierenberg and Janovic, 1979). You can, to the best of your ability, explain and describe to the child what lies in store.

Yet there is a problem with discussing medical matters with children: No matter how clearly a parent explains them, children will tend to misinterpret. Judith Nierenberg and Florence

Janovic in their very helpful book about coping with hospitals, *The Hospital Experience* (Nierenberg and Janovic, 1979, p. 36), tell about a little girl in a Washington, D.C., hospital who was informed that she was going to have dye shot into her veins. The girl misunderstood the word "dye," thinking it meant "die." She thus thought the doctors were going to inject her with death and she became appropriately hysterical. Another little boy in a New York hospital thought that he was going to be killed by the doctors because they took so many blood samples from his arm. "Soon I won't have any left!" he cried.

All you can do is correct whatever misapprehensions come up as you go along. Speak simply to children, and address their particular level of comprehension. Do not expect them to understand everything you say. But do not underestimate their intuitions either. They will quickly get the picture that something is very wrong, and that what is coming up is serious business. Assure them that you will be there all the way and promise them that if you have to leave at any time during the hospitalization, you will always, *always,* come back soon.

Many hospitals today have preentry programs to help both the parents and the child adjust. In Children's Hospital of Orange County, children who are about to undergo surgery are invited to a "pre-op party" several weeks before the operation. Here stuffed animals wearing surgical gowns are on display, together with stretchers, bandages, scalpels, masks, and all the paraphernalia of the operating room. Leaders of these parties show slides of the room where the surgery will occur and provide children with preliminary descriptions of how the operation works. Children admitted to this program, studies have determined, show fewer postoperative aftereffects and tend to recover more quickly from the anesthesia than do children in other wards.

Not many hospitals are as far-thinking as this, though some are now offering question-and-answer sessions for parents, together with "Get-To-Know-Your-Child's-Surgeon" meetings, preoperative home visits by professionals, and various publications to answer the most commonly asked questions. Inquire about these in advance. There are, moreover, specific organizations which provide volunteer help for parents with children in the hospital. These include:

Children in Hospitals, 31 Wilshire Park, Needham, MA 02191. (There are branches of this organization in many states.)

Family Centered Parents, 348 Paper Mill Road, Newark, DE 19711.

Parents for Family-Centered Health Care, 546 Wallkill Road, Walden, NY 12586.

Can a Parent *Insist* That He or She Stay Overnight with a Child in the Hospital?

According to George Annas, author of the American Civil Liberties Handbook, *The Rights of Hospital Patients* (as quoted in Nierenberg and Janovic, 1979, p. 37), you can. Writes Annas:

"Parents may not be able to give fully informed consent for their children if they are not able to be with them constantly to monitor their reactions, which they can interpret better than anyone else because of their experience with their children. Also, parents have the right to withdraw their consent to treatment at any time, and this right can only be meaningfully exercised if the parent is continuously present with the child to determine that circumstances have not changed to such an extent that consent should be withdrawn. Parents whose requests to stay with their children are refused can always condition any consent they are asked to give, or form they are asked to sign, with being permitted to stay with their children. If they are thereafter denied the right, their consent terminates, and the hospital can no longer treat the child."

In other words, by trickery, knavery, and the bully stick, parents can usually inveigle it so that they remain nights with the child, even if it is "against hospital policy." Nierenberg and Janovic, moreover, suggest that as added ammunition, a parent get the doctor to write a note telling the hospital how important it is that the parent stay in the child's room. "This," remark the authors, "then becomes 'doctor's orders,' a sacred document in hospitals."

If the Hospital Refuses to Allow the Parent to Stay with the Child, or If the Hospital Staff Is Generally Uncooperative, Can a Parent Transfer the Child to Another Hospital?

The parents are the boss; the parents are in charge. If they feel that a particular hospital does not provide a congenial atmosphere for their child, they can move the child elsewhere. The same goes for treatment, or for the choice of doctors. If the parents find that the hospital is providing substandard care, or if they are dissatisfied with the way the doctor handles the case, it is their privilege to change.

Remember, though, it is the child who must go through the drudgery and disorientation of moving to a new hospital and adjusting to a new physician. It is best to take such bold steps only if they are drastically warranted.

Should a Child Be Told That He or She Is Dying?

A surprising number of children already know. Others hint around the subject, playing the question out with adults, anxious to get a definitive answer, yet frightened of it, too. As with so many questions about death, it is impossible to provide final answers about whether or not a child should be directly informed. Many professionals who have spent a good deal of time around dying children, however, have come to what amounts to a kind of consensus: They feel that the best way of handling a child's death awareness is to allow the child to set his own limits.

What does this mean exactly? First, let the child initiate the questions. Answer them as carefully and clearly and as sincerely as you can, until the child stops asking. Then do not push the matter. Allow the child to move at his own pace.

If the child does not ask these questions, or seems reluctant to know the truth, do not force the issue. Chances are that he has not asked for a very good reason—he does not want to know. Fine. Many children are perfectly satisfied with partial explanations together with assurances that the doctors are doing their best to make them feel better. Among many serious and well-meaning professionals, there is a credo that a child (or for that matter, a person of any age) must *always* be informed that his illness is fatal. But this is big medicine, especially for the fragile ego of a child, and as any doctor knows, medicine that cures one person may kill the next. Better not to apply formulas blindly. Better to treat each child as the separate being that he is.

Many children, by the same token, prefer the dynamic of what is called "mutual pretense": "I understand that I'm dying, and you understand that I'm dying, but to ensure an easy flow between us, we'll both pretend that neither of us knows." This may seem a mature concept for a child to master, but it is not, really. The child simply acts as if everything is fine, and the adult responds in kind. It takes no great sophistication to implement such a game.

Children tend especially to favor mutual pretense if the surrounding adults are reluctant to speak of death or to admit that death is imminent. First and foremost children wish to appease their elders. They want above all to be liked by important authority figures. So, although the child himself may not have much difficulty facing up to his fate, he adopts the charade of mutual pretense in order to avoid (so he thinks) being scolded or chided or otherwise alienated from the grownups.

In reference to mutual pretense, Bluebond-Langner suggests that both mutual pretense and open awareness have their place. "I would suggest that the best approach to psychological management of terminally ill children would be one that allows a child to practice mutual pretense with those who feel comfortable in that context, and open awareness with those who feel most comfortable in that context. One should not use an either-or approach in these cases any more than in the case of sex" (Bluebond-Langner, 1977).

Who Does the Child Usually Ask If He Wants to Know If He Is Dying?

Generally, the doctors and the nurses. The child is less likely to confront his parents, knowing they are already upset about his sickness and not wishing to risk their disapproval (or even abandonment) with such a loaded subject.

Parents should thus keep in touch with doctors and nurses concerning the kinds of questions their sick child asks. If it turns out that a young patient has been peppering the staff with queries centering on what disease he has, will he survive, and so on, but has not once broached the subject to mother or father, this may mean that it is time for the parents to initiate conversations with the child directly, demonstrating to him by voice tone and choice of words that the topic of death is not taboo.

If after giving the child a number of openings to reveal feelings about his terminal ailment, he still prefers to keep mum and indeed insists on it, probably the truth is that he needs to keep these issues between himself and the staff, and that his relationship with his parents will be more harmonious if kept free of anxiety-provoking matters. All children have their own requirements in this matter.

What Is the Dying Child's Greatest Fear?

All dying children cannot be spoken for, of course, but as a generalization the thing children fear most often is abandonment, followed closely by pain. This is especially true in the beginning, when a youngster begins to realize that something is grossly wrong with his health and that all the treatments are not making him any better.

At this point the child has many questions that relate to both these concerns: Will I be operated on? How deep will they cut me? How much will it hurt? Do I have to go on that noisy machine? Will there be lots of blood? Will my parents be with me? Will it be dark in the hospital? Will there be other children around? Will I have a big scar? Will it make me look funny? How long will it hurt? Will I lose my legs? Will my friends stop liking me? Will my parents be mad at me if I do not get better?

A good doctor and nurturant parental team working together can calm the child's worst fears of pain and abandonment, first by advising him in general terms what will take place during the test—the medical procedure, the operation. (A good part of the pain, with children as much with adults, comes from the suspense of not knowing what to expect.) Second, by telling him that whatever may be done to him, there are medications and drugs that will stop it from hurting; and third, by assuring him that he will not be deserted at any time *no matter what.*

How Does One Answer a Child When He or She Asks "Why?"

There is only one answer really: I don't know. There are many ways of expressing this, however, through the glass of religion, or mystery, or ignorance, or wonder.

Isn't the Child's Real Question, "Why *Me?*"

Perhaps. But the answer is still the same. As Kübler-Ross suggests, it may be pointed out to the dying person that the question "Why not me?" is just as valid. For everyone dies sooner or later—and although this disclosure may be of small consolation to the dying child, it may also talk to some secret spot in her heart, and perhaps help a little bit.

Do Children Pass through the Same Stages of Dying—Denial, Anger, Bargaining, Depression, and Acceptance—as Adults?

Generally speaking, they do. But, of course, as children, not as adults. Their anger is a child's anger, their acceptance is a child's acceptance. There are also indications that children who know they are dying pass through the stages rapidly, whereas those kept ignorant rarely get past the point of anger, with its concomitant feelings of confusion, abandonment, impatience, and denial.

A girl of 9, for instance, was slowly dying of leukemia. For periods of time she was able to attend school and work with a therapist. But in these early days her parents were incapable of dealing with the reality of the disease. Each time the child asked what was wrong with her, and why people treated her so differently all of a sudden, they ignored her questions or tried to deflect them.

The girl became sicker. Her friends stopped coming to see her and she no longer had the strength to attend school. Over and over she would ask: "What's wrong with me? People treat me differently than before! What's wrong?" But no one would tell her. She was being "spared."

The result of this terrible mercy was that the child started to believe that she had done some horrible unnamed thing and that everyone was punishing her for it. She began to develop paranoid rationales to explain it all. Her family was not really feeding her, she decided, that was why she was getting so thin. Perhaps they were secretly trying to kill her for that terrible "thing." Along with her friends. Even in the last days when she had been ravaged into a wasted skeleton, no one would admit that anything was wrong. She passed away angry, guilty, and very innocent.

How Does a Child's Age Affect the Way He or She Deals with Death?

Very young children, say 2 to 5, do not have the ego development of older children and are likely to accept death with less fear than older children. This is, moreover, the age when the child is particularly likely to feel guilty for his illness and to believe that it is a form of punishment for bad thoughts.

Children from 5 to adolescence realize that death is final and also *unusual* for someone their age. They feel singled out, picked on, separated from other children. They sense the unfairness of it, in a way that younger children do not. They also feel more afraid and disoriented than do 4- and 5-year-olds. John E. Schowalter (in Schoenberg et al., 1970, pp. 62, 63) gives a lucid and poignant description of the particular problems faced by the dying child during puberty and the early teenage years: "The child is faced with regression, loss of control, and the need for external help in performing even the most basic body functions. For the adolescent who until recently was beginning to realize real autonomy and independence, such deterioration is devastating. Youngsters with this age group who become ill are especially susceptible to feelings of disgrace and lack of prestige. This feeling of shame is unique to this older group of children. The problem of separation experienced by the younger child in terms of *physical* separation becomes for the adolescent the problem of *emotional* separation of the self from others. . . . To then be aware that one is going to die triggers what Solnit and Green have perceptively noted is one of man's deepest fears—death before fulfillment. It has been shown that dying patients turn away from the future and gain solace from the past. The adolescent often sees little in his past to comfort him. Although adults often find it hard to believe, a substantial number of teenagers describe childhood as a necessary evil orientation imposed on them as preparation to join the freedom and happiness of grown-up life. For these adolescents death means not only that there is nothing in their future, but that the time spent in growing up was wasted."

Schowalter sums up the question of a child's response to dying at different ages in this way (p. 65): "Under the age of three, death is not yet a fact, but separation is, and the child's reaction is exquisitely sensitive to the caliber of mothering he receives. The dying preschool child recognizes the fact of death but does not understand it. Although he may express less death anxiety than children in other groups, and no longer responds to his illness purely with separation anxiety, he commonly believes his illness is a retribution for bad thoughts or actions. If the child accepts his guilt, he often becomes passive and withdrawn. If he denies guilt and projects it onto others, he may become angry and rebellious. This complicated interaction between guilt, denial, projection, passivity, and aggressivity will continue to be seen at all ages.

"During his early primary school years, the child begins to comprehend the permanency of death. The concept of *terminal* illness first makes its impact, and death anxiety is greatest during this period. The severity of the recently formed superego and its self-punishing characteristics increase the child's fear of physical procedures, and he conceptualizes death as an external force which will malevolently stop his life. Religion begins to play a more important role, positively or negatively, with this age group, and although some children realize they are dying, they may be reluctant to voice these fears to their parents but rather confess to the staff that 'I'm not supposed to know.'

"After age ten or eleven most children intellectually understand the universality and permanency of death. This is also the time of life when physical and sexual maturation, self-identity, and independence begin to develop. Most terminally ill adolescents know they are dying and may be overwhelmed by the despair and resentment of unfulfillment. Shame, guilt, anticipatory mourning for oneself, and depressive symptoms are not uncommonly seen."

Is It True That Most Children Know They Are Dying Even If They Are Not Told?

Some people attribute to children an almost mystical ability to *know*, without anyone telling them directly. But the ways in which a child learns the truth about such matters is usually far more practical.

That is, after a certain amount of time spent in the hospital, being buzzed around by a galaxy of specialists, after hearing parents whisper worried medical things in the hall outside the room and noting the new and deferential ways people now treat her; after having suffered pain, taken medicines of every description, gone through lab tests and bizarre medical treatments, having talked with other children in the hospital and watched medical shows on television and overheard the doctors and nurses speaking of her case and witnessing other children disappear from the ward and never return—after all this, even the younger child is likely to decide that something is seriously wrong and that perhaps nobody may *ever* be able to fix it.

If a Child Knows That He Is Going to Die, Will He Talk about It Much?

Again, it depends on the atmosphere that has been established around him. If the adults are committed to an open awareness, the child will talk. If not, he probably won't. Even if awareness is kept open, however, many children will not voluntarily bring the subject up but will discuss it in a covert or symbolic way.

Are Dying Children Different from Other Children?

They are usually more mature than their less experienced peers and more capable of comprehending ideas—emotional ideas in particular—that are too sophisticated for normal youngsters. This is especially true of children who have suffered drawn-out chronic diseases and who have gone through much pain and trauma. Such children often develop both a world-weariness and a knowing patience which is unusual, even in mature adults.

For Many Parents There Is a Tendency to Indulge and Over-coddle a Very Sick Child.

It is natural, of course, but too much is destructive. Suddenly to become the center of everyone's concern, with piles of toys and games appearing from nowhere, with members of the family magically dancing to the child's beck-and-call, with solicitous phone calls from friends of the family who seemed hardly to have noticed the child in his healthy days, with behavior patterns that were once greeted by a hefty "No!" suddenly smiled upon indulgently—all this is not only confusing to the young mind but overwhelming. It is *too much power for children to handle*. It can cause them to regress to an infantile stage where demands become insatiable and where behavior becomes rebellious.

The fact is that an overindulged child must *invariably* misbehave. Then a bad situation is made worse when the parent gets angry at the child for acting out, or spoils the child even more in a futile attempt to appease him. Round and round they go as the child becomes more intractable, more demanding. The vicious circle twists, with both parties caught in the middle.

Therefore—although the tendency is strong to spoil sick children and to withhold discipline, parents should struggle against this impulse. The best gift they can give the child is normalcy, regularity, and consistency. Here is where the child's real security lies: in the peace of life's everyday routines.

How to do this? Ordinary methods of discipline and reward must be maintained. Bedtimes should be honored (for children still functioning and at home) as well as homework tasks and household chores. In the hospital children should be required to maintain proper respect for their family plus civility toward the staff. They should not be allowed to fly into tantrums whenever a visiting friend or relative arrives without a present. Too many gifts come to be taken for granted, then expected, then demanded. Limits should be set and kept.

To overindulge a dying child, although a very human impulse, ultimately works against the better interests of everyone involved.

The Parents of Dying Children Must Often Feel Guilt over Their Own Impatience.

Taking care of a chronically ill child is a time-consuming and exasperating enterprise. Most parents have their limit, like all of us, and when they pass it they get angry over the incessant demands, the endless hours, the money spent, and perhaps most of all, the frustration that never goes away: the child simply *will not get well.*

Now since it is taboo to become directly angry at a dying child, a parent's anger may be projected elsewhere, onto innocent bystanders, onto the doctor perhaps, or the nurse, or the spouse, or the dying child's brothers and sisters. The sickness of a child is an enormously disturbing event in the equilibrium of family affairs, especially between husband and wife. It is not unusual for a marriage to break up shortly after a child has died, especially if the marriage was in jeopardy before the event. It is not unusual for family members to become openly hostile.

Taking all these possible circumstances into consideration, one is tempted to say that it should be a mandatory obligation on the part of parents to realize that they *are* under an impossible strain, that their relationships with other people, even loved ones—especially loved ones—*will* get frayed, and that anger at a sick child is not only a natural by-product of this struggle but an inevitable one.

Guilt only breeds guilt; it has never contributed to the nursing process. A parent should be urged to shun such emotions, if not for their own sake, then for the better interests of the child. In the face of self-recrimination, feelings of inadequacy, anger at one's impatience, even the belief that one was somehow responsible for the child's sickness in the first place ("If I'd only not been so cheap and left the heat up in Tommy's room, this might not have happened"; "If I'd only listened to what Jenny was telling me about her throat instead of poo-pooing it . . .")— in the face of all these concerns it becomes the parents' job to forgive themselves, remember that they are only frail human beings, and get on with the job of caring for their child.

While the Parents Are Going through the Experience of Nursing a Dying Child, Are There Times When They Feel Incapable of Going to the Hospital? Is It Unusual for a Parent to Feel that He or She Simply *must* Get Away from the Child for a While?

For parents of dying children there sometimes comes a peculiar feeling of drawing back, of detachment. It might be supposed that sickness would bring the parent closer to the child's bedside, but this is not always the case.

When a father in his early thirties discovered that his twin sons had the same rare and fatal disease, his first reaction was to quit his job—he was a furniture stripper—and spend all his time at the hospital with the children. After several months it became apparent that the disease they suffered from was progressing very slowly and that much physical pain was involved.

Soon thereafter the man found himself making excuses for not going to the hospital, and his wife, who was now the sole breadwinner, had to leave her job and go in his place. As more time passed, his visits continued to decrease, from once a day to several times a week, to once a week. Then less than that. The twins died a year and a half later, within several hours of each other. Their father, it turned out, happened to be in New Mexico when the deaths occurred–on business, he explained to everyone at the funeral.

In fact, what was really taking place, and what happens

frequently with parents of dying children, is that the day-to-day trauma of watching a child die becomes too great, and the parents subtly, or not so subtly, withdraw. The accompanying guilt and self-loathing that results from this behavior makes the process even more convoluted and more difficult to deal with after the child has died.

Such withdrawal is a form of anticipatory grief, but one given literal expression. If this withdrawal becomes too common, the abandoned child soon comes to act listless and zombie-like. The parents rationalize their behavior in any number of ways, a favorite being that they are leaving the job of taking care of the child to the medical staff, who know better than they about such things.

At some point almost all parents of dying children experience the urge to withdraw. Sometimes it is a wise urge, and a short vacation may be the only thing between the self and sanity. At other times it becomes necessary to invoke such protection simply to gain the strength to continue. Parents, however, must keep close watch on this impulse, making sure that they are not truant too often, or that they are not being neglectful in the name of high-sounding purposes. Too much withdrawal from a sick child is a bad idea. Permanent withdrawal is disastrous. It will almost certainly ensure that this child will die suffocated by feelings of abandonment and lack of love.

How Can One Help the Parents of a Dying Child?

Judith Stillion and Hannelore Wass in an article on children and death ("Children and Death," in Shneidman, 1980, pp. 251ff.) suggest that the physician attending a dying child should adopt the following course of behavior when dealing with the stricken parents. Although written for the professional, this list is helpful for anyone on any side of the dying-child dilemma:

1. "Recognize the depth of shock and despair the parents must be feeling."

2. "Explain the basis for the diagnosis and the nature and type of disease."

3. "Explain the fatal outcome and type of therapy to be undertaken. Make every attempt to gain parental support in both the physical and emotional care of the child."

4. "Assure parents that medical support will always be available in times of need."

5. "Try to help parents anticipate problems involved in the initial telling of others and during the child's illness. Go over possible reactions of siblings (e.g., anger, jealousy, fear, guilt)."

6. "Discuss causes of the problem, with emphasis on relieving possible parental guilt."

7. "Emphasize any hope possible. If there is hope for remission, dwell on that. If there is not, discuss scientific research going on, if appropriate. If nothing is available, emphasize the support the child will get throughout the illness from the medical staff. While the good physician will discourage excessive optimism, parents must be allowed some hope, especially during the early stages of the disease."

8. "Discuss anticipatory grief both as an attempt to educate parents about their own feelings in the coming days and to prepare them to recognize stages their child may be passing through."

9. "Stress the importance of maintaining continuity in raising the child. It is essential that parents assume the child will live to adulthood and raise him or her consistent with their prior values and ideas. The alternative is that parents in their grief and guilt will indulge the child, who in turn will become confused and often test new limits until parents are forced to discipline him or her. This often leads to greater feelings of guilt both for the child and the parents. Children need the security of consistency in their parents' behavior."

10. "Try to assess family's strengths and weaknesses and encourage building on the strengths. It is important to ask

each parent how the other will accept the death, thus encouraging empathy and visualizing problems in advance."

11. "Next, there is evidence that a follow-up talk after the death of the child is often appreciated by the family in order to provide closure for the family and to permit them to express feelings after the death."

Another list of Do's and Don'ts for helping bereaved parents, put together by Lee Schmidt, R.N., of the Parent Bereavement Outreach Association and quoted in Katherine Fair Donnelly's book on parental bereavement (see Donnelly, 1982, pp. 125, 126), makes the following suggestions:

DO'S

- "Do let your genuine concern and caring show."
- "Do be available . . . to listen, to run errands, to help with the other children."
- "Do say you are sorry about what happened to their child and about their pain."
- "Do allow them to express as much grief as they are feeling at the moment and are willing to share."
- "Do encourage them to be patient with themselves, not to expect too much of themselves and not to impose any 'shoulds.' "
- "Do allow them to talk about the child they have lost as much and as often as they want to."
- "Do talk about the special endearing qualities of the child they've lost."
- "Do give special attention to the child's brothers and sisters— at the funeral and in the months to come (they too are hurt and confused and in need of attention which their parents may not be able to give at this time)."
- "Do reassure them that they did everything that they could, that the medical care their child received was the best, and whatever else you know to be *true and positive* about the care given their child."

DON'TS

- "Don't let your own sense of helplessness keep you from reaching out to a bereaved parent."
- "Don't avoid them because you are uncomfortable (being avoided by friends adds pain to an already intolerably painful experience)."
- "Don't say you know how they feel (unless you've lost a child yourself, you probably don't know how they feel)."
- "Don't say 'you ought to be feeling better by now' or anything else which implies a judgment about their feelings."
- "Don't tell them what they *should* feel or do."
- "Don't change the subject when they mention their dead child."
- "Don't avoid mentioning the child's name out of fear of reminding them of their pain (they haven't forgotten it!)."
- "Don't try to find something positive (e.g., a moral lesson, closer family ties, etc.) about the child's death."
- "Don't point out that at least they have their other children (children are not interchangeable; they cannot replace each other)."
- "Don't say that they can always have another child (even if they wanted to and could, another child would not replace the child they've lost)."
- "Don't suggest that they should be grateful for their other children (grief over the loss of one child does not discount parents' love and appreciation of their living children)."
- "Don't make any comments which in any way suggest that the care given their child at home, in the emergency room, hospital, or wherever, was inadequate (parents are plagued by feelings of doubt and guilt without any help from their family and friends)."

The following suggestions, taken from a self-help brochure published by a bereavement group known as The Compassionate Friends (you will find the address at the end of the chapter), are especially for doctors and nurses, although anyone can profit from reading them:

- "Prepare patients and siblings for what they will see *before they see it.* Explain beforehand the machines, tubes, needles, etc. Clean and bandage all you can before they come in."

- "If parents really want to watch, let them see what you are doing with their child. Let them lead in that decision. (They don't see the same things you see.)"

- "Anticipate their questions as much as possible. Avoid complicated terminology, but don't 'talk down' to families either."

- "*Always tell the truth!* Tell them everything you *know* about their child's condition. Be honest about what you don't know. Tell them the numbers, i.e., blood pressure, temperature, pulse, etc."

- "Let parents 'parent'—they need to participate in the care of their sick child as much as possible. Later they need to be able to say, 'I helped'!"

- "Give parents permission to talk about their feelings, to be extremely tired, to *cry*. Cry with them if you are truly sad. Don't hide your feelings to protect them. You are in a position of authority and your permission (modeling) gives their feelings validity."

- "Parents may not be accepting of bad news, and may cope by denial. Do be patient with parents as denial is a form of emotional protection, and will disappear when an individual is ready. Everyone is on a different timetable. Recognize that sometimes there is a need to repeat the same explanation or information several different times; parents in stress may only absorb a little of what you thought had been explained to them."

- "Reassure families that everything possible is being done. They won't automatically know or assume that. *Keep* on reassuring them that no measure will be left untried in the attempt to save their child's life."

- "Take pictures of newborns who die and put them in the

file in case parents want them in future weeks or months. (Many will.)"

- "Make *every effort* to arrange for parents to be with the child at the moment of death *if they want to be there.* Please don't 'protect' parents from this opportunity. It will be extremely important in their later healing."

- "Refer to the child by name—especially after death."

- "Remember the two things which concern parents most: 'Was my child in pain?' and 'Was my child afraid?' Be prepared to reassure as honestly as possible about these questions."

- "Treat parents equally in giving information and breaking news. Fathers need as much support as mothers."

- "Families judge you by your caring levels, as well as your medical skills. Convince them their child is special to you, that this is not 'just a job.' "

- "Allow parents as much time as they need to be with their child (alone if they want) after death. This is vital in their healing process."

- "At the times of informing parents that their child has died, tell them what steps to take next. They are in shock (and disbelief) and will be confused and need direction and guidance. There is no such thing as an 'expected death' when it happens!"

- "Express your personal frustrations: 'We try so hard, but sometimes nothing works.' 'He was such a wonderful child.' 'It hurts us, too, that we couldn't save him.' "

- "Touching is our most basic form of comfort and communication—put your hand on their arm, or your arm around their shoulder."

- "If possible, go to the visitation or funeral. It means more than you can imagine. Families will really appreciate your *showing* your caring!"

- "Most of the parents we've talked with have appreciated being asked about organ transplants. Parents who weren't asked felt left out or even insulted. However, parents need reassurance that their child's body will be treated with respect and dignity."

- "Don't expect the parents of a dying child to be logical or objective. Runaway emotions have left logic at the starting gate, and it will take quite a while to catch up!"

- "Don't 'hit and run.' If you must break sad news, don't rush away immediately. If you can't handle the situation sensitively, send or take along someone who can."

- "Don't assume all anger is 'displaced.' Some of it is, but some of it is justified and needs to be ventilated and examined."

- "Don't try to give parents rationalizations about their child's death, such as: 'Your child would have been a burden to you as he was,' or 'She just would have suffered if she had lived.' (This is the 'You're really lucky he died' routine.)"

- "Don't say 'You ought to be feeling better by now,' or anything else which implies a judgment about their feelings."

- "Don't point out that they can always have another child, or suggest that they should be grateful for their other children. Children are not interchangeable—they cannot replace each other."

- "Don't suggest 'busy work' as grief therapy. Bereaved people know they need to have something to do, but they are extraordinarily tired for a long time, and whatever they do needs to have meaning and importance."

- "Don't be in a hurry to offer medication. There is a big difference between profound sadness and true depression. *Sad* people are often medicated for depression unnecessarily!"

Remember: As you treat the patient *in* the bed, you must be careful not to create patients *around* the bed!

Are There Other Ways in Which Parents of a Dying Child Can Help Themselves?

There is some sound advice on this matter, also from The Compassionate Friends. It includes:

- "Grief, with its many ups and downs, lasts far longer than society in general recognizes. Be patient with yourself."
- "Each person's grief is individual. You and your spouse will experience it and cope with it differently."
- "Crying is an acceptable and healthy expression of grief and releases built-up tensions for mothers, fathers, brothers and sisters. Cry freely as you feel the need."
- "Physical reactions to the death of a child may include loss of appetite or overeating, sleeplessness, and sexual difficulties. Parents may find that they have very little energy and cannot concentrate. A balanced diet, rest, and moderate exercise are especially important for the whole family at this time."
- "Avoid the use of drugs and alcohol. Medication should be taken sparingly and only under the supervision of your physician. Many substances are addictive and can lead to a chemical dependence. In addition they may stop or delay the necessary grieving process."
- "Friends and relatives may be uncomfortable around you. They want to ease your pain but do not know how. Take the initiative and help them learn how to be supportive to you. Talk about your child so they know this is appropriate."
- "Whenever possible, put off major decisions (changing residence, changing jobs, etc.) for at least a year."
- "Avoid making hasty decisions about your child's belongings. Do not allow others to take over or to rush you. You can do it little by little whenever you feel ready."
- "Parents may feel they have nothing to live for and may think about a release from this intense pain. Be assured that many parents feel this way but that a sense of purpose and meaning does return. The pain does lessen."
- "Guilt, real or imagined, is a normal part of grief. It surfaces in thoughts and feelings of 'if only.' In order to resolve this guilt, learn to express and share your feelings, and learn to forgive yourself."
- "Anger is another common reaction to loss. Anger, like guilt,

needs expression and sharing in a healthy and acceptable manner."

- "Children are often the forgotten grievers within a family. They are experiencing many of the same emotions you are, so share thoughts and tears with them. Though it is a painful time, be sure they feel loved and included."

- "Holidays and the anniversaries of your child's birth and death can be stressful times. Consider the feelings of the entire family in planning how to spend the day. Allow time and space for your own emotional needs."

- "A child's death often causes a parent to challenge and examine his faith or philosophy of life. Don't be disturbed if you are questioning old beliefs. Talk about it. For many, faith offers help to accept the unacceptable."

- "It helps to become involved in a group of parents having similar experiences; sharing eases loneliness and promotes the expression of your grief in an atmosphere of acceptance and understanding."

- *"Bereaved parents and their families can find healing and hope for the future as they reorganize their lives in a positive way."*

What Organizations Exist to Help Bereaved Parents or Parents of Dying Children?

Many of these are mentioned in Chapter IX (see pp. 259–263). The following list includes organizations specifically dedicated to providing help for bereaved parents and families. Contact an organization at the address given concerning information on local chapters."

Amend (Aiding Mothers' Experiencing Newborn Death), 4023 Towhee Drive, Calabasa, CA 91302.

Barr-Harris Grief Groups, 180 North Michigan Avenue, Chicago, IL 60601.

Bereavement Clinic King's County Hospital, 451 Clarkson Avenue, Brooklyn, NY 11203.

The Candlelighters Foundation, Suite 1011, 2025 Eye Street, NW, Washington, DC 20006.

The Compassionate Friends, Inc., National Headquarters, P.O. Box 1347, Oak Brook, IL 60521.

The Grief Institute, P.O. Box 623, Englewood, CO 80001.

Hand, P.O. Box 3805, San Francisco, CA 94119.

Hopes (Helping Other Parents Experience Sorrow), P.O. Box 1143, Lutz, FL 33549.

National Self Help Clearing House, 33 West 42nd Street, New York, NY 10036. (Serves as a free referral service for the bereaved.)

National Self Help Resource Center, 2000 South Street, NW, Washington, DC 20009. (Offers the same services as the preceding organization.)

National Tay-Sachs and Allied Diseases Association, Inc., 122 East 42nd Street, New York, NY 10017. (Provides information and other services to parents of babies.)

Parent Bereavement Outreach, 535 16th Street, Santa Monica, CA 90402.

Parents of Murdered Children, 1739 Bella Vista, Cincinnati, OH 45237.

Share (Sources of Help in Airing and Resolving Experiences), St. John's Hospital, 800 East Carpenter, Springfield, IL 62769.

Sudden Infant Death Syndrome Association. Contact any one of the following:

• The National Clearinghouse for SIDS, Suite 600, 1555 Wilson Boulevard, Rosslyn, VA 22209.

• National Headquarters Council of Guilds for Infant Survival, P.O. Box 3841, Davenport, IA 52808.

• The National SIDS Foundation, 2 Metro Place, Suite 205, 8240 Professional Place Landover, MD 20785.

Support Group for Bereaved Parents, Department of Social Services, Brigham and Women's Hospital, 221 Longwood Avenue, Boston, MA 02115.

8

Home Care

Is It Better in General, for Adults As Well As Children, to Have Home Care?

It depends on many factors, not the least being whether the person's condition is chronic or acute. As mentioned previously, hospitals are acute-care-oriented institutions. They usually will not allow a patient to register unless he is in a crisis situation. It is thus not always a patient's prerogative to enter a hospital at will, even if he or she is suffering from a fatal disease. Even a fatal disease must be in an advanced or crisis state. As far as the terminally ill are concerned, hospitals are places where one goes to die.

Where Do Most People Prefer to Die?

A majority of people die in hospitals. A majority of people would *prefer* to die at home. Even if a person thinks that he desires home care, moreover it is not unusual for the family, or for the person herself, to develop a case of cold feet at the last minute and race off to the nearest health care institution.

Nor is it unusual for such patients, exposed to the sudden excitement and anxiety of the ambulance ride, to die in the back of the vehicle on route to the "safety" of the hospital.

If People Prefer to Die at Home, Why Do So Many End Up in Health Care Institutions?

For many reasons. A doctor may automatically send a patient to the hospital when the patient's condition becomes acute, without her knowing that other options are available. A person may be rushed to the hospital for emergency measures and die on the premises without the question of home care ever becoming an issue. The patient's family may be unprepared or unwilling to provide home care. Or there may simply be no one at home to do the caring, or not enough space. The patient may demand hospitalization out of fear or habit, even when it is evident that hospital care cannot prolong life any more than home care, nor make it more comfortable. A person's insurance may only cover medical care when administered in a hospital—and since all third-party payment insurance is institution-oriented, people in this situation are financially forced to die in a medical care establishment. It is a complex issue.

Does Medical Insurance Cover Home Care?

It depends on the policy. Some of the better policies, the so-called "medi-gap" policies such as Major Medical, will cover unlimited home care, but they are commensurately expensive. Other policies offer home care as an option, or they provide minimal coverage, a hundred visits a year, say. This looks like a lot of visits on paper. But consider how often a professional would be needed in the case of a patient suffering from a slow degenerative disease. The hundred-visit-a-year clause is used up in no time and the family is then financially on their own.

How Much Will Medicare and Medicaid Help with Home Care?

Medicare will pay for a number of home care services. These include part-time nursing, speech and occupational therapy, home aids, and a limited line of health care and rehabilitative equipment. There are several catches, though. The first is that these services must be provided by a home health agency that is officially certified by the U.S. Department of Health and Human Services. The second is that the rules governing who can get what and when are exceedingly complex. A booklet called *The Medicare Handbook* explains these complications in relatively plain English. It can be picked up at any Social Security office.

Benefits for Medicaid differ from state to state. Those states that do provide Medicaid home services are obliged to provide recipients with part-time nurses and homemakers, some medical supplies, and some equipment. Although for years just how much of the above was due the patient has been unclear, new legislation has made an expanded home care program available to needy patients in thirty-eight states. Check with a local department of social services or with the Social Security office in your area to see if your state is among these.

What about Veterans' Benefits?

Some home care benefits are available for veterans who are suffering from service-connected sicknesses or disabilities. Check with the closest Veterans' Administration office for particulars.

What Are the Advantages of Home Care?

Home care can be an advantage for several reasons. These include:

1.   Most people feel more comfortable and secure in their own homes. Hospitals are by and large impersonal, anonymous places. Statistics indicate that people cared for at home live longer than those in nursing homes and hospitals.

2.   A patient is more likely to get loving, careful attention at home than in a hospital, especially if the family has some training in home care and if a resident nurse is on the premises. Generally speaking, both doctors and nurses in hospital situations dislike working with terminal patients and often, due to

a complex mixture of futility and denial, fail to give dying patients the attention they need. With a good home care program this is not the case.

3.   In instances where a person has no hospital insurance or has limited funds, home care is far less expensive than hospital care, even when a resident nurse is employed. Home care also releases hospital beds that might otherwise be occupied by those needing immediate care for acute illnesses and thus helps reduce overcrowding in health care institutions.

4.   The costs of some home care goods and services are tax deductible. See IRS Publication 502, *Medical and Dental Expenses*, for specifics.

5.   Home care is especially appropriate when the home is located a good distance from the hospital, or when local hospitals are overcrowded or offer inferior health care.

6.   Home care allows the entire family to participate, to do their part for the dying person, to truly help the loved one up to the end. If there are children in the household, they will gain the privilege of witnessing the dying process from close up, without the nonsense of sugarcoating and denial. From this experience they will hopefully gather lessons to deal better with death as grown-ups.

So Home Care Is Right for a Person Only When the Family Is Willing, Able, and Pleased to Take On Care Responsibilities?

Generally, yes. Family members should be in sync with the patient and with each other. They should function as an harmonious unit, at least in terms of its activities toward the patient. Otherwise, home care probably will not work very well.

Is This Always the Case?

It is impossible to be absolute on the subject. Generally speaking, the more enthusiastic and involved family members are, the better home care will work.

Don't Family Members Need Professional Help Taking Care of the Homebound Patient?

It is certainly better this way, and there are many organizations that offer this kind of help. For instance, one of the largest home care institutions in the United States is the Visiting Nurse Service (or Visiting Nurse Association as it is known in some areas). In New York City alone the Visiting Nurse Service works with a million homebound patients a year.

Are Most Doctors Agreeable to Home Care Programs?

Doctors are usually agreeable to home care as long as a patient's case does not involve too much paperwork. When, for whatever reason, it becomes apparent that hours of paperwork in triplicate will be required, a doctor often refers the patient to the hospital, where the red tape can be done by others.

Many doctors do not yet realize the benefits that can accrue to them, both in time and services, by encouraging home care. Others are simply not informed of the home care resources available in their community and thus never think of suggesting it in the first place. Like the health care services they work with, doctors are very institution-oriented.

How Do Visiting Nurse Services Usually Operate vis-à-vis the Patient's Doctor?

It should be clearly understood that home care is not a substitute for a doctor's care. It is a complement to it. A patient treated at home by a visiting nurse will almost always remain simultaneously under the jurisdiction of a regular doctor.

This means that from the start the doctor must be agreeable to working with a patient who requests home care and must be willing to cooperate with home care professionals. Not all doctors are friendly to home care programs. It is best to inquire about this on the first visit to any physician.

In the preliminary stage of home care the visiting nurse enters the patient's home, often accompanied by a social worker or other health care professional. Together they make a total assessment of the domestic situation. Then they devise a plan for home care operation and send their proposal to the doctor. The doctor reads it and gives suggestions. He may specify how many visits he believes the patient should receive, or he may leave this up to the nurse. He may draw up a schedule of specific treatments to be provided by a specialist; or he may prescribe a routine care plan that can be supplied by paraprofessional home health aides.

Once the final plan is drawn up and discussed among all participants, the program becomes official. From this point on, the doctor, the nurse, and the nursing service will work closely together in the patient's home environment until the job is completed.

Today It Is Rare for Doctors to Make House Calls. What Is the Doctor's Role in Times of Emergency?

This depends entirely on the relationship that a physician has with the patient and with the family. Sometimes programs are worked out ahead of time in which it is agreed that the doctor will make regular calls, or that he will be available for home visits in time of crisis. In other instances the doctor will agree to work with a home care patient, but only on the understanding that the nurses do the actual in-house medical care and that he remains in an overseer's position.

Does the Home Nurse Provide All Health Care Services Herself, or Does She Have Help?

Most of the better visiting nurse services provide a full repertoire of health care professionals to supplement and support their team of registered and licensed practical nurses. Their staff may include both professional and paraprofessional workers: occupational therapists, physical therapists, nurse's aids, homemakers, dieticians, nutritionists, home companions, social workers, housekeepers, speech therapists. The service will also often provide access to clinical nurse specialists who can be called in for consultation specific to certain problems, cancer care, say, or colostomy care, neurological disorders, or psychiatry.

A visiting nurse, in other words, comes to the home of the sick person backed up by an entire staff of trained professionals, a staff capable of providing services that more or less match those available at a hospital. *Home care is not a substitute health service; it is an alternative form of health service.*

What Other Home Care Associations Exist besides the Visiting Nurse Association?

Many home care programs are directly operated by hospitals. Those interested should inquire with the local hospital administrations.

If the hospital does not have such a program, there will usually be a discharge coordinator on the staff whose job is to link patients with outside home care agencies. Many medical facilities keep an entire discharge planning team on staff to help outgoing patients determine acceptable home care strategies.

Most hospitals have either a home care program or a relationship with a visiting nurse service of some kind. Today, if a person wants home care, he or she can almost always get it.

How Will Patients Know Where Home Care Resources Are Available?

As mentioned, most hospitals have access to this information and will help make arrangements. Social workers specialize in referrals of this type. Phone books, especially the classified sections, are full of listings for home nursing organizations.

At the same time, the patient must learn to be aggressive in this matter. If requested, social workers will gladly inform the patient about the specifics of available home care. If they are not asked, they may not think to mention it. *The truth is that if home care is desired, the patient must be the one to initiate the questions and to follow up on the leads. As yet, American health care services do not volunteer this information as a matter of course.* If all else fails, there are two national groups which represent the home health care industry and which will provide local referrals on request. They are:

National Association for Home Care,
311 Massachusetts Avenue, NE,
Washington, DC 20002.

National HomeCaring Council,
235 Park Avenue South,
New York, NY 10003.

Further sources of information for families considering home care include the following:

Center for Medical Consumers and Health Care Information,
237 Thompson Street,
New York, NY 10012.

Homemaker's Home and Health Services,
3651 Van Rick Drive,
Kalamazoo, MI 49001.

National Council for Homemaker and Home Health Aid Services,
67 Irving Place,
New York, NY 10003.

National Voluntary Organizations for Independent Living for the Aging,
1828 L Street, NW,
Suite 504,
Washington, DC 20036.

Visiting Nurses, National League for Nursing,
10 Columbus Circle,
New York, NY 10019.

If a Patient or a Patient's Family Opts for Home Care, Will the Visiting Nurse Help Train Them in the Basics of Nursing?

Part of the nurse's job is to teach the family how to help them help the patient. A good nurse will involve the *entire* family in patient care, children included, and will instruct them in fundamental methods of health care, such as changing sheets, checking vital signs, bathing the patient, and so on.

Could You Describe in a More Detailed Way Some of the Specific Nursing Techniques That a Home Care Nurse Might Teach to Family Members?

The family will learn to take the patient's vital signs. These include oral and rectal temperature, blood pressure and blood pressure record information, pulse, pulse record keeping, and breaths-per-minute respiration checks.

Families may also be trained in treating bed sores and various ulcerated skin conditions; in watching for symptom changes that indicate improvement or emergency situations; in detecting and treating dehydration; in dietary and exercise methods for relieving constipation; in moving the patient from room to room; in dressing, feeding, and washing the patient; and in overseeing the patient's toilet activities.

Sometimes bandaging techniques will be learned, as well as recognition and treatment of minor irritations such as itching, bad odors, mouth dryness, headache, and so on. Specific instruction for avoiding accidents may be communicated, together with systems of hygiene specific to the sick person, range-of-motion exercises which ensure that a patient's joints will be moved through all their possible directions at least once a day, and methods for home entertainment and recreation. The use and maintenance of adaptive devices such as wheelchairs, artificial limbs, walkers, traction equipment, and so on, may be explained. Each case is different and requires different specific consultation.

Does This Mean That at a Certain Point the Family Takes over Patient Care Duties from the Nurse?

No, the family remains a complement to the nurse. The role of the visiting nurse in the patient's home is that of supervisor-facilitator. She oversees all care practices and works directly with the doctor, the patient, and other professionals to make sure that the best service is provided. She serves as liaison between the family and physician, watches over the whole process of nursing and medicalization, and besides all this, takes care of the patient. The sum adds up to a global task, one that requires too much time and too much training to be handled fully by the family.

What Are Some of the Other Functions That a Visiting Nurse Performs When Working with a Terminally Ill Person?

In terminal cases a home nurse's job is primarily one of maintenance rather than cure. If she is well trained, she will approach this task in a holistic manner, watching over the patient's social and psychological processes as well as his physical ones.

Let's take the example of home nutritional care. Here a nurse will, of course, make sure that the patient is fed at the proper hours and that he receives a balanced and wholesome diet. She will also help feed the patient, oversee the preparation of the food and administer intravenous feedings should they be scheduled.

Besides this, in certain cases the nurse will join forces with the social worker, devising special arrangements for the acquirement of food stamps, say, should the patient's finances require them, or making arrangements for certain foods to be stocked at a neighborhood grocery store. Sometimes she will make suggestions to the family on how to improve food quality or how to present it in a more attractive way. She may encourage the family to move their eating area into the sick person's room. In this way the communal social climate that eating is associated with is restored, and the patient feels part of things once more.

The visiting nurse may work with a nutritionist to plan a dietary program, with a doctor to construct a bowel training plan for an incontinent patient, with a physical therapist to devise exercise programs to keep the person's alimentary muscles in working order, or with a psychiatric worker to oversee problems the patient may have in accepting or rejecting food. The nurse's job, in other words, is multifaceted, overlapping areas of other professionals and requiring administrative as well as technical skills.

What Does a Family Practicing Home Care Do If There Is an Emergency?

They call the nurse and, if necessary, the nurse calls the doctor. The problem, really, is how to distinguish a real emergency from a false one.

In fact, a good home care nurse will educate the family in emergency measures long before such a situation occurs. One nurse who has worked with home care cases for many years describes her approach to this matter in the following way: "Families get very nervous about what constitutes an emergency, and when they should call the doctor. My approach is to go over with them all the possible bad things that might happen. The way I do it is, I sit there and ask them if they ever get panicky that something is going to happen and they won't know what to do? They always say yes. Then I'll ask them the specific things that come to mind, the things that really make them nervous. They will give me their list. I'll write them down. Then I say we should go over these points and talk about: number one, how big is the possibility of it happening; number two, what will it look like when it happens; number three, who should you call and what should you do.

"We then go down the list, even over the crazy and improbable things they're scared of. I explain the procedures that might be used in each case. Usually this helps tremendously. It prepares the persons ahead of time and helps lessen a lot of their fears. Now they have a plan. It's there before them in writing and if anything happens they can refer to it."

In a Hospital There Is Always a Nurse or Doctor Somewhere in the Vicinity. At Home This Is Not Always the Case. How Does One Keep Track of All the Sick Person's Symptoms and Report Them Correctly When the Nurse or Doctor Does Arrive?

Both homebound patients and their families can easily become frustrated over the matter of remembering what to tell the doctor. By the time the doctor and nurse arrive, everyone in the family, it seems, has forgotten what they wished to say and what they wanted to ask. Until, of course, the doctor and nurse leave, and then it all returns.

"As a nurse what I used to do," another visiting nurse tells us, "is keep a memo pad on the wall in the kitchen, and another by the patient's bed. As questions and problems come up they get written down. Right away. Anyone who has a sick relative at home should keep written records—*written*—because probably you will not remember it all in your head. I knew one patient who had a tape recorder and would talk into it and leave messages for his family and for the nurse. That's a good system too."

Doesn't the Patient Often Feel Like an Encumbrance to His Family and to Those around Him If He Is at Home?

Yes. But feeling like a burden is not exclusive to home care patients. Many terminally ill people in hospitals are equally apologetic, both to their families and to the staff. Indeed, if one has characteristically felt like a burden to others throughout life, this is probably part of one's emotional disposition; that person will probably feel like a burden again when he is dying. Those who die at home have no monopoly on this sentiment.

But Sometimes the Patient Will Be an Undeniable Drain on the Household; and the Family, despite Themselves, Will Signal Their Irritation in Subtle and Nonsubtle Ways. Can't This Build Up Resentments and Friction among All Concerned?

Yes, it can, and it is one of the many real concerns with which those involved with home care must deal. Home care, for better or for worse, is looked on by many as the definitive "natural" alternative to the medico-hospitalization machine, a sort of cure-all against all the ills of institutionalized medicine. As such it is equated with other homespun alternatives too, such as home birth or unorthodox healing techniques, and like both, its value and effectiveness are often overestimated. In reality, home care is to be looked on simply as an alternative to hospital care—a better one in many situations, a worse one in some.

As to friction at home: In cases where a great deal of conflict arises between patient and family, it is best to consult the visiting nurse, social worker, or therapist. Often the problems boil down to basic areas of dissent, and a trained professional can get to the heart of the matter.

It might be added, moreover, that the question of whether or not the family feels put upon by home care is often an ambiguous one. Take the case of an elderly couple from the midwest. The man was dying a slow, disintegrative death and the woman, equally old, was in the best of health. Forced into a caretaker role, the wife never ceased complaining about her invalid husband, often in front of the husband himself.

At the same time, when the actual hour arrived for the woman to bathe or change or exercise her bothersome charge, she became quite a different person. Even an outsider could perceive the lovingness with which she tucked him in, helped him around the room, fed him, rubbed his limbs. A great deal of the woman's deeper emotions were communicated through the bed bath, through feeding, through care with the hands. What the woman said and what she did—and felt—were, in other words, two quite different matters.

So in a Home Care Situation One Should Expect Both the Family and the Patient to Have Mixed Feelings?

How could it be any other way? Home care is difficult. It puts a lot of responsibility on everyone. A caretaker may feel enormous exasperation at having to feed and change a grumbling, bedridden, foul-smelling invalid. It is only human nature to react this way. However, this does not mean that the caretaker loves the dying person any the less, or that he would have things any other way. It is well within the perimeters of human feelings to simultaneously look on our burdens with the upmost resentment and the deepest love.

What Can Be Done When a Dying Person Wants Home Care but the Family Refuses?

Investigation must be done to discover *why* the family feels this way. In some cases the family may suppose that they have neither the time, patience, nor wherewithal to care for a home-bound patient, even if helped out by a home nursing service. The responsibility is indeed a sizable one, and frequently work situations or complicated family dynamics make the shoulder-ing of added pressures impossible. If this is the case, the family's wishes should, of course, be honored. Without willing partici-pation, home care inevitably ends up in a shambles.

In other instances, a family may feel that there is not enough physical space to accommodate the sick person. Assessments by a trained social worker may be helpful in this instance, to show how home care can be done in a limited area, perhaps even in areas as small as a single room. Again, though, sometimes it *is* true; the space may be too small, and hospitalization then be-comes the better alternative.

In still other cases, if the truth be told, families simply do not like the dying person (for whatever reasons) and make little effort to hide the fact that they can't *wait* until he or she passes on. The relative, meanwhile, unless she is thick-skinned or non compos mentis, will probably be aware of the loveless climate at home and will suffer miserably for it. If home care is initiated in such a situation, or forced on the family by whatever powers that be, prior experience has demonstrated that the family will use the least available excuse to dump the patient in the hospital, usually via the ambulance through the emergency room. Every-one is ambivalent about home care to a certain degree, and in some cases negative feelings outweigh positive ones. Home care should never be attempted in such an instance. It will wind up with hurt feelings, sudden rides to the hospital, a lot of triplicate forms being filled out, all with no benefits to either family or patient.

Still another difficulty arises when families worry that home care patients will not receive the kind of top-quality medical care available in hospitals. Such an attitude usually comes from lack of knowledge about what home care really is, and ignorance of the resources available to homebound patients. Consultations with visiting nurses services, with hospital liaison coordinators, nurses, social workers, and sometimes physicians will provide specifics on the many services available through home care proj-ects.

Of all reasons for the avoidance of home care, however, the one most commonly seen in families is fear of their own incompetence. Consider the example of the elderly woman with a broken hip and cancer of the pancreas who was hospitalized for three months when her hip condition became acute. While in the hospital her family came every day and stood by the bedside watching while the nurses and aids took over, ordering the family not to touch the old lady—they would do it—not to move her—it was their job—not to feed her—the dietician would see to that. All the family could conclude from this, naturally, was that the professionals knew everything, and that they knew nothing.

Then, suddenly, the old woman was sent home. She was no longer in need of crisis treatment, the hospital announced, and it was now the family's turn to take over: without training, without equipment or support, and with deep-rooted inferiority feelings concerning their ability to provide health care of any kind. No wonder they were frightened. And this is a common scenario throughout the country.

The remedy can be worked out in several ways. First, by advanced planning. The family can procure the required equipment—wheelchair, adjustable bed, special foods, and so on— before the person returns from the hospital. Either patient or family may suggest that assessment of home and patient be made *ahead of time* by the visiting nurse service, while the patient is still in the hospital, so that when the patient is brought home all preliminary work is taken care of. They can, as well, make advance arrangements with a nursing service to avoid overlap between the patient's return and her treatment. They can also seek training in the fundamentals necessary for care of a shut-in. This training is available through various health care training courses offered in many communities, and occasionally through the visiting nurse service itself. Finally, there are many excellent books on the subject of home care which offer much practical information. See the bibliography which follows.

Cherkasky, M., I. Rossman, and P. Rogatz, *Guide to Organized Home Care.* Chicago: Chicago Hospital Research and Educational Trust, 1961.

Covell, Mara, *Your Guide to Better Health Care.* Merit Books, 1981.

Duda, Deborah, *A Guide to Dying at Home*. Santa Fe, N. Mex.: John Muir, 1982.

Howell, Mary, *Healing at Home*. Boston: Beacon Press, 1978.

Stewart, Jane. *Home Health Care*. St. Louis: C. V. Mosby, 1979.

Stolten, Jane Henry, *A Guide to Family Nursing*. Boston: Little, Brown, 1975.

What If the Family Attempts Home Care and Simply Finds It Too Difficult to Sustain? Does This Mean That the Patient Must Go Back to the Hospital?

Not necessarily. There are many resources that can be tapped before the family gives up. Remember, with home care and visiting nurse services we are not just talking about a single domestic helper but a large backup organization of experts. If things become difficult, social workers may be called in to help solve personal problems, or psychiatric counselors, or even homemakers, should the work load become too great and cleaning or cooking services be required.

As well, think of community services. In every town and city there are volunteer groups, many of them set up to ease the burden of families. Senior companion programs, for instance, send elderly visitors to the home of an ill person, providing diversion for the shut-in and allowing family members to get out for a while, to go to the supermarket or to a movie, to take a breather. There are also neighborhood center programs in many urban areas. These provide a multitude of vital services, such as a meals-on-wheels program, telephone reassurance programs, search and care programs, shopping aids, escorts, and psychiatric treatment.

Religious organizations are deeply involved in social services, and many offer outreach programs designed specifically for the homebound. There are, for instance, church-based volunteer helpers who come to one's home for, say, three 4-hour periods a week; and driving services which provide transportation to a meal center or to the doctor. These services are ordinarily free, or are available at low cost. The participant's task is to find out about them by inquiring at religious institutions or local social centers.

How Do Medication and Prescription Programs Work for the Homebound?

The doctor prescribes the medications, the family or nurse picks them up at the drugstore, and the nurse or sometimes the family gives them to the sick person. It is more or less the same system used by doctors and patients everywhere.

What If Injections Are Necessary?

The nurse can teach family members how to give injections. The family will then administer shots when the nurse is not present.

Is It Legal for Nonmedical Professionals to Give Injections?

It depends on the substance being injected. Diabetics inject themselves all the time. If a nonnarcotic substance is required, family members or the patient herself can inject them directly. If narcotic substances are involved, they must be given by a doctor or a nurse.

What Can Be Done to Make a Dying Person's Immediate Home Environment More Comfortable?

Establish regular routines, regular rhythms: meals at a certain time of day, naps at a certain hour, visits at specific time periods. These regularities have security and reassurance built into them. Reduce stressful input, loud noises, sudden interruptions, unexpected visits from unwanted visitors, tiring demands.

The sick space: Make the patient as physically comfortable as possible. If feasible, she should have her own room or at least her own well-defined area of the house or apartment. Lighting should be cheerful, and adequate for reading. A bell or buzzer system may be set up to call for aid, especially if the patient is sequestered in a far corner of the living area. It would also be handy, for both the family and the patient, to place an equipment shelf near the patient's bed to hold common medicinal supplies such as mouthwash, towels, medicines, tape, massage oil, bedpans, enema apparatus, talcum powder, hot water bottle, thermometer, Kleenex, ointment tubes, Q-tips, cotton, and so on. Comfortable chairs can be arranged around the patient's bed so that visitors are pleasantly accommodated. If the patient is permanently bed-bound, a backrest will encourage sitting up and will help vary the monotony of supine postures. A telephone near the bed may be useful, and the patient might be provided with a handy night table on which to keep personal items as well as glasses, books, tissues, pen and paper, newspaper, and so on. Room temperatures should be well controlled. If the area is underwarmed, an extra space heater will make up the difference. If the patient is allergic or if she suffers from lung ailments, air conditioning and air purifiers will make breathing easier.

The bed: This is a central part of a sick person's universe, and everything possible should be done to make it as accommodating as possible. The mattress should be adequately firm. Overly soft mattresses cause back pain. The sheets should be fresh and should be changed as often as possible. Underpadding is important. It should not be lumpy or too thin. The blankets should be correctly matched to the seasons: heavy blankets for winter, light blankets for summer. Provision of comfortable pillows will be welcome, especially if the person enjoys propping herself up while reading or conversing.

Meals: These take on both a social and a physical importance for the dying patient. Make sure that the patient is served the kind of food she enjoys, and honor all special requests as long as they fit into the dietary regime. Surprise dishes, coveted desserts, and old culinary favorites will all sweeten the convalescent's day.

As far as possible, the patient should be included in regular family meals. If it is not feasible to move her into the dining area for at least one meal a day, the focus can be shifted to the person's room, where the entire family can gather around her bed to take food.

Social and psychological considerations: These are much the same as those we would provide a dying person under any circumstances. Let the person know that she is loved and valued;

keep her active and involved—unless, of course, she chooses voluntarily to withdraw, at which point allow her the space to be private. Help the homebound patient not to feel helpless or like a burden. This means allowing her to do limited chores around the house, should she wish, and permitting her to live life as normally as possible.

What about Pain Relief at Home?

Pain relief programs more or less follow the same lines as at a hospital. The medicine is prescribed by the physician, injections are given at regular intervals, and dosages are geared to an amount and frequency that allows the patient to remain pain-free.

What Major Costs Are Involved in Home Care?

The most expensive home services are those purchased from private or hospital-based programs. The least expensive are provided by government agencies or by visiting nurse associations. Upjohn HealthCare Services, the largest private home care organization in the United States, charges from $13 to $25 an hour for home visits by a registered nurse. Licensed practical nurses cost from $10 to $20 an hour. Paraprofessionals such as homemakers and companions charge from $6 to $10 an hour. The highest expenses are for specialists. A single home visit from an occupational therapist or psychiatric social worker can cost from $40 to $60, and sometimes more. The average cost of a single home health care visit in 1982—this includes professionals and paraprofessionals—was $39 per visit.

Do Patients Undergoing Home Care Usually End Up Dying in Their Homes? Or at the Last Moment Do They Usually Go to the Hospital?

As sometimes happens, dying patients at the last moment will panic and opt to go to the hospital. The truth of the matter is that the hospital can usually do no more for a terminal case in crisis than can be done at home, which is basically to control the pain and maintain a level of comfortability. But force of habit breeds hope. Whether or not a person chooses ultimately to go to the hospital at the last moment is a personal decision, and one which a dying person should, if possible, ponder carefully before the moment arrives. Dying at home is a commitment of sorts, one which, to the best of one's ability, should be reached before the moment of truth becomes imminent.

When Is Home Care Not Advisable?

If the relationship between the patient and the family is conflicted and the family objects to having the patient at home, this is a primary reason for *not* having home care. If home care is to work it must, by definition, be a team effort. Without this effort home care may end up driving both the family and the patient to distraction, and will ultimately make the patient's last days miserable.

Other considerations have already been mentioned: There may not be enough space in the living space for home care; working conditions may force family members to be absent from the home during the day; the family may not be able to afford a visiting nurse service and may feel incompetent to take on the job themselves; the patient may prefer hospital care or insurance may demand it; the family may not like the patient. Families and patients must weigh the alternatives and decide for themselves.

What Is the Most Important Thing That a Person Should Know Ahead of Time about Home Care?

Probably this: that home care exists, that it is available, and that it is feasible.

At risk of being redundant, we will say again that the most significant reason why people do not take advantage of home care today is because they do not yet recognize it as a workable option.

Surveys show that the majority of people would prefer to spend their last days surrounded by loving faces and familiar settings. Yet most die hospitalized. Unless we ourselves take the initiative and learn what home care is and what home care resources exist in our community, the sad truth is that this is the way it will remain.

9
Sources of Help

Besides the Immediate Family, Friends, the Physician, and the Social Worker, What Other Sources of Support Exist for a Dying Person?

There are several. The first is personal religious counsel. The second is psychological/psychiatric counsel. The third consists of organizations dedicated to group-oriented self-help work with the dying and their families. Naturally, there is much overlap between the three.

Which of These Supports Is Most Consistently Successful in Helping People Cope?

All three have their degree of success and failure. How much they help and which helps best is always a question of individual need. An atheist, obviously, will not receive much solace from theological lectures by a cleric. A loner will not be comfortable at group discussions.

Note, however, that there is no reason why a person cannot simultaneously avail herself of several means of aid. Personal religious counseling can be made richer by attendance at a hospital self-help group. Work with a therapist may add new perspectives to the understanding of those already involved with a religious counselor.

Must a Person Be Religious in Order to Work with a Chaplain?

No. The chaplain is perhaps the most misunderstood of all professionals working with the sick and dying. Although schooled in religious teachings, he ordinarily receives training in practical helping techniques as well as in sacerdotal dogma, and his role extends far beyond the borders of religion per se. His job among the dying is to administer secular as well as religious help, and to make it available to *all* men and women regardless of their spiritual opinions. This is part of *his* religion, and he does it— ideally speaking, at any rate—as much for altruistic reasons as for reasons of gain.

These are important considerations. They should be noted by the patient's family as well as by the patient himself: that the chaplain is on duty to serve all persons, and that his presence— in essence—is a voluntary mercy. This sets him apart from other hospital professionals; under the right conditions it allows his relationship with the sick person to take on a particularly sweet and unique quality.

A good cleric, for example, will be a sympathetic listener as well as a ready advice-giver. Any compulsion, any terror, any bad dream, any unspeakable urge, all the antisocial impulses that cannot be confided in doctor or lawyer or husband will be heard by a wise chaplain and accepted with a sense of com- passion and nonjudgmentalness. His primary job is to show the patient that somebody sympathizes, that someone's regular vis- its can be counted on, and that someone will stand up for him, can be trusted and knows the score, and cares. In the deper- sonalized corridors of the hospital ward there is no way to describe how much such an ally can come to be valued.

Beyond this the cleric serves as a liason between the patient and his family, or between the doctor and the patient. In many cases it is he who brings the message of the inoperable cancer or the failing heart. It is he who leads the self-help program for dialysis patients, or who trains laypersons in the art of counseling the dying. And, of course, for the actively religious, he is there to discuss questions of the soul and to hold the patient's hand when silence is the best religion.

This All Sounds like a Difficult Model to Live Up To. Is Every Chaplain Capable of Playing Such a Demanding and Sensitive Role?

Of course not, no more than every doctor can live up to the image of the divine physician or every nurse can be Florence Nightingale. As in all professions there are the geniuses and the duds and those who fit somewhere in between. What we describe here is the ideal.

It is worth remembering, though, that those who join helping professions like the clergy usually do so out of a humanitarian conviction; and hence they are somewhat more inclined toward unselfish activity than those who seek fortunes in the more self-serving professions.

Does Every Hospital Have an Affiliated Chaplain?

Almost all do, and most have chaplains available for people of different religions: priests for Catholics, rabbis for Jews, ministers for Protestants, and so on.

How Does One Link Up with Clerical Help at a Hospital?

Information is available from the administrative office when checking into a hospital. Social workers can be consulted and will help make outside arrangements with one's personal religious counselor.

Must One Pay for a Chaplain's Services?

Usually not. One may, of course, be asked for a donation, and after a patient has died it is considered etiquette for the family to make a contribution if the chaplain was particularly helpful.

What If One Is a Member of a Minority Religious Group and Religious Help is Not Available through the Hospital?

Again, the administration and the hospital social worker will help. It is wise in such cases to alert one's religious counselor before checking into the hospital and to make advance arrangements so that regular visits can begin as soon as the patient is ready to receive.

Can a Hospitalized Patient Receive Visits from Her Own Religious Counselor As Well As from the Chaplain Connected to the Hospital?

Usually this is encouraged by the hospital chaplain. Family and hospital clerics will often work together, spelling each other on visits and collaborating with one another to make the patient's situation as tolerable as possible.

One of the Reasons Patients Are Reluctant to Consult a Chaplain Is That They Fear They Will Be Lectured to, Made to Feel Guilty, or Suffocated with Homilies—When What They Really Want Is Simply to Get Relief from Fear and Stress.

Some chaplains are guilty of countering their own death phobias with sermons about how "God is testing you" or how "you must learn to accept His Will." This is true.

Whether or not such statements are valid is beside the point. What is to the point is that these phrases may be used as a kind of smoke screen, invoked by the chaplain to separate himself from the patient's real emotional needs—and from his own fears of death. It is the cleric's form of denial.

This does not always have to be the case, however, and in fact there is really a more subtle mechanism at work behind the reluctance many people have toward requesting clerical guidance. After all, *if* one is religious in the conventional Catholic, Jewish, Protestant, Moslem, Hindu, Confucian way—whatever—one would be hard put to deny that however unfairly life may be treating one, God ultimately knows what He is doing, and things doubtless are unfolding as they should, and must. For believers this must be a fundamental tenet of belief.

The problem arises when such counsel is given by a person who does not really believe it himself, or who does not understand it. The admonition not to fear death, to surrender to God's will, to repent of one's sins, when delivered by a representative of the church who is quite obviously distant from such achievements himself, is a travesty. The dying are particularly sensitive to hypocrisy, and are quick to discern empty words. No wonder they turn away when lectured to by those who speak as experts concerning things they do not feel or understand. At the same time, however, it is this very sensitivity that allows a patient to recognize real spiritual vitality when it is present, and to be comforted by it. The same words that die as clichés on the tongue of a nonentity chime out their truth when delivered by a person of spiritual maturity. Those who have experienced the difference are familiar with the contrast.

In the sense of spiritual counsel it is therefore not so much the words that are spoken by the chaplain but the silent sense of being that he radiates—or does not radiate—that decides how much a patient will profit. It is on these grounds that the value of spiritual guidance should be judged.

Do Chaplains Provide Patients with Medical Advice or with Help concerning Physical Problems?

No, this is not the chaplain's job. It is good manners on the part of the patient to refer all medical considerations to the doctors or nursing staff, and to avoid involving the cleric in such matters.

Do Dying Patients Frequently Become Religious?

There is some research (Fichter, 1954, p. 73) to indicate that those who have been brought up with a strong religious background and who have forsaken their religion often return to it at the time of death.

In general, it can be said that at the point of death, as with the other key points along life's journey, a person acts in character. Religious people become more religious, agnostics more agnostic. Dramatic conversions are rare. Changes of heart are the exception, not the rule, and the norm remains the norm up to the end.

Do Deeply Religious People Have Less Fear of Death Than Nonreligious People? Do They Tend to Die More at Peace with Themselves Than Agnostics and Athiests?

This question has been raised many times and a great deal of academic effort has been expended to determine the answer. The result has been a mass of data, much of it contradictory. To quote E. Mansell Pattison (Pattison, 1977, p. 76): "Where direct tests of relationship have been made, three studies report that religion has a negative influence . . . five studies report a positive influence . . . and four studies found no religious differences in attitudes and behavior. . . . In separate comprehensive reviews, both Lester (1972) and Spilka, Pelligrini, [and] Daily (1968) conclude that religion per se is not a critical factor in the person's response to dying or to death. People for whom religion has had no importance will usually not turn to religion when they are dying; people whose lives have been imbedded in a religious context will deal with dying within that religious context. In effect, people will use religion in their dying as they have used religion throughout their lives. They may use religion destructively or constructively. Father André Godin (1972) sums up our conclusions: 'The anxious person finds new reasons for anxiety in his religion; the more serene person also derives from his religion the means of justifying his serenity.'"

The problem with such surveys, of course, is the question of defining the word "religious." Is a person who attends church every Sunday *ipso facto* religious? How does one measure faith? What religion are we talking about anyway?

Religious commitment is declining in Europe and the Americas, and to a large degree, religion in the West has been reduced from a great faith to a simple morality with acts of charity such as singing in the choir, being nice to your neighbor, and giving money to the poor serving as the highest sacraments.

No doubt such observances are valuable; but when practiced in and of themselves without reference to God, they become acts of secular altruism rather than religion. Many forms of Western religion, as a result, euphemize death or ignore it completely, cooperating with the modern antireligious spirit, where flight from the recognition of mortality becomes an inviolable rite of its own. Meanwhile, the more ancient notion of religion as a vehicle through which one attempts to know God and—more to our purposes—as a tool to help prepare one for the coming of death is now much neglected.

Keeping all this in mind, it is entirely unrealistic to suppose that anyone can pay religion mere lip service all their lives, tip their hat to ritual formalities, and then have their religion suddenly become a luminous light in the final hours.

No other interaction in life works this way. Why should religion?

Religion affords the dying person solace in direct ratio to the intensity of her commitment. In fact, there is much evidence to show that while people with deep faith do meet death squarely and peacefully, those with lukewarm belief have an even harder time dying than does the complete nonbeliever (Hinton, 1967, pp. 83–84). A little faith thus becomes tantamount to no faith at all, or less than none. As Elisabeth Kübler-Ross writes: "Only the few true genuine religious people have accepted death with great peace and equanimity, but in our counseling we have seen very few of these people, because we are usually called for consultations to the patients who are troubled. I would say that about 97 percent of our patients that we have studied have been a little bit religious, but not genuine and authentic. They then have the additional concern about punishment after death, regrets and guilt about missed opportunities. . . . Truly religious people with a deep abiding relationship with God have found it easier to face death with equanimity. We do not often see them because they aren't troubled, so they don't need our help" (Kübler-Ross, 1974, pp. 162–163).

For many thousands of years, in societies innumerable, for people uncountable, religion has been a mighty bulwark in the hour of death. That such is now no longer the case is perhaps more a comment on what religion has become in our times than it is about the value of faith per se.

Some People Are Shy about Asking for Help from a Chaplain, Especially If They Have Never Gone to Church or Have Left the Church.

Generally speaking, chaplains are easy people to approach. They are easy to talk with, easy to get along with. Being approachable is part of their job. A person should not be shy about asking for their help.

Don't Many Hospitalized Patients Believe That the Presence of a Chaplain by Their Bed Means They Are Receiving Last Rites or That They Are About to Die? Doesn't This Discourage Many People from Making Use of Clerical Counseling?

Only further education will help dispel this myth. Chaplains are a regular part of the health care team in any hospital and their services are for people in all stages of sickness and health. They are, as mentioned, trained to help people with everyday problems as well as with spiritual ones, and as such their visits should in no way be interpreted as a sign that the final hours have come.

What If a Family Wishes to Call In the Services of a Chaplain but the Patient Objects?

The patient's wishes should be honored. It is, after all, the patient's own body and soul that are in question.

What If a Family Has Firm Religious Beliefs and Wishes to Have Rites Performed for an Unconscious Dying Patient, but the Patient Has Previously Indicated That She Prefers to Avoid Any Religious Service?

This gets into a gray area. Generally speaking, it is usually considered good policy to honor a patient's last wishes, even if they run counter to what the family feels is right. Questions such as these are extremely sensitive and are best discussed with the chaplain.

Do Members of Any One Particular Religion Meet Death with Greater Peace Than Members of Other Religions?

The surveys done on this question are conflicting. One interesting study (Vernon, 1970, p. 193) shows that the greatest decrease of death fear due to religious conviction is reported by members of the Mormon Church. To the question: "Have your religious experiences in general served to increase or decrease fears towards your own death?" 85 percent said that it decreased them; only 4 percent said that it increased them. Lutherans were next: 64 percent said "decreased" and a rather high 17 percent said "increased."

The descending order in the "decrease" category runs as follows: Jewish (61 percent decrease, 8 percent increase), Presbyterian (60 percent decrease, 6 percent increase), and Methodist (59 percent decrease, 8 percent increase).

In terms of Catholic-Protestant groupings, an in-depth study (Jepson, 1967) shows that:

1. Catholics tend to define death in more negative terms (that is, hellfire, damnation) than do Protestants.

2. Catholics have a slightly greater conviction than Protestants that fear of death increases with age.

3. Slightly more Catholics than Protestants report fear of dying, as well as fear of the dead (cemeteries, bodies, and so on).

From further studies (mentioned in Vernon, 1970, pp. 195–196), it is also apparent that death per se is more of a pivotal concern for Catholics than for Protestants, that Catholics are introduced to death issues earlier in life than are non-Catholics, that death is more openly discussed and considered by Catholics than by Protestants, and that during life, greater emphasis is placed on preparing for death by Catholics than by Protestants.

Can a Person Receive Religious Help from a Chaplain without Participating in Religious Rites and Ceremonies?

Yes, to whatever degree is preferred. Those not inclined to ritual and ceremony may simply ask that these be omitted.

But a Chaplain Will, at the Same Time, Always Be on Hand to Administer Last Rites Should They Be Requested?

Almost all hospitals have chaplains on call who are available for the administration of last rites. If last rites are a particularly important request for the dying person or if the patient wishes a particular family chaplain to preside, it is best to arrange such services in advance. Do this by staying abreast of the chaplain's schedule, keeping him informed concerning the patient's state of health, knowing where he can be reached day and night, and so on.

How Beneficial Are Last Rites and Rituals for the Dying? Don't Many People Feel That They Are Pointless?

There is much evidence that on a subliminal level ritual serves to validate an important rite of passage, especially if the dying person has been brought up with a religious faith. "Perhaps we do not fully understand the therapeutic function of religious rites and sacramental procedures offered traditionally to terminal patients," writes Margaretta Bowers (Bowers, 1964, p. 9). "Probably many things done in the name of religion have more meaning on the subconscious level than we are aware of. Sacraments may have important emotional meaning in overcoming the feeling of separation. They *may*, in a language deeper than words, make the person feel related to an institution and tradition that are sources of faith. He may feel 'in the company of the saints.' Psychotherapists are becoming increasingly aware of the importance of symbolic acts as means of saying much in little time."

Bowers goes on to discuss the matter of ritual, with specific reference to the Catholic rites of Extreme Unction: "Roman

Catholic priests point out that reactions to Extreme Unction fall into three categories. First, the patient may become resigned to death. Aware of the fact that the Church has taken official notice of his impending demise, he gives up and dies easily and quickly. Second is the release from anxiety, apprehension, and feelings of guilt, which often produce physical relaxation, with an attendant relief of pain and other conditions associated with spasticity and tension. Third is the production of subtle changes in body chemistry which produce a change in the medical picture. It is not unknown for persons to experience what is medically referred to as 'a spontaneous regression' of the malady following a sacramental act or deep emotional experience. That these religious rites serve deep and important psychological as well as spiritual needs is verified by the fact that comparable acts with a non-religious setting often produce similar results."

Do Highly Religious People Pass through the Same Stages of Denial, Anger, Bargaining, Depression, and Acceptance As Those Who Are Not Religious?

Kübler-Ross (Kübler-Ross, 1974, p. 163) claims they do, but more rapidly and with less turmoil.

Is It Wise for a Patient to Receive Counsel from a Chaplain and from a Psychiatrist or Psychologist at the Same Time? Will the Conflict between These Viewpoints Be Too Confusing?

It depends on how sympathetic the psychiatric professional is toward religion and/or how oriented a chaplain is toward psychotherapy. If there is room in the philosophy of both to allow for the counsel of the other, if neither makes a point of countermanding the other's advice, and if the patient feels no conflict between the two points of view, it would seem an acceptable way of approaching guidance.

Although religion and psychology were once considered mutually exclusive (perhaps because Freud himself was an unbeliever), in past decades the two disciplines have made genuine attempts to learn from each other, often with favorable results.

Indeed, certain psychiatrists today now round out their practice with emphasis on spiritual growth, meditation technique, and the search for an afterlife; and the practice of many chaplains can be said to come closer to psychotherapy than to religion.

A good rule of thumb is: If it helps, use it.

Does a Person Have to Be Technically Trained to Counsel the Dying Successfully?

Just as there are professional principles for counseling children, or war veterans, or criminals, so there are principles essential to caring for the dying.

These principles have been tested in real life. They work. At least they work much of the time. They are learned through training, through hours in the field, and through focused dedication. They must be respected, even if they are not entirely understood by those outside the field.

It is thus something of a mistake to suppose that anyone can work with the dying any time without at least some minimum preparation, and that compassion alone will get one through. With dying people mistakes can be made, sometimes big mistakes, and there is precious little time to rectify them. In this area wisdom and experience are needed just as intensely as good intentions.

The fact is that everyone has a part to play. The involved bystander acts toward the dying from a compassionate, "gut-level" place. This is good. The professional acts toward the patient as her training and professional intuition tell her. This is good, too. Both are part of the helping team.

Do Most Hospitals Maintain Mental Health Professionals on Their Staffs?

Yes, or they at least have access to trained personnel.

Can a Dying Person Use His or Her Own Private Therapist When in the Hospital?

As mentioned, not every mental health professional is keen over the prospect of counseling the dying. Persons who have had a long-term relationship with a particular psychiatrist or psychologist may be shocked to discover that now, when they are most needful, their beloved doctor is strangely unavailable. In such an instance a patient may be obliged to make use of a staff psychologist.

How Can One Get Psychiatric Guidance in a Hospital If One Wishes It?

A doctor will often recommend psychiatric help if the patient's condition calls for it. Patients can make requests for psychiatric aid through the doctors or via the nursing staff, the social worker, or office administration.

Does a Dying Patient Necessarily Have to Be Neurotic or Psychologically Unstable to Require Therapeutic Work?

Work with the dying is different from other kinds of counseling. It is not necessarily addressed to neurosis or pathology but to a very sane, very real fear of pain and death. As such, anyone who feels the need for aid against these feelings would do well to seek professional help.

But the Person Is Dying. Of What Real Help Can a Psychologist or Psychiatrist Be?

This question is often asked, and the answer is that a good mental health professional can help the dying patient in several profound and sometimes unexpected ways. This does not mean that psychological counseling inevitably works wonders, of course. It rarely works wonders per se, but it often helps, and as such is well worth the attempt. The following are some of the representative goals which good psychological counseling can help the patient attain:

1. *The therapist can help the patient accept death.* Often it is not an abstract terror that haunts the patient but a very specific, very addressable problem: a person is afraid his wife will not be able to cope when he dies; he fears the damnation of hell; he is phobic about needles; he is compulsively regretful con-

cerning how he behaved toward members of his own family; and so on.

Sometimes these fears are rooted in childhood experiences, or in fantasy, trauma, or unresolved relationships. By confronting them through therapy it becomes possible to loose these ancient knots and help the person let go in a conscious and willing manner.

2. *The therapist can help the sick person find purpose in his past, and a pattern to his existence.* Since the dying patient is often exhausted and depressed, with little prospect for the future and limited energy to enjoy what remains, the past begins to look as impoverished as the present. A wise therapist can help patients salvage nuggets from the ashes of an existence that seems wasted or incomplete—meaningful motifs are present in everyone's past, even in the most evil or pathetic of lives. The therapist then guides the person to take pride in these accomplishments and to see a design in it all, perhaps even a message.

A 69-year-old man dying of renal failure had spent the first part of his life in petty criminal activity and the last as a semi-derelict in a suburban section of Boston. When first admitted to the hospital as a *pro bono* case his psychological state altered between deep depression and sudden fits of anger and violence.

Work with a student psychologist demonstrated that there was indeed much pathology in this man, and that it was exacerbated by a profound sense of aimlessness and self-loathing. Sessions with the man further revealed that in his early twenties he had been married and that this union had produced one child, a girl. Although he walked out on his wife several months after the child was born, in the beginning he maintained contact with both mother and daughter, and occasionally sent them gifts and money.

Focusing conversation on this relatively bright area, the student was able to elicit from the man feelings of love and concern for his daughter (she now lived with her large family in Indiana), and as a result was able to trigger more intimate discussions concerning his past in general.

The man grew calmer and less depressed. Some fragments

of meaning and dignity had been restored to his last days, both because genuine attention was being paid him by the young therapist and because the therapist skillfully balanced the man's feelings of pride concerning his daughter with his feelings of remorse for having deserted her. The human spot in the man had been touched. Things of value, long forgotten, became important for him again.

Together the patient and the student composed a letter to the daughter—he had not communicated with her in several decades—and in it he rather elegantly said his goodbyes. They also drew up a will, making the daughter beneficiary of the man's meager finances, and then composed another letter for her to read after his death. In this second letter, under the direction of the student, the man set down an abbreviated autobiography, describing the events that had been important in his life, explaining why he had acted as he did, and asking for his daughter's forgiveness.

At one point the man even toyed with the notion of telephoning his daughter directly, although he was not able to go through with it. He also expressed hopes that she would answer his first letter, although she never did. Nonetheless, these activities added zest to the patient's last days, during which he and the student would spend hours excitedly discussing the particulars of what he would do if he and his daughter met face to face.

In these simple ways the man was comforted, and a kind of meaning was forged for him from the sad shambles of a life.

3. *The therapist can help the dying person's family.* The therapist often spends as much time with family members as with the patient, guiding them through their bouts of anticipatory grief, helping them with whatever conflicting feelings they may have about the patient, mediating as they meet their own fears of death. To witness the physical and mental states of degeneration a loved one must pass through is an indescribably difficult experience. For many it is simply too dispiriting: The husband of a dying woman may withdraw into his work, avoiding regular visits, eating his heart out in the process. The child

of a dying person may concoct any number of excuses for not coming to the hospital, all out of fear rather than neglect.

Such withdrawal is common, especially in the last days when a patient starts the enervating slide toward death. It then becomes the therapist's job to work at both ends, with the neglected patient and with the guilt-ridden relative. In whatever ways he can he helps both confront their demons.

Later, when it is all over, the therapist may start bereavement counseling with the family, helping them through their mourning. If he is not qualified for such work, he may refer them to another professional who specializes in post-death therapy.

4. *Therapy can help a dying person resolve whatever negative feelings she may have toward herself and others.* While a patient's family may sincerely wish to speak honestly with the patient concerning importat problems, they often have neither the tact nor the objectivity to turn such conversations into healing experiences. Indeed, relatives or close friends are often part of the problem, and their probing only makes matters worse.

The therapist, on the other hand, is a benevolent outsider. He is trained in helping people verbalize hidden parts of themselves and in hearing it all with a nonjudgmental ear. He bolsters up the patient's sagging ego, resolves unsavory feelings of self-hate, and works in psychological territories where those closer to the patient might only flounder.

The primary tool here is dialogue. Problems that go unverbalized turn into poison. The patient is encouraged to discuss unresolved emotions and to examine them. A good therapist brings these hostilities into the open, and in a sense exorcises them with the light of day. In many cases just expressing them brings relief.

5. *The therapist is a friend and support.* A good patient-therapist relationship is always a caring relationship. First and foremost. The doctor presents herself not only as a transference figure but as a friend. While the patient may feel deserted by family members who are busy processing their own anticipatory grief, and by friends who suddenly become so very busy, the therapist remains steadfast. She is there, she is available. Dying

alone without care or support, as Ivan Ilyich described it in Tolstoy's famous story, *The Death of Ivan Ilyich,* is like a stone falling into a black, bottomless well, faster and faster: rank alienation. It is the therapist's job to see that the patient does not feel like a falling stone.

Is Therapy Advisable for a Person Who Does Not Yet Know That He Is Dying?

One of the first things that must be determined in terminal therapy is how much the patient knows about his condition. If his diagnosis is fatal and he does not know it, the therapist can help him reach, shall we say, an accommodation to his ignorance.

For some this accommodation means forcing the fact, bringing the truth into the open and working from there. Many patients who have been kept in the dark concerning their real diagnosis feel relieved when told the facts. Now at least they know what the enemy really is, and where they really stand.

For others a kind of quasi-acceptance is more appropriate, one masked in symbolic language and nonverbal acknowledgments. For still others it means no acceptance at all, yet an increased willingness to speak frankly concerning one's doubts and anxieties. Whatever accommodation a patient is most capable of, a good therapist will sense it and guide things in this direction.

So the Patient Does Not Have to Know That He Is Dying to Be Helped by Therapy?

No. Sometimes it may be better if he does not know. The therapy may work better that way, influencing the person on a "gut level," reducing anxieties from the unconscious out, as it were. In certain cases it would be cruel to force open awareness. Each person's therapy is different.

Does This Mean That in Certain Instances Therapy Can Be Dangerous for the Dying Person?

Perhaps. But dying is dangerous, too, and one must weigh the advantages against the disadvantages. It is true that pent-up feelings can be released in therapy and that they may turn destructive. But a good therapist is adroit at sizing up a patient's tolerances during preliminary sessions, and at sensing his or her limits of ego strength. A good therapist does not give a patient more than the patient can handle.

It is, moreover, a truism among psychologists that patients hear what they wish to hear. The bad news filter comes built in. Although this filter may keep patients oblivious to truths concerning themselves, it also acts as protection. One of the arts of therapy is knowing how much to push at this shield, and when to back away.

But What If You Don't *Have* a Good Therapist?

It is the same as having or not having a good doctor, and as with a doctor—or dentist, or lawyer, or accountant—it pays to look around.

Talk to people who have dealt with the therapist before. Ask about his reputation at local medical societies and consumer groups. Is he accredited? How long has he been in practice? Is he is affiliated with a hospital, what do other patients say about him? How close does he come to meeting some of the standards we have mentioned in the last few pages? Have other patients been helped?

Go with your own experience. If after several sessions you feel compatible with the therapist and think he knows his stuff, stay with him. If you get a sense of incompetence, or if you simply do not like him, find someone else.

What Answers Might a Therapist Give to a Terminal Patient Who Has a Particular Fear of Dying?

Therapists do not give answers. Not as a rule. Especially answers to such imponderables as fear of death. The therapist helps the patient face his situation. She helps him out of mental ruts and over psychic blockages and around emotional fantasies. She deals less in information, more in insight.

At its best, therapy can give a person the understanding and courage to deal with death from his own resources. The therapist is a catalyst and friend and is there when needed. She is neither a magician nor a prophet.

Is There Group Therapy for the Dying?

Yes, and this gets into our third category of psychosocial services for the dying: group help organizations.

Today, for example, some hospitals run group programs especially for the dying. These groups may be presided over by a trained psychiatric professional, and they are especially designed to help patients voice their worries about any number of problems. The modus operandi of each differs, of course, but generally speaking, meetings are centered around voluntary discussion. Mutual support is encouraged, along with honest, open discussion. Experiences are shared, sometimes psychological exercises are practiced, and leaders may lecture on subjects pertinent to patients' needs.

How Does a Person Make Contact with Such Groups?

By making inquiries with the doctor, the nursing staff, the social worker, or the liaison medical services at a hospital. If none of these can help, which is unlikely, you can find out about support groups from friends, other patients, messages on local bulletin boards, and in the newspaper. A comprehensive list of well-established local and national support groups, with names and addresses, is given at the end of this chapter.

Are They Open to Everyone?

It depends on their focus of interest. A self-help group for patients with leprosy will obviously not be of interest to those with heart conditions. Aside from this obvious consideration, support groups are almost always nonsectarian and open to those who need them.

How Do These Groups Help?

Help groups for the chronically ill (as well as groups for the bereaved, families of the dying, and so on) work on several levels. On the one hand, they offer fellowship. On another they help people realize they are not alone, that others are going through similar crisis situations. They also provide direct answers to practical concerns. (Legal questions: "What happens to our joint bank account if my husband dies?" Medical questions: "My doctor refuses to answer me in plain English when I ask him about my condition. Does anybody else here have this problem? What do you do about it?" Emotional questions: "Why me?") Finally, a good support group subtly directs the person to the realization that he does not have to be a victim, that attitudes toward one's situation *affect* one's situation, and that, in more ways than we realize, they affect the *outcome* of that situation.

Do Discussion Groups Talk about Death Directly?

It depends on the type of group of which we are speaking. Organizations cater to different specific needs.

At a typical meeting, say one for women who have had mastectomies, discussion will center on topics of immediate concern: the pros and cons of chemotherapy, reactions to recurrence, sexual problems, the cost of cosmetic surgery, and so on. Discussion is not directly about death but about practical methods of adjusting to present problems. At the same time, concern with death is obviously at the backs of many people's minds, even if it is not brought up within the forum of discussion.

Are There Self-Help Organizations for Families of the Dying?

Yes, and they are becoming increasingly common. Many hospitals now sponsor discussion groups especially for families of cancer patients, say, or for relatives of patients who are in a kidney dialysis program. Consult with a social worker or the hospital administration about linking up with such a group.

What Groups Exist to Counsel Dying Patients and Their Families?

First there are the numerous local organizations which specialize in helping people through difficult times. These can be contacted through hospitals, senior citizens' centers, community aid groups, family service groups, social service agencies, social workers, and so on. There are also the following groups, many of which have both nationwide and statewide chapters.

The American Cancer Society, Director of Service and Rehabilitation, 777 Third Avenue, New York, NY 10017. (Offers many supports for cancer patients and their families; literature available; many helpful aids.)

American Heart Association, 44 East 23rd Street, New York, NY 10011. (Provides help for people with severe heart conditions and for those recovering from heart surgery.)

Ars Moriendi, 7301 Huron Lane, Philadelphia, PA 19119. (Provides help for dying and bereaved patients.)

Arthritis and Rheumatism Foundation, 23 West 45th Street, New York, NY 10036.

Bereavement and Loss Center, 170 East 83rd Street, New York, NY 10028.

Big Brothers/Big Sisters of America, 220 Suburban Station Building, Philadelphia, PA 19103. (Local agencies in different states offer volunteer Big Brother programs for children who have lost one or both parents.)

Cancer Care, Inc., One Park Avenue, New York, NY 10016. (Part of the National Cancer Foundation, this group provides counseling help for cancer patients and their families. Its services are usually free.)

Cancer Information Service, Memorial Sloan-Kettering Cancer Center, 1275 York Avenue, New York, NY 10021.

Candlelighters Association, 123 C Street, SE, Washington, DC 20003. (A group for parents of children with cancer.)

Children in Hospitals, 31 Wilshire Park, Needham, MA 02191.

Clear Light Society, P.O. Box 219, Boston, MA 02123. (Offers nondenominational programs that train people to help the dying through guided meditation techniques; also provides emergency training to families of the dying.)

Concern for Dying, 250 West 57th Street, New York, NY 10107. (Provides educational materials on the right to die.)

The Dying Project, P.O. Box 1725, Santa Fe, NM 87501. (Provides spiritually oriented help for the terminally ill; interested parties are invited to send their phone number and permission to call collect to the address above and consultation will be provided; workshops and lectures are also conducted. A catalog of audio tapes on the subject of death and dying is available on request.)

Forum for Death Education and Counseling, P.O. Box 1226, Arlington, VA 22210. (An organization to promote skills in death education and counseling.)

The Foundation of Thanatology, 630 West 168th Street, New York, NY 10032. (The emphasis of this group is on education in the field of death and dying.)

I Can Cope, American Cancer Society, Director of Service and Rehabilitation, 777 Third Avenue, New York, NY 10017. (A branch of the American Cancer Society with local chapters to help people deal with cancer diagnosis; classes and literature are available. Contact the American Cancer society for information.)

The International Association for Near-Death Studies, Box U-20, The University of Connecticut, Storrs, CT 06268. (Provides counseling and study for people who have had near-death experiences; magazine and educational literature available.)

International Association for Suicide Prevention, 2521 West Pico Boulevard, Los Angeles, CA 90006.

Make Today Count, 218 South Sixth Street, Burlington, IA 52601. (A self-help group for the terminally ill and their families.)

The Multiple Sclerosis Society, 257 Park Avenue South, New York, NY 10010.

Muscular Dystrophy Association, 1970 Broadway, New York, NY 10019.

National Association of Patients on Hemodialysis and Transplantation, 505 Northern Boulevard, Great Neck, NY 11021.

National Burn Victim Foundation, Metcalf Building, 308 Main Street, Orange, NJ 07050.

National Foundation of Sudden Infant Death, 1501 Broadway, New York, NY 10036. (Has local chapters; provides guidance for families that have suffered early and sudden loss of a child.)

National Institute for the Seriously Ill and Dying, Henry Avenue and Abbottsford Road, Philadelphia, PA 19129.

National Save-a-Life League, 20 West 43rd Street, Suite 706, New York, NY 10036. (Provides counseling for potential suicides.)

The National Sudden Infant Death Syndrome Foundation, 310 South Michigan Avenue, Suite 1904, Chicago, IL 60604. (Provides consultation and volunteer aid for grieving parents, and research and service programs for families. Educational pamphlets are available.)

Pain Consultation Center, Mount Sinai Medical Center, 4300 Alton Road, Miami, FL 33140. (Provides help with pain control.)

Pain Treatment Center, Scripps Clinic and Research Foundation, La Jolla, CA 92037. (Provides help with pain control.)

Parents Concerned for Hospitalized Children, 26 Danbury Circle, Amherst, NH 03031.

Parents of Murdered Children, 1739 Bella Vista, Cincinnati, OH 45237.

Parents without Partners, 7910 Woodmont Avenue, Washington, DC 20014. (Provides help for widowed parents; lectures, discussions, recreational activities, self-help groups, and so on. There are chapters in most states.)

Ray of Hope, 1518 Derwen Drive Iowa City, IA 52240. (Provides help for the families of suicides.)

Shanti Nilaya, P.O. Box 2396, Escondido, CA 92025. (Provides help and spiritual counseling for the dying and the living; project headed by Elisabeth Kübler-Ross.)

Shanti Project, 218 South Sixth Street, Burlington, IA 52601. (Sends volunteers to the homes of sick persons to provide counseling on medical, psychological, or legal problems.)

Silent Unity, Unity Village, MO 64065. (800) 821-2935 (toll free). (A religious group that will pray for anyone upon request.)

The Society of Compassionate Friends, P.O. Box 3247, Hialeah, FL 33013. (Provides guidance for bereaved parents.)

Society of Military Widows, P.O. Box 254, Coronado, CA 92118. (Provides assistance to the wives of deceased veterans.)

Suicide Prevention League, 815 Second Avenue, New York, NY 10017. [Call (212) 736-6191 for help.]

Theos Foundation, Inc., 306 Penn Hills Mall, Pittsburgh, PA 15235. (A Christian self-help fellowship for the bereaved.)

U.S. Catholic Conference, Family Life Division, 1312 Massachusetts Avenue, NW, Washington, DC 20005.

Widowed Persons Service, 1909 K Street, NW, Washington, DC 20049. (Offers special help for bereavement in the first few months following death of a mate; direct work with volunteers. There are many chapters.)

Widows' Consultation Center, 136 East 57th Street, New York, NY 10022.

Widow-to-Widow Program, Needham Community Council, Needham, MA 02192. (This and similar "widowed-to-widowed" programs are found in many cities; they are designed to bring widows together to discuss problems of living alone, coping, and so on.)

10

The Hospice

Is a Hospice in the Category of Help Groups?

Yes and no. Technically, a hospice is set up somewhat along the lines of a group support organization. It is, however, a considerably more inclusive and holistic organization; it really operates as much as a principle as a program.

The *Discursive Dictionary of Health Care*, published by the Subcommittee of Health and Environment of the Committee on Interstate and Foreign Commerce, the U.S. House of Representatives, provides the following useful and rather inclusive definition of a hospice (quoted in Rossman, 1977, p. 240):

"*Hospice*: a program which provides palliative and supportive care for terminally-ill patients and their families, either directly or on a *consulting* basis with the patient's physician or another community agency such as a Visiting Nurse Association. Originally a medieval name for a way station for pilgrims and travelers where they could be replenished, refreshed, and cared for; used here for an organized program of care for people going through life's last station. The whole family is considered the unit of care, and care extends through the mourning process. Emphasis is placed on symptom control and preparation for and support before and after death, full-scope health services being provided for by an organized interdisciplinary team available on a twenty-four-hour-a-day, seven-days-a-week basis. Hospice originated in England (where there are about 25) and are now appearing in the United States. As one example of their human- and cost-saving effects, 61 percent of one hospice's patients died at home (compared with 2 percent of all American deaths which occur at home).

HOSPICE GOALS

1. "Keep patient at home as long as possible"
2. "Supplement, not duplicate, existing services"
3. "Educate: health professionals, lay people"
4. "Help patient to live as fully as possible"
5. "Keep costs down"

As mentioned, a hospice is a place that practices a principle—either a ward on an existing hospital or a building of its own—where a sick person goes quite specifically to die. There is no subterfuge concerning this fact, no "euphemism-speak," but neither is there an atmosphere of hopelessness—patients sometimes end up leaving the hospice via a remission or recovery and return home to resume active lives. Nonetheless, the hospice is first and foremost a place where one goes to prepare oneself for death and to pass through the experience in the best and most dignified of ways.

This means many things: for one, that the hospice is patient-oriented, not medicine-oriented or even cure-oriented. What counts most is that the patient is physically comfortable and psychologically at ease. To assure this, close contact between staff and patient is encouraged. It is not an unusual sight to see a hospice doctor or nurse seated on a patient's bed in the middle of the day, chatting about politics or the latest fashions, or about the meaning of life and death. Intimacy is quite consciously fostered here. It is a rule of the house.

The hospice plan, contrary to many hospitals where families

of the dying are thought to be a necessary evil at best, is to encourage family members to become part of the daily routine on the ward, to get to know the doctors, nurses, the other patients, to attend symposiums and group discussions, to share in the medical information imparted to the patient, to spend as much time with the patient as is practically feasible, to be part of the helping team; friends, children, even pets, all are welcome on the hospice floor as long as they live up to the golden rule of the house: The patient's welfare comes first.

The hospice philosophy of keeping patients both alert and pain-free through the careful balancing of narcotic medications has already been discussed (see page 106). These techniques are complemented by careful avoidance of the green-walled "hospital look," by allowing patients to bring precious possessions into the hospital and to decorate their own rooms, by supplying patients with a full-scale choice of personal services, including a dentist, an occupational therapist, a dietician, a pharmacologist, and so on. As well, all efforts are made to welcome newcomers when they first arrive and to maintain a family feeling; all efforts are made *not* to reduce identities to bed numbers, or to demean patients with such titles as "the kidney case in room five."

What Are the Costs of Hospice Care?

It depends on the hospice and on one's particular situation. In many hospices care is based on a "what you can pay" program. In others the costs are set. It is best to inquire directly.

If there is a set fee, hospices usually cost less than regular hospitals. Since hospice doctors do not employ high-tech therapies, do not run up specialists' fees and laboratory bills, and do not prescribe rare, expensive drugs, the hefty prices of specialized medicine are not an issue. This difference alone reduces medical bills considerably. So does the fact that volunteers form a large part of the hospice staff, and that some hospices are aided by private funding.

As of 1978, according to Sandol Stoddard in her book, *The Hospice Movement*, average costs were in the range $400 to $500 per month. Although prices are higher today, sometimes twice as high, they are still bargain basement compared with standard hospital fees. One of the principles of the hospice program is that good terminal health care should be available to everyone despite their yearly earnings. By and large, they stick to their guns on this matter.

Won't a Place Where People Come to Die Be Pretty Gloomy and Depressing?

By the time one gains admittance to a hospice any dissimulation concerning the fact that one will—by all educated opinion—soon be dead, has ceased. The question is no longer "Will I die?" but "How will I die?" The answer is that one can die in the hospital in a highly structured and fairly regimented way, or one can spend the last days partly at home with one's family and partly in a hospice setting, where a premium is placed on a patient's comfort and importance and where the concept of spiritual well-being is not considered a naive indulgence. There is rarely any way that one can totally escape the gloom of death. The gloom *can* be minimized by availing the patient of the specialized caring techniques used in hospice programs.

Don't Many Hospice Programs Also Offer a Home Care Plan?

Yes they do, and this is central to the hospice notion of keeping the patient and family together throughout the terminal period.

For example, if there are, say, 50 patients living in a hospice, another 100 or 150 patients may be enrolled in the same program but will be living temporarily or permanently at home, maintained on a regular basis by a hospice home care team and enjoying many of the services supplied at the hospice.

Hospice home care services maintain a full staff of professionals on call seven days a week, twenty-four hours a day. The staff is available both to people who have gone home for the weekend and to patients who wish to stay home throughout the term of their illness.

Visits are made to the patient's house at scheduled times,

and the staff is on alert at all hours should an emergency arise. The visiting member of the hospice staff, morever, will work closely with a visiting nurse or with other home care personnel, the goal being to maximize the patient's resources and provide support from as many areas as possible.

Is the Hospice Staffed Entirely by Professionals?

Professionals form the backbone of the hospice. Most organizations include doctors, nurses, aids, orderlies, social workers, pastors, and so on. But hospices also encourage volunteer programs. Volunteers are, of course, trained, and their ranks often consist of relatives of patients who have lived and died in the hospice, and who, during their experience with the hospice, have felt so much a part of things that they returned to continue the work.

In What Ways Do the Volunteers Help?

First, by simply talking to the patients and keeping them company. Second, by providing logistical aid such as transportation to and from a patient's home. Third, by helping out with hospice administrative duties—typing, photocopying, writing letters, and so on.

Does the Hospice Provide Further Services to the Families of Deceased Patients after the Patient's Death?

The hospice provides what is known as "bereavement follow-up service." In this program counselors are dispatched to the home of the grieving family after the patient's death, and psychiatrists and social workers are made available as a regular feature of the program. Part of this counseling is done by staff members who participated in the patient's care and who may have maintained a warm personal relationship with the patient during his ordeal. This person will obviously be a familiar figure to family members by now and perhaps a much cared for one as well. Such a bond between family and counselor allows the process of grievance counseling to flow more easily and to cut through many formalities.

Do People Really Die "Better" Deaths at Hospices?

No one finds the last days a bed of roses exactly. Generally speaking, though, by helping the patient develop a reflective attitude toward death and by creating an atmosphere of support and love, it is possible to considerably improve his quality of life before death *and* to help him face it with greater composure, courage, and reserve.

How Does a Person Gain Admittance to a Hospice?

At present there are very few hospices in the United States, and the admittance standards are rather strict and perhaps even arbitrary. For example, hospices are usually restricted to people suffering from a single disease—cancer.

Only those in advanced stages of this disease are admitted, moreover, the reason being that most hospices are not equipped to house patients for many months at a time. Hospice home care programs take up the slack to a certain extent, but not all of it.

Also, the patient's doctor must give his consent for the patient to become part of the hospice plan. Translated, this means that the doctor must be sympathetic to such a program and must be willing to cooperate fully with hospice staff members.

Further, to qualify, a patient must live within the general area of the hospice. A cancer patient in Los Angeles will not gain admittance to a hospice in Cleveland.

Finally, the patient's family must live within the immediate vicinity of the hospice so that home care will be feasible should the opportunity arise. The family must be willing to care for the patient at home when and if the time comes, and they must be sympathetic to the hospice philosophy in general.

So As It Stands Today, Hospices Are Only for People Suffering from Advanced Stages of Cancer?

By and large this is the case. In the future hospice programs may broaden their acceptance programs.

What Is a Palliative Care Unit?

A PCU is a hospice type of care unit set up within the environment of a larger hospital. It operates, more or less, on hospice principles but with a bit more emphasis on research and teaching.

Could You Sum Up in Outline Form the Basic Principles of the Hospice That Make It Different from Regular Care?

Parker Rossman in his book *Hospice* (Rossman, 1977, pp. 226–227) has done an admirable job in this department. We quote him:

- "The patient needs to be as symptom-free as possible so that energy can be used to live. The goal of skilled health care is optimum relief of noxious symptoms so that the patient and family can be alert, comfortable, and themselves."

- "Terminal illness upsets the equilibrium of the family group. Help is available to all involved, whether patient, relative, or friend."

- "The patient/family life-style is disrupted by multiple change. Continuity of care shall be sustained by the same health-care team regardless of locale."

- "The patient/family thrives best when its own life-style is maintained and life philosophies respected. The structure of the care system must provide multiple options available to the patient/family under the care of the same health team in different settings."

- "Loneliness and isolation are significant sources of anguish to patients who are dying. Care-gives must always be available *where* and *when* the patient needs them."

- The varied problems and anxieties associated with terminal illness can occur at any time, day or night. Therefore 24-hour-a-day care must be available for the patient/family whatever the program may be."

- "The patient/family are needed in making decisions. Education and counseling of the staff and patient/family are required to facilitate communication, share knowledge, and reach decisions."

- "No one person can fully meet all the needs of the terminally-ill patient. Care requires collaboration of many disciplines and persons, working as a health-care team."

- "The problems of the patient/family facing terminal illness include a wide variety of issues—psychologic, legal, social, spiritual, economic, and interpersonal. Teams must be custom-made and call upon persons and institutions in the community in addition to patient/family hospice staff."

- "Caring for the patient/family as human beings affects the psychologic state. The staff shall integrate humanistic care with expert medical and nursing care."

- "Those who face separation and the end of life need spiritual support. The religious, philosophic, and humanistic components of care are as essential as the medical, nursing, and social work components."

- "The patient/family facing death needs someone who cares, and this requires emotional investment on the part of the staff. Such involvement by the staff must be fostered, and the staff given support so that it can sustain involvement."

- "Caring involves receiving as well as giving. The patient/family and staff will be educated to act within this principle."

- "Emotional investment will cause staff to grieve at the time of loss. Replenishment must be provided through mutual support."

- "The environment affects the individual's course in health and disease. The milieu will be designed to make the patient-family condition optimal."

Since Hospices Seem to Be a Healthy and Practical Alternative to Hospital Ward Service, Why Hasn't the Movement Caught On with More Enthusiasm?

Any new notion that works against the entrenched establishment will meet resistance. This is a law of human behavior. More to the point is the fact that for many years insurance companies and government health services would not cover the costs of hospice care.

Very recently this has changed. Now, for example, Medicare will assume coverage for hospice programs; and large insurance programs such as Blue Cross/Blue Shield will provide some coverage for home care. Because of these and other imminent modifications in policy, we can probably expect to see a healthy proliferation of hospice services across the United States within the next ten years.

How Can One Find Out More About Hospices?

There are several good books and articles on the subject, including:

Buckingham, Robert, *The Hospice Guide*. New York: Harper & Row, 1983.

Dubois, Paul, *The Hospice Way of Death*. New York: Human Sciences Press, 1980.

Holden, Constance, "Hospices: For the Dying, Relief from Pain and Fear." *Science*, 193 (July 30, 1976), 389ff.

Rossman, Parker, *Hospice*. New York: Fawcett (Columbine Books), 1977.

Saunders, Cicely, "Dying They Live: St. Christopher's Hospice." In Herman Feifel, (ed.), *New Meanings of Death*. New York: McGraw-Hill, 1977.

Saunders, Cicely, "St. Christopher's Hospice." In Edwin S. Shneidman (ed.), *Death: Current Perspectives*. Palo Alto, Calif.: Mayfield, 1980.

Also, contact the National Hospice Organization at:

National Hospice Organization, 1750 Old Meadow Road, McLean, VA. 22101.

Where in the United States Is Hospice Care Presently Available?

The following list, based on the information provided by Deborah Duda in her valuable book, *A Guide to Dying at Home* (Duda, 1982, pp. 280–286), provides the names and addresses of many hospices presently operating in the United States. Hospices are arranged alphabetically under each state by the name of the *town* in which they are located.

ALABAMA

Hospice, Baptist Medical Center-Princeton, 701 Princeton Avenue, *Birmingham*, AL 35211. (205) 783–3022.

Hospice of the Baptist Medical Centers, 800 Montclair Road, *Birmingham*, AL 35213. (205) 592–1059.

House Call, Inc., Suite 101, Oakmont Building, 956 Montclair Road, *Birmingham*, AL 35213. (205) 521–5085.

Villa Mercy, Inc., P.O. Box 1096, *Daphne*, AL 36526. (205) 626–2694.

Hospice of Montgomery, Inc., P.O. Box 1882, *Montgomery*, AL 36103.

ARIZONA

Hospice of the Valley, 214 East Willetta Street, *Phoenix*, AZ 85004. (602) 258–1572.

Oncology Life Enrichment Program, St. Joseph's Hospital, P.O. Box 2071, *Phoenix*, AZ 85001. (602) 277–6611.

Hillhaven Hospice, 5504 East Pima Street, *Tucson*, AZ 85712. (602) 886–8263.

ARKANSAS

Northwest Arkansas Hospice Association, P.O. Box 817, *Fayetteville*, AR 72701. (501) 521–7429.

274   LIVING WITH DYING

Hospice of the Ozarks, Inc., 906 Baker Street, *Mountain Home*, AR 72653. (501) 425–2797.

CALIFORNIA

Mission Hospice, Inc., of San Mateo County, 530 El Camino Real, Suite B, *Burlingame*, CA 94010. (415) 347–1218.

Hospice at Parkwood, 7011 Shoup Avenue, *Canoga Park*, CA 91307. (213) 348–0500.

Hospice of the Monterey Peninsula, P.O. Box 3193, *Carmel*, CA 93921. (408) 625–0666.

South Bay Hospice, 10863 Stevens Creek Boulevard, *Cupertino*, CA 95014. (408) 252–3110.

The Elisabeth Hospice, Inc., 336 South Kalmia Street, P.O. Box 891, *Escondido*, CA 92025. (714) 741–2092.

Hospice—Granada Hills, 10445 Balboa Boulevard, *Granada Hills*, CA 91344. (213) 360–1021.

Hospice of Contra Costa, 49 Knox Drive, *Lafayette*, CA 94549. (415) 934–5380.

Hospice Orange County, Inc., 24953 Paseo de Valencia, No. 16B, *Laguna Hills*, CA 92653. (714) 837–6500.

V. A. Wadsworth Medical Center Palliative Treatment Program, Wilshire and Sawtelle Boulevards, *Los Angeles*, CA 90073. (213) 478–3711.

The Visiting Nurse Association of Los Angeles, 2530 West Eighth Street, *Los Angeles*, CA 90057. (213) 380–3965.

Modesto Community Hospice, 1320 L Street, *Modesto*, CA 95354. (209) 577–0615.

Inland Hospice Association, Inc., 5156 Holt Boulevard, *Montclair*, CA 91763. (714) 624–4759.

Kaiser Permanente Hospice Program, 12500 South Hoxie Avenue, *Norwalk*, CA 90650. (213) 920–4525.

Mercy Hospice of St. John's Hospital, 333 North F Street, *Oxnard*, CA 93030. (805) 487–7861.

Mid-Peninsula Health Services Home Health Agency, 385 Homer Avenue, *Palo Alto*, CA 94301. (415) 324–1964.

Hospice of Mercy, 4001 J Street, *Sacramento*, CA 95819. (916) 453–4545.

Hospice of San Francisco, 14th Avenue and Lake Street, *San Francisco*, CA 94118. (415) 668–2673.

Hospice of the Valley, 349 South Monroe, Suite 2, *San Jose*, CA 95128. (408) 985–1640.

Vesper Hospice, 311 MacArthur Boulevard, *San Leandro*, CA 94577. (415) 351–8696.

San Pedro Peninsula Hospital, 1300 West Seventh Street, *San Pedro*, CA 90732. (213) 832–3311.

Hospice of Marin, 77 Mark Drive, No. 19, *San Rafael*, CA 94903. (415 472–0742.

Hospice of Santa Barbara County, Inc., 330 East Carrillo Street, *Santa Barbara*, CA 93101. (805) 963–8608.

Visiting Nurse Association, Inc., of Santa Clara County Hospice Program, 2216 Alameda, *Santa Clara*, CA 95050. (408) 244–1280.

Hospice of Santa Cruz County, Inc., 115 Maple Street, P.O. Box 6–1248, *Santa Cruz*, CA 95061. (408) 426–1996.

Home Hospice of Sonoma County, P.O. Box 11546, *Santa Rosa*, CA 95406. (707) 542–5045.

Valley of the Moon Hospice, Sonoma Valley Hospital District, P.O. Box 600, *Sonoma*, CA 95476. (707) 938–4545.

Hospital Home Health Care Agency Hospice Care, 23228 Hawthorne Boulevard, No. 11, *Torrance*, CA 90505. (213) 373–6373.

Hospice of Tulare County, Inc., P.O. Box 781, *Tulare*, CA 93274. (209) 733–7090.

National In-Home Health Service, 6850 Van Nuys Boulevard, *Van Nuys*, CA 91405. (213) 988–7575.

COLORADO

Boulder County Hospice, Inc., 2118 14th Street, *Boulder*, CO 80302. (303) 499–7740.

Hospice of Metro Denver, Inc., 1719 East 19th Avenue, No. 256, *Denver*, CO 80218. (303) 839–6256.

CONNECTICUT

The Connecticut Hospice, Inc., 61 Burban Drive, *Branford*, CT 06405. (203) 789–1509.

DISTRICT OF COLUMBIA

Hospice Care of the District of Columbia, 1828 L Street, NW, No. 505, Washington, DC 20036. (202) 223–9270.

The Washington Home Hospice, 3720 Upton Street, NW Washington, DC 20016. (202) 966–3720.

FLORIDA

Hospice of Boca Raton, 162 West Palmetto Road, *Boca Raton*, FL 33432. (305) 395–5031.

Hospice of Broward, Inc., 3700 Washington Street, No. 208, *Hollywood*, FL 33021. (305) 963–5410.

Hospice of Northeast Florida, Inc., 1503 Oak Street, *Jacksonville*, FL 32204. (904) 353–8211.

Methodist Hospital Hospice, 580 West Eighth Street, *Jacksonville*, FL 32209. (904) 354–2071.

Hospice of Palm Beach County, Inc., 130 North Dixie Highway, *Lake Worth*, FL 33450. (305) 832–6363.

Hospice, Inc., 111 Northwest 10th Avenue, *Miami*, FL 33128. (305) 325–0245.

Gold Coast Home Health Service, 4699 North Federal Highway, Suite 205, *Pompano Beach*, FL 33064. (305) 785–2990.

Good Shepherd Hospice, Inc., P.O. Box 1183, *Winter Haven*, FL 33880. (813) 294–6837.

Hospice Orlando, Inc., P.O. Box 449, *Winter Park*, FL 32790. (305) 647–2523.

GEORGIA

Hospice Atlanta, Inc., 5665 Peachtree-Dunwoody Road, *Atlanta*, GA 30342. (404) 256–7271.

ILLINOIS

Hospice of Madison County, 2120 Madison Avenue, *Granite City*, IL 62042. (618) 798–3399.

Hospice of Highland Park Hospital, 718 Glenview Avenue, *Highland Park*, IL 60035. (312) 432–8000.

Northern Illinois Hospice Association, 106 North Main Street, *Rockford*, IL 61101. (815) 964–0230.

Mercy Hospice Care Program, 1400 West Park, *Urbana*, IL 61801. (217) 337–2115.

Hospice of the North Shore, 520 Glendale Avenue, *Winnetka*, IL 60093. (312) 441–9150.

INDIANA

Methodist Hospital of Indiana, Inc., 1604 North Capitol Avenue, *Indianapolis*, IN 46206. (317) 927–3083.

IOWA

Hospice Care Group, Inc., 2501 East Pleasant, *Davenport*, IA 52808. (319) 355–6120.

KENTUCKY

Community Hospice of Lexington, Suite 109, 465 East High Street, *Lexington*, KY 40508. (606) 252–2308.

Hospice of Louisville, Inc., 233 East Gray Street, Suite 800, *Louisville*, KY 40202. (502) 584–4834.

MAINE

Hospice of Maine, 32 Thomas Street, *Portland*, ME 04102. (207) 774–4417.

MARYLAND

Church Hospital Corporation Hospice-Care Program, 100 North Broadway, *Baltimore*, MD 21231. (301) 732–4730.

MASSACHUSETTS

Hospice of the North Shore, Inc., 315 Topsfield Road, *Ipswich*, MA 01938. (617) 356–0457.

MICHIGAN

Good Samaritan Hospice Care, Kellogg Community College, 450 North Avenue, *Battle Creek*, MI 49017. (616) 965–1271.

Hospice of Greater Grand Rapids, Inc., 1715 East Fulton, *Grand Rapids*, MI 49503. (616) 459–5976.

MINNESOTA

Hospice–Duluth St. Luke's Hospital, 915 East First Street, *Duluth*, MN 55805. (218) 727–6636.

Fairview Community Hospitals, 6401 France Avenue South, *Edina*, MN 55435. (612) 920–4400.

Abbot-Northwestern Hospital, 2727 Chicago Avenue South, *Minneapolis*, MN 55407. (612) 874–6717.

St. John's Hospital Hospice Program, 403 Maria Avenue, *St. Paul*, MN 55106. (612) 228–3222.

St. Mary's Hospital Hospice Program, *St. Paul*, MN 55454. (612) 338–2229.

MISSOURI

Hospice Care of Mid America, 1005 Grand Avenue, Suite 743, *Kansas City*, MO 64106.

St. Luke's Hospital Hospice, 5535 Delmar Boulevard, *St. Louis*, MO 63108.

NEW JERSEY

Northwest Bergen Hospice Program, c/o Valley Hospital, *Ridgewood*, NJ 07450.

Hospice Home Care Department of Overlook Hospital, 193 Morris Avenue, *Summit*, NJ 07901.

NEW MEXICO

Hospital Home Health Care, Hospice Program, 500 Walter NE, Suite 316, *Albuquerque*, NM 87102.

NEW YORK

Cabrini Hospice, 227 East 19th Street, *New York*, NY 10003.

Calvary Hospital, 1740 Eastchester Road, *Bronx*, NY 10461.

Hospice of St. Luke's, St. Luke's-Roosevelt Hospital Center, Amsterdam Avenue at 114th Street, *New York*, NY 10025.

Hospice Buffalo, Inc., 2929 Main Street, *Buffalo*, NY 14214.

OHIO

Hospice of Cincinnati, Inc., P.O. Box 19221, *Cincinnati*, OH 45214.

Hospice of Dayton, 908 South Main Street, *Dayton*, OH 45402.

PENNSYLVANIA

The Bryn Mawr Hospital Hospice Program, Bryn Mawr Avenue, *Byrn Mawr*, PA 19010.

Philadelphia Geriatric Center Home Health Services Program, 5301 Old York Road, *Philadelphia*, PA 19141.

Forbes Health System Forbes Hospice, 500 Finley Street, *Pittsburgh*, PA 15206.

TEXAS

Dallas VNA Home Hospice, 4606 Greenville Avenue, *Dallas*, TX 75206.

Community Hospice of St. Joseph, 1401 South Main, *Fort Worth*, TX 76104.

Visiting Nurse Association of Houston, Inc., 3100 Timmons Lane, Suite 200, *Houston*, TX 77027.

VIRGINIA

Hospice of Northern Virginia, 4715 North 15th Street, *Arlington*, VA 22205.

WASHINGTON

Hospice of Seattle, 819 Boylston Avenue, *Seattle*, WA 98104.

Hospice of Tacoma, 742 Market Street, Suite 201, *Tacoma*, WA 98405.

WISCONSIN

Bellin Hospice at Bellin Hospital, P.O. Box 1700, 744 South Webster, *Green Bay*, WI 54306.

Milwaukee Hospice, Inc., 1022 North Ninth Street, *Milwaukee*, WI 53233.

11

An Appropriate Death

Is It Really Possible to Die, As They Say, a "Good Death?" A Death with Dignity?

Since death is under permanent veto in present society, few among us have witnessed the actual process close up. Thus we really do not know *how* most people die, whether with courage, apathy, or terror, whether with a bang or with a whimper. In a civilization where the dying are herded to terminal wards and hidden from the world and from other patients alike, there is little wonder that the only witnesses to a patient's final hours are the professional staff and the next of kin. For the former this dying process is a routine affair. For the latter it is mostly too private to discuss. So ignorance of the matter endures.

In the past several years, thanks to the work of pioneers like Kübler-Ross, Avery Weisman, Edwin Shneidman, and others, it has gradually become quasi-public knowledge that people die in all kinds of ways, not all of them unpleasant. Some leave with bravery or with joyful resignation, even with humor and stateliness; or with an ironic wink, a cry of impatience, a sigh of relief. Many die in a manner that Wiesman has termed "an appropriate death."

What Does an Appropriate Death Mean Exactly?

An appropriate death is the death each of us would die if given the choice. For one person it is dying in sleep, for another dying surrounded by loving family members, for another passing away entirely without pain, for another dying like a martyr, for still another dying in a way that inspires others. It is the best way to die according to the needs and ideals of each particular person.

Avery Weisman's definition depicts appropriate death as a situation in which "there is reduction of conflict, compatibility with the ego ideal, continuity of significant relationships, and consummation of prevailing wishes." To help a person die in this manner, says Weisman: "He should be relatively pain-free, his suffering reduced, and emotional and social impoverishments kept to a minimum. Within the limits of disability, he should operate on as high and effective a level as possible, even though only tokens of former fulfillments can be offered. He should also recognize and resolve residual conflicts, and satisfy whatever wishes are consistent with his present plight and with his ego ideal. Finally, among his choices, he should be able to yield control to others in whom he has confidence. He also has the option of seeking or relinquishing key people" (Weisman, 1972, pp. 36–41).

Doesn't This Description of an Appropriate Death Represent a Lofty Ideal? Isn't It Doubtful Whether Many People Can Achieve It?

Some can and some cannot. However, a little is a lot in this instance, and even small efforts toward making death a more purposeful event is a gain.

The point of formalizing such a notion as appropriate death, moreover, is to advertise the point that, as Weisman writes, "our preconception that death can *never* be appropriate may be a self-fulfilling idea. If we believe that death is bad, and dying people, by a magical contagion, are tainted, then appropriate deaths are never possible."

For a patient simply to be exposed to the ideal of dying purposefully, to realize that the possibility *exists*, can, as it were, give him something to live for until he dies. Even if he cannot ultimately determine the way he will die, the very act of thinking about it and planning for it represents a positive action in the face of a seemingly unchallengeable passivity.

What Are Some of the Ways a Person Can Be Helped—and Can Help Themselves—to Die a More Meaningful Death?

A list might include:

1. Ensuring that the sick person—to the best of her ability—takes care of unfinished emotional business. This means that any practical matters which might later cause hard feelings are resolved; that disputes are settled among friends and family members; that loving words which have never been spoken and which should be spoken *are* spoken. It is, furthermore, best to attend to these issues *now*, or at least in an appropriate amount of time, and this pertains both to the sick person and to his close associates. Good intentions not acted upon are of scanty value once the opportunity has passed. There is no greater matter for regret than remembering things you wished to say to the dying person after that person has died.

2. Make certain that all paperwork is completed, that a will has been drawn up, that insurance matters are under control, that inheritances have been decided among all involved, that items such as deeds, mortgages, personal debts, outstanding bills, IOUs, and so on, have been properly resolved.

A patient can, in fact, compose a checklist of the final details to be settled and check off each as it is finished. The small but relevant details might include:

• Composing a guest list of people to be invited to one's funeral or last rights. Pallbearers can be designated and music picked out for the service. Some people like to compose compositions to be read at their own funeral.

- Making necessary phone calls; paying last visits to those who should be visited; making final contributions to favorite charities; performing final good works of whatever kind.

- Taking care of religious duties; attending Mass for the last time; performing certain prayers and rituals; making last contributions.

- Making certain that all borrowed items are returned.

- If a burial plot has been procured, double-checking that everything has been taken care of: payments, provisions for maintenance, and so on. Also, if a pre-need funeral plan has been purchased, making sure that the executor and relatives know about it.

- Making certain that the whereabouts of all important items are revealed to the proper parties. At the time of death and thereafter, possession of these items by survivors may be of the utmost importance. Such items can include:
  - Hidden keys
  - Combinations to locks and safes
  - Private bank accounts
  - Hard-to-find files
  - Insurance policies
  - Personal documents (such as citizenship papers, birth certificate, marriage license, divorce papers, military discharge papers, important documents pertaining to one's children, and so on)
  - Safe-deposit box
  - Stashed money
  - Diaries (together with directions as to their disposal after death)
  - Car registration, driver's license, auto insurance cards, and so on.
  - Devotional objects, keepsakes, gems, coins, stamps, and so on.

- Making note of last instructions or final statements on any subject, philosophical or practical.

- Overseeing completion of all personal projects and hobbies; taking care that beloved items—a library of collected books, a garage full of tools, a good set of golf clubs, a selection of recordings—go to the person who wants/needs/requests/deserves them.

• If there are pets, making certain that plans have been made for their welfare.

3. The dying person should be secure in her knowledge that she will pass her final days free of pain, that she will not be exposed to dehumanizing treatment at home or in the hospital, and that she will be protected from unnecessary tests, painful experiments, or dubious medical intrusions. If she does not wish to be kept alive via heroic means on life-support machinery, now is the time for these wishes to be voiced and for a living will to be drawn up (see p. 139).

4. Patients should be surrounded by the environment they most prefer. Many opt to be at home. Some prefer the security of a hospital room. Some wish to be encircled by friends and relatives, others ask for privacy and solitude. The person's choice should be carefully honored.

5. Patients should not be sedated more than necessary unless they request it. A dying person should be allowed to maintain the degree of consciousness or unconsciousness most agreeable to his needs.

6. For those who wish it, appropriate religious rituals should be provided. In most religions, last rites are a scheduled part of the dying person's journey from this world. In a way determined by centuries of deathbed experience, they provide a chronology of confession, repentance, release of anxieties, final instructions, and last blessings. For some people these procedures may not be necessary. For others they are vitally important, and to die without them would be tantamount to dying in spiritual pain.

7. The dying person should say goodbye to actual objects or events from the past as well as to particular people. Saying one's farewells, mentally if not in person, registers a period or exclamation point on a life fully lived. The affair is now officially over. Nothing is left hanging. If a person dies today she dies with the knowledge that matters are concluded with that one individual, with that one remembrance, and this becomes one less string to keep her bound.

What Creative and Artistic Methods Can a Dying Person Use to Make His Death More Purposeful?

There are a variety of these, and most do not require elaborate equipment or large areas of space. An obvious example is painting and drawing. This is a pastime which chronically ill people can take up at home or in the hospital, and which for many becomes a means of saying in symbols what they cannot put into words. Sculpture, a musical instrument, decoupage, calligraphy, the study of literature, stamp collecting, modeling, sewing, quilting, all are highly creative arts which can be done in a small area. So is poetry. In Japan it is traditional for a dying person to write a "death poem," where in a few pithy couplets he or she makes a definitive statement about his or her life and about existence in general. Sometimes these poems are written spontaneously. In other cases many hours of careful thought go into them. After death they are read. Sometimes they are recited at the funeral or memorial service.

Akin to this is the keeping of a diary. In it one person writes of sufferings, another of insights and understandings, another of the day-to-day events at the hospital. Patients compose such documents for many reasons, one of the important ones being that it will be read after their death and that it may help others prepare for their own dying journey.

12

Practical Preparations

How Can One Plan for One's Own Funeral While Still Alive?

By first deciding what type of funeral one prefers: whether large or small, inexpensive or lavish, religious or nondenominational. To this list can be added the people one wishes to invite, which funeral home to employ, what type of ceremony is preferred, and where one's remains are to be laid.

All of these facts should be written down and typed up neatly. One copy should be given to the executor of the will, the other kept in a safe place where family members can find it quickly. (Some people go to elaborate lengths drawing up provisos about their funerals, then hide the papers so thoroughly that even the next of kin have no idea where to look.)

Funerals can be prepaid and preplanned by the patient himself. When this is done, the financial burden on relatives is considerably reduced, as is the number of chores they must shoulder when the time of death arrives. When funeral arrangements are made quietly beforehand, without the reckless pressures that death imposes upon the bereaved, financial choices of coffin, burial, and so on, are likely to be accomplished more carefully than those done later in a state of grief.

Speak with the funeral director of your choice about terms, procedure, and so on, and make sure that you receive an itemized paper stating all the services your prepayment plan is purchasing. If you then decide to go ahead with the plan, make certain that members of your family know where the papers, receipts, and so on, pertinent to the agreement are located. The average cost of a funeral is presently around $2000 and getting more expensive all the time. Check your insurance to see if it covers any part of these costs. Occasionally, it will. Some people keep a special policy to cover burial expenses alone. For more information on preplanning, you can write for the following booklets:

The Pre-arranging and Pre-financing of Funerals. Write: National Funeral Directors Association, 135 West Wells Street, Milwaukee, WI 53203.

Pre-planning the Funeral—Why? Who? How? Write: Consumer Information Bureau of the National Selected Morticians, 1616 Central Street, Evanston, IL 60201.

The following preplanning checklist, based on one compiled by the National Funeral Directors Association, can also be filled out in advance and put on file with relatives and the executor(s) of your will.

1. Full and legal name: _____

2. Legal residence: _____

3. Telephone: _____

4. Date of birth: _____

5. Place of birth: _____

6. Date and city of baptism: _____

7. Date and place of confirmation: _____

8. Sex: _____ Single: _____ Married: _____

    Widowed: _____ Divorced: _____

a. If married, give full name of spouse: ——————
Date and place of marriage: ——————————

b. If widowed, give full name of spouse and date and place of death: ————————————————
Date and place of marriage: ——————————

c. Previous marriages [give name of former spouse(s) and dates of termination of marriage(s)]: —————

9. Name and birthplace of father (address and phone, if still living): ————————————————————

10. Name and birthplace of mother, including maiden name (address and phone, if still living): —————————

11. Name, address, and phone of brothers and sisters (if deceased, indicate and just list name): —————————

12. Name, address, and phone number of children (if deceased, indicate and just list name): —————————

13. Name, address, and phone number of other significant friends and relatives. ——————————————

14. If you are a veteran, please complete the following:

    a. Date and place of enlistment: ————————

    b. Date and place of discharge: —————————

    c. Rank or rating: ——————————————————

    d. Service number: —————————————————

    e. Organization or outfit: ——————————————

    f. Commendations received: ————————————

    g. Location of copy of discharge: ————————

    h. Flag desired to drape casket: ————————

15. Educational background, including name of high school and year of graduation and college(s) attended and degrees received and year(s) received: ——————————

16. Occupations and past positions of employment (give names of employers): _____

17. a. Religious affiliation (including name of church):

       _____

    b. Membership in professional, religious, veteran, fraternal, and other organizations: _____

    c. Would you like one or more of the organizations in your funeral service? Which one(s)? _____

18. Awards received: _____

19. Name, address, and phone of person with legal right to handle your funeral and other postdeath arrangements:

    _____

20. Name, address, and phone of funeral director you desire:

    _____

    a. If any prearrangements have been made, please indicate, including statement as to whether all or some of the prearrangements have been prepaid:

       _____

21. Location of will: _____
    Executor/trix: _____

22. Location of safety-deposit box and key: _____

23. Name, address, and phone of your attorney/bank trust department:

    _____

24. Listing of all checking and saving accounts: _____
    a. Location of checkbooks and passbooks: _____

25. Listing and place of insurance policies and their respective numbers: _____

26. Credit cards and charge accounts to be canceled: _____

27. If you have a cemetery plot, where is it and what is the lot number and location of the grave in the plot? _____

    a. If you do not wish to use your presently owned cemetery plot (or do not have one), where do you wish to be buried? _____

28. What kind of grave monument or marker do you wish if you do not have one? _____

29. If you own a mausoleum space, where is it? Identify your crypt: _____

    a. If you do not own a mausoleum space and would like to be entombed, where do you wish such entombment?

_____

30. Do you wish to be cremated and, if so, what do you wish to have done with your cremated remains? _____

31. Instructions concerning selection of casket and vault:

    a. Casket—wood, metal, other: _____

    b. Vault—concrete, metal, other: _____

32. Do you suggest your survivors have "calling hours" or a visitation? _____

    a. If yes, where: _____

    b. If yes, should the casket be opened or closed: _____

33. List anything special you wish to wear or have buried with you: _____

34. Is the service to be public or private? _____

    a. Place of service: _____

    b. Type of service: _____

    c. Any special instructions: _____

35. Name, address, and phone of clergypeople or other officiant in lieu of or in addition to a clergyperson: _____

36. Special requests for service, (hymns, other music, readings): _____

37. In addition to flowers, do you wish donations made in your memory? Where? _____
    a. Do you wish to omit flowers? _____
    b. If "omit," do you want the money donated to charity? _____

38. Name, address, and phone of persons you would like to have as casket bearers: _____

39. Anything special you wish to have placed in your obituary and/or paid death notice? _____

40. Newspapers in which your obituary and/or paid death notice is to be placed: _____

41. Are you donating your body or any part thereof to medical science? _____
    a. If so, where is the permission card, what part (or all) of your body is donated, and who should be notified (list name, address, and phone)? _____

42. Any additional information, special requests, or other personal desires not covered in this checklist? _____

Can Plans Which a Person Makes concerning His Own Funeral Arrangements Be Changed by His Relatives after His Death?

Laws differ in different states. In most the next-of-kin have legal control over the body of the deceased and can dispose of it any way they see fit. This may occur, for instance, when financial or emotional contingencies force relatives to scale up or scale down disposition plans made by the deceased. Usually, however, if the deceased wishes his remains handled in a certain way and communicates this fact clearly to his family, they will honor his wishes.

Must One Make a Prepaid Funeral Arrangement Exclusively with a Funeral Home?

No. It can also be purchased from a special firm that specializes in prepaid plans for funerals and cemeteries and which acts as an intermediary between the customer and the funeral home or cemetery. Their term for such agreement is a "pre-need plan."

What Happens If a Person Purchases a Pre-need Funeral Package from a Particular Undertaker on the Installment Plan— Many Are Paid Off This Way—and Then Dies before Having Paid It All Off?

Unless the heirs hold credit life insurance, they become responsible for assuming the remaining costs. The heirs may, as a rule, opt to change the plan and purchase a cheaper funeral.

What Happens If a Person Prepays for a Funeral and Later Decides to Terminate the Agreement?

Legally, the money must be returned to the purchaser. In most states there are laws to cover this contingency. If such laws do not exist, it is suggested that the prepayment agreement between customer and funeral director include a provision for a trust fund composed of all monies paid in advance for funeral services, and that the person purchasing the agreement maintain control of this fund. Further, the person controlling the trust fund should be the agreed-on recipient of interest accruing from this money, and he or she should have the option of using the interest at any time to offset the increased funeral costs which inflation invariably brings. Finally, it should be stipulated in the prepayment agreement that this contract can be terminated at any time without incurring a financial penalty, especially in the event that the person who has paid for it leaves the area.

Is Purchasing a "Pre-need" Program Recommended?

According to Consumer Union's report on prepaid funeral plans (see *Funerals: Consumers' Last Rights*, 1977), it is not generally recommended. The Union tells us that there are now so many legal and emotional pitfalls connected with pre-need plans that most are ultimately not worth the effort. State laws controlling sales of pre-need plans vary widely, the Union reports, door-to-door hucksterism of pre-need plans has given them a bad name, and because of inflation and possible problems with the financial arrangements, pre-need services do not always end up saving people money in the long run.

Not everyone agrees with this assessment, however, for despite the potential problems of pre-need plans, the peace of mind that comes from taking care of such matters in advance goes a long way toward counterbalancing the drawbacks. Whatever one believes, the best approach is to look into the matter in depth before deciding. The following points are all worth checking on prior to any decision:

- That the funeral home from which the plan is purchased is stable enough to warrant confidence that it will still be in business at the time of the person's death.

- That provisions be made for a refund in case the buyer changes his residence.

- That provisions be made for cancellation of the contract, or for switching to a lower-cost funeral program.

- That the buyer knows in advance whether a penalty will be charged for late payment of monthly installments.

- That the buyer knows if credit insurance is available as part of a pre-need plan and what the costs are for this coverage. (Credit insurance plans guarantee that if the purchaser dies before the prepaid plan is fully paid up, the remaining costs will automatically be covered by the insurance company. Some funeral homes offer this coverage option as part of the contract; some do not.)

- That the buyer knows how much time survivors will be given to pay off the balance of a prepaid plan should he die before it is paid in full. Also, whether survivors have the option of transferring the original plan and the monies so far spent into a cheaper funeral plan.

- That it is determined exactly which items and services the pre-need contract covers, and that each is itemized. Also, that the kinds of goods and services supplied be described in as much detail as possible: what kind of coffin will be provided, the clothes that will be provided the deceased, which transportation costs will be paid, and so on.

- That everything included in the contract is in agreement with local and state laws.

What Are Guidelines for Donating One's Body (or a Particular Organ in One's Body) to Medical Science?

The Uniform Anatomical Gift Act of 1968 defines the legal and moral considerations of body donation as follows:

1. Any person 18 years of age or older can donate all or part of his body after death for transplantation, research, or placement in a tissue bank.

2. A donor's valid statement of gift supersedes the rights of anyone else, unless a state autopsy law prevails and has conflicting requirements.

3. If a donor has not acted in his lifetime to specify a wish to donate, his survivors may do so, in a specified order of priority (spouse, adult son or daughter, either parent, adult brother or sister, guardian, or any other person authorized or under obligation to dispose of the body).

4. Physicians who accept anatomical gifts, relying in good faith on documents provided to them in such cases, are protected from legal action.

5. Where a transplant is planned, the fact and time of death must be determined by a physician *not* involved in the transplant.

6. The donor has the right to revoke the gift, and it may be rejected by those for whom it is intended.

What Are the Necessary Procedures for Donating One's Body?

A person's body can be used after death in two ways: (1) The particular organs can be removed and employed for transplants, stored in organ banks, or used for experimental programs and research; or (2) a person's entire body can be donated to a medical school, where it will be used for teaching, research, and dissection.

If a person wishes to give her remains to a particular institution for either of these purposes she should first contact the institution directly. They will help work out the arrangements. As well, a document called a Uniform Donor Card should be procured and filled out. The card can be attained from the institution itself or by writing to any of the following:

American Medical Association, Order Department, 535 North Dearborn Street, Chicago, IL 60610.

Eye-Bank Association of America, 3195 Maplewood Avenue, Winston-Salem, NC 27103.

Living Bank, P.O. Box 6723, Houston, TX 77005. (They will send you a donor's card and will put your name and particular instructions on record in their files.)

Medic Alert, P.O. Box 1009, Turlock, CA 95380.

Northern California Transplant Bank Institute for Medical Research, 751 South Bascom Avenue, San Jose, CA 95128.

Once signed in front of two witnesses, the Uniform Donor Card becomes a legal document and is to be carried on one's person at all times. If possible, the word "Donor" or "Organ Donor" should also be recorded somewhere on the person's driver's license in case of sudden death.

After receiving and processing the card, a letter should then be written to one's lawyer, doctor, and the institution receiving the donation, as well as to the executor of one's will and to immediate family members and friends, clearly specifying one's wishes to be a donor. The letter may read as follows:

Dear

In the event of my accidental or normal death, please be informed that I wish to donate my body [or the following body parts _____] to [state institution if you have a particular one in mind, or simply say "medical science"]. I am presently carrying a Uniform Donor Card on my person on which specific instructions are listed. Please make sure that these instructions are carried out at the time of my death. If by chance this card is lost, destroyed, or overlooked, please see that the proper authorities are informed of my last wishes in reference to body donation. You may use this letter as proof of my intentions.

Sincerely,

Date

Next, in case one is hospitalized for a serious illness or operation, or if death seems imminent, the hospital adminstration should be informed that the patient is a donor, as should the immediate attending staff, especially the doctor. Following the moment of death, physicians must often remove a donated organ with incredible swiftness and transfer it to the proper storage facilities. Even a few hours delay can be fatal in this regard, and it is extremely important that the doctor be kept up to date concerning one's plans for donation.

Finally, a perspective donor can contact any of the following organizations for more information concerning donation of specific organs. Some of these organizations will help in making the appropriate arrangements.

American Heart Association, 7320 Greenville Avenue, Dallas, TX 75231.

UNIFORM DONOR CARD

of _____
(print or type name of donor)

In the hope that I may help others, I hereby make this anatomical gift, if medically acceptable, to take effect upon my death. The words and marks below indicate my desires.

I give: (a)   ☐   any needed organs or parts

       (b)   ☐   only the following organs or parts

_____

Specify which organ(s) or part(s) for the purposes of transplantation, therapy, medical research or education;

       (c)   ☐   my body for anatomical study if needed.

_____

LIMITATIONS OR SPECIAL WISHES, IF ANY

Signed by the Donor and the following two witnesses in the presence of each other.

_____

Signature of Donor   Donor's Birthdate

_____

City & State where signed   Date signed

_____

Witness   Witness

THIS IS A LEGAL DOCUMENT UNDER THE UNIFORM ANATOMICAL GIFT ACT OR SIMILAR LAWS

American Medical Assocation Committee on Transfusion and Transplantation, 535 North Dearborn Avenue, Chicago, IL 60610.

Deafness Research Foundation, 336 Madison Avenue, New York, NY 10017.

Eye Bank for Sight Restoration, 3195 Maplewood Avenue, Winston-Salem, NC 27103.

Living Bank, P.O. Box 6723, Main Street, Houston, TX 77005.

Medic Alert, P.O. Box 1009, Turlock, CA 95380.

National Burn Victim Foundation, Metcalf Building, 308 Main Street, Orange, NJ 07050.

National Kidney Foundation, 116 East 27th Street, New York, NY 10010.

National Pituitary Agency, Suite 503–9, 210 West Fayette Street, Baltimore, MD 21201.

National Temporal Bone Banks Program, Massachusetts Eye and Ear Infirmary, 243 Charles Street, Boston, MA 02114.

New Eyes for the Needy, Short Hills, NJ 07078.

The New York Firefighters Skin Bank, 525 East 68th Street, New York, NY 10021.

The Tissue Bank, Naval Medical Research Institute, National Naval Medical Center, Bethesda, MD 20014.

Transplantation Society, State University of New York, Room 040, T–19, Stony Brook, NY 11794.

Is an Organ Donor's Body Badly Mutilated When the Organ Is Removed?

It depends on whether a single organ is donated or if the whole body is given. If a single organ is taken, there is usually very little damage, sometimes only a small incision. If the entire body is given, the cadaver will often be heavily disfigured.

If a Body is Donated, Will It Ultimately Be Returned to the Family for Burial?

If the family requests it, a school or institution will usually return the remains of a person's body in a sealed coffin for funeral or cremation. If the request is not made, the institution cremates the remains.

How Long Must the Family Usually Wait for an Institution to Return a Donor's Body?

If organs are to be removed, the delay is usually no longer than a day or so. If an entire body is donated to medical education, the waiting period may be much longer.

Can a Family Receive the Ashes of a Body If It Has Been Cremated by the Institution?

Yes, if they request them in advance.

What Specific Organs and Parts of the Body Might One Wish to Donate?

The following organs are all put to use, some with more success than others: the kidneys, the eyes, the skin, the liver, the temporal bones (the bones that contain the inner ear), the teeth, the skeleton, the heart, the pituitary glands, the lungs, the bone marrow; also, various structural tissue from the circulatory system, bone structure, muscular system, and so on.

Must an Institution Accept One's Organ or Body Donation?

Not in certain cases. For example, if a person dies from cirrhosis of the liver, the hospital or medical school will obviously not be keen on receiving that liver via donation. The same is true of any organ that has been damaged or has been reduced via a degenerative disease. Most institutions do not accept bodies of persons who have died of contagious diseases or who have suffered diseases of the blood. A body that has undergone an autopsy or one that has been badly disfigured due to accident, surgery, and so on, will usually be rejected.

Can One Sell His or Her Body to an Institution?

No, a person can donate his or her body or body organs, but selling it is illegal.

Are There Any Costs Involved for an Organ Donor?

The receiving institution usually takes care of any costs that may arise for transportation, preservation, and so on. Occasionally, however, charges will be made to the donor's family if a body must be transported over a long distance. Be sure to inquire about such considerations *in advance*, to spare survivors unexpected expenses.

What Are the Advantages of Donating One's Body to Science?

Besides the obvious fact that donation helps medical science, donation helps reduce postdeath financial expenses. The heirs are spared heavy funeral costs plus the onerous burden of having to arrange it all. Many people become donors for this reason alone.

What If after Going on Record as a Donor a Person Changes Her Mind?

Technically, all she must do is destroy her Uniform Donor Card. It is also advisable, however, that she notify the institution involved, both as a courtesy and to prevent any mistakes being made after death.

Don't Certain Religions Object to Organ Transplantation and the Mutilation of the Body?

Protestants and Catholics by and large approve of organ donation. Orthodox Jews, Muslims, Hindus, and some fundamentalist Christian sects oppose it.

Certain objections are based on traditional practices of hygiene, others on the eschatologic notion that the physical body continues for a certain time to play an invisible part in the journey of the soul. In both instances, disfigurement of the corpse is believed to interfere with the afterlife of the deceased and hence is discouraged. Check with your spiritual leader for information on your religion's policies toward body donation.

Should One State One's Wishes to Be a Donor in a Will?

There is nothing wrong with this per se. The problem is that by the time a person's will is read much time has elapsed since death, and the body may no longer be in usable condition. Do not rely on the will alone. Make sure that the proper people are officially informed in advance, the proper documents on file, and so on, as mentioned above.

What Is a Memorial Society? What Services Do They Provide to a Perspective Funeral Buyer?

A memorial society is a local consumer-oriented group organized to help people plan for a simple funeral at a reasonable cost. It works on a nonprofit basis, is staffed by volunteers, and is often affiliated with a church, union, coop group or civic organization. There are big memorial societies and small societies, but all operate on the same premise, that funeral expenses are too high, that the funeral ceremony itself is overelaborate and personally exploitative, and that alternatives should be available to those who wish them.

Although the Memorial Society Movement started with something less than a bang in 1939 as a project sponsored by a Congregational church in Seattle, Washington, it has gained both power and prestige through the years. Today, the Memorial Society Movement is instrumental in overseeing undertaking industry practices. It has also been active in lobbying for better funeral regulation.

Who Can Join a Memorial Society? Is Membership Restricted by Religious Affiliation?

Memorial societies are open to everyone. They are non-denominational and unrestricted.

What Are the Joining Fees?

The one-time membership fee is no higher than $20 in most areas and usually less. A "record change" of $10 to $15 may also be levied on members when extensive use is made of the society's resources. Remember, the memorial society is a nonprofit organization and is largely run by its own membership. Their primary concern is to help people get a fair deal from the funeral industry. Their costs to the consumer are commensurately fair.

What Is the Point of Joining a Memorial Society? How Do They Help?

A memorial society does not provide direct interment or disposition services. What they do depends on whether they work as (1) a contract society, (2) a cooperating society, or (3) an advisory society:

1. A *contract society* serves as an official intermediary between the customer and the funeral home. The society and mortician, operating on a contractual basis, work out various simple and inexpensive funeral packages between them in advance, and these are then offered to members. Average costs for these funerals run from $400 to $800. Their low price reflects the fact that simple wooden coffins are used instead of bronze, minimal funeral services are featured, and so on. The memorial society serves as a kind of liaison between the customer and the mortuary. In the event that any disputes should arise between the two parties, they serve as mediator.

2. A *cooperating society* has a relationship with local undertakers but on a less formal basis than the contract society. At the time of need, a member contacts this society and the society refers the member to one or more local funeral homes which are known to offer low-cost funeral programs and which have a proven track record of honest, reliable service with other society members.

3. An *advisory society* acts mainly as a guide for customers and as a referral service, providing names and addresses of funeral homes that offer inexpensive funerals and competent service.

What Is the Attitude of the Funeral Industry toward Memorial Societies?

At one time it was openly hostile, and there are many incidents of funeral directors being boycotted by their associates for cooperating with a memorial society. Although many undertakers are still far from friendly to this innovation in funeral practice, many others are beginning to cooperate with plans for low-cost deposition. By and large, the memorial society seems to be an institution whose time has come.

What If One Dies Far from Home and Hence from One's Memorial Society?

Memorial societies are almost all members of the same parent organization, the Continental Association of Funeral and Memorial Societies (see address below), and hence offer reciprocal services between local chapters. If a member dies in a distant locale in the United States or Canada and his survivors opt to bury him there, they should get in touch with the local chapter of the society and make arrangements through them. If the family wishes to transport the body home, local chapters will provide help in making these plans.

What Other Services Do Memorial Societies Provide?

Memorial societies help the family of the bereaved plan for a memorial service in place of a formal funeral. They provide educational materials. They keep the family informed concerning cost changes in the funeral industry and they report any questionable practices to the public. Detailed information on the subject can be found in the very valuable book, *A Manual of Death Education and Simple Burial*. It is available for $2.50 from several sources, including:

Continental Association of Funeral and Memorial Societies, 1828 L Street, NW, Washington, DC 20036. (202) 293–4821.

Or directly from the publisher:

Celo Press, Route 5, Burnsville, NC 28714.

How Can One Join a Memorial Society?

There are literally hundreds of local societies in the United States. The Continental Association of Funeral and Memorial Societies listed above will provide information on an association in your particular area. You can write them directly. Participating funeral directors will provide information on locally based societies. In Canada the address to contact is:

Memorial Association of Canada, Box 96, Weston, Ontario, M9N 3M6, Canada.

There Has Been Some Publicity over the Possibility of Deep-Freezing the Body of a Person Who Has Died from an Incurable Disease, Keeping the Body in Storage for an Indefinite Length of Time, and Then Someday, Should a Remedy Be Discovered for That Disease, Resuscitating the Body and Curing It. What Is This All About?

This practice is called cryonics, cryogenic interment, or cryobiology. It is the science of preserving life at low temperatures.

What happens is this: As soon as a person dies, all the blood is drained from his or her veins and is replaced with a preservative such as dimethyl sulfoxide. The body is then netted in a shroud of crushed ice and granulated salt, wrapped in special aluminum dressings, and quick frozen—"freeze-dried" as champions of the method enjoy calling it—at laboratory temperatures of around $-320°F$. Like something out of a science fiction caper, the body is then planted in a capsule-shaped storage vault where liquid nitrogen and helium keeps it on ice in "cryonic suspension" for an indefinite period of time—until the cure is found for whatever disease, and the corpse is brought back to living land. There are presently a half-dozen cryonics societies in the United States.

Is the Method of Cryonic Burial Perfected?

Far from it. At low temperatures ice crystals damage human viscera even as they preserve it. No one knows for certain whether life is actually preserved by this method, or whether it is the inanimate flesh alone that endures, like the body of a mastodon quick-frozen in ice many thousands of years ago. True, various body parts such as blood, corneas, sperm, kidneys, veins, and so on, have been chilled, stored, and then later reused by doctors. Also true is the fact that during intricate surgery, vital parts of living patients have from time to time been kept in deep hypothermia for hours and then rewarmed. But the freezing of a whole human being is something quite different. No mammal of any kind has ever been deep-frozen and then successfully brought back to life, and not a single human being has undergone this experience and been revived to tell the tale.

Have Many People Been Stored Cryonically?

At present there are probably some seventy persons—give or take a few—who are in cryonic storage, or who are enrolled for future freezing.

Why So Few?

The process is very expensive. The deluxe treatment can cost from $7000 to $10,000, and this just for the initial freezing. Then there is a yearly upkeep cost that ranges from $2000 to $3000 per year. Cryonic burial is for the wealthy few.

Moreover, there are an inordinately large number of practical and ethical problems surrounding this very modern idea. Suppose that a cure for a particular disease is achieved, but in many years to come. Who will be here to revive the frozen soul? Who will care? What about the person himself? Might he not find it intolerably painful to reorient himself to the world minus his family, his possessions, his friends, everything? Is life such unmitigated pleasure? Is death so terrible?

More particularly, if a person's organs are damaged during the course of his disease, as they often are, what are the chances that discovery of a cure will guarantee renewal of these organs? To be fully effective, moreover, cryonic freezing should start *before* the person has actually died, when cell damage is still minimal. How will *that* work?

What about the person's heirs? Do they still inherit the deceased's estate? When? If not, what happens to the estate while the frozen owner dangles in cold vitro? Can the surviving mate marry? Is it bigamy to have one living mate and one whose state of aliveness or deadness is undefined? What about taxes? Who becomes liable, the body or its heirs? And insurance? Can relatives make claims for someone who is not exactly dead but not quite alive either? Must they wait to know if the revival is successful before they can collect? Must *they* then be frozen to ensure that they will be around for the other person's thawing?

Can retirement benefits, Social Security, and pension be claimed by the survivors? What about state record keeping: Is the person officially dead as far as the state goes, or officially alive, or officially on hold? Just what is "dead," anyway? There are also, of course, religious considerations: For those who believe in the immortality of the soul and its passage from the body after death, the prospect of cryonic storage represents a nightmare beyond any that might be hatched by M.G.M., that of an immortal soul captured indefinitely in cold suspension between heaven and earth. "For those who have confidence in the human spiritual nature," writes Elaine Vail in *A Personal Guide to Living With Loss* (Vail, 1982, p. 172), "cryonics presents a special dilemma. Does the soul remain 'trapped' in a frigid shell of a body or is it 'released' at the moment of death? If it is released, will it return to the body at the moment of reanimation? Or will another spirit inhabit the body as if it were a newborn? These questions may be of little significance to the scientist embroiled in issues of optimal temperature and cryobiology, but there are many for whom these considerations bear great importance."

How Can One Get in Touch with a Cryonics Organization?

By contacting any of the following addresses:

ALCOR Society, Box 282, Verdugo City, CA 91406.

The Cryonics Association, 24041 Stratford, Oak Park, MI 48237.

The Cryonics Society of San Diego, 4791 50th Street, San Diego, CA 92115.

Hartman Help, Inc., Stuart, IA 50250.

The Manrise Corporation, Box 731, La Canada, CA 91001.

A magazine called *Life Extension Magazine,* published by the Society for Life Extension, Inc. (663 West Barry, Chicago, IL 60657), also features information on cryonics and the latest in life-prolonging news.

Besides Funeral Planning through a Memorial Society, Donation of One's Body to Science, and Fringe Options Such As Cryonics, Are There any Other Alternatives to Conventional Disposition?

There is one. It is termed "immediate disposition" and it is designed, according to the Telophase Society (they were first to sponsor this method of disposal), to "bypass both the mortuary and the cemetery."

In brief, immediate disposition offers just what the name advertises. The company picks up the body, does all the necessary paperwork, cremates it quickly, then returns the ashes to the family for final interment. The complete price of the service is usually below $500.

How Does One Find an Immediate Disposition Society?

Direct disposition has been fought by the funeral industry with great gusto, and as a result only a few are in operation. Two organizations that can be contacted directly are:

Neptune Society, 4922 Arlington Avenue, Riverside, CA 92504.

Telophase Society Plan, P.O. Box 33208, San Diego, CA 92103.

The Telophase Society charges a membership fee of $15 per person and $25 per couple, plus expenses incurred for services at the time of death. The Neptune Society's joining fee is approximately the same. Neptune also provides a scattering-of-the-ashes-at-sea ceremony for an additional small fee.

What about Purchasing a Cemetery Plot in Advance?

There are innumerable cemeteries in this country, and costs differ widely. Some offer minimum services for the price, just a plot of ground, sometimes without even grave-opening and grave-closing expenses included. Others provide a certain number of years of upkeep or perpetual care, scheduled deliveries of flowers, aboveground crypts, and so on. With cemeteries, as with everything, one gets what one pays for.

Pre-need selection of a cemetery plot is heavily encouraged by the cemetery industry, and a large number of burial plans are available, many with attractive financing. Often, these plans are sold door-to-door by representatives of a funeral home or the cemetery itself. Sometimes guilt-provoking strong-arm sales tactics are used: "You *owe* it to your loved ones to prepurchase a burial plot! Do you want to burden them the more with burial expenses!"—and this, not only at the consumer's doorway but through mass mailings and telephone solicitations (one cemetery in California reaches thousands of potential customers via a computerized voice synthesizer). Over the past years cemetery canvassing has gotten a rather bad name, and many outright scams have been reported.

Nonetheless, prepaid cemetery plots deserve their place, especially if one wishes to spare the loved ones this difficult job. But the buyer should watch for pitfalls, most of them similar to those related to pre-need funeral programs (see pp. 293–295).

Be aware, for example, of the finance rate levied for installment buying, especially if the initial down payment is low. Anything above 12 to 15 percent will prove mightily expensive in the long run. Make sure that you know exactly what services are being purchased. When the time of death comes there will be many so-called incidental interment expenses that most of us would never consider: sod to cover the grave, grass-seeding supplies, canopy rental, the price of a concrete vault to line the grave, chair and podium rental for graveside services, use of cemetery urns to hold flower arrangements, light and electricity costs for nighttime ceremonies, music fees for recorded hymns, and many more. Find out which of these items are covered in the pre-need plan and which are not. Make sure that they are put into the agreement. Get an itemized list.

"Apart from specific abuses and deceptions in cemetery sales," reports the Consumers Union report on funeral and cemetery practices (see *Funerals: Consumers' Last Rights*, 1977, pp. 147, 148), "There are a number of misconceptions on the part of consumers about buying cemetery plots on a pre-need basis. Many buyers look upon the purchase of a plot as something of a modest real estate investment. In case they move away or otherwise cannot use it, they reason, it can be sold, and probably for more than it originally cost. This is seldom the case. Because the owner of a plot is not, in a landholding sense, the real owner, many cemeteries will not buy back plots from purchasers. In certain states, the law prohibits cemeteries from buying back plots. Plot owners, therefore, must try to sell their grave sites on their own or through a cemetery broker. (And when the transfer is made, there is sometimes a cemetery charge—about $20—for recording the change in ownership of the plot.) In some states, such as New York, selling plots at a profit is against the law. Some cemetery sales agreements stipulate that the buyer may not sell the plot to anyone. In such cases, only the buyer can use the plot; a buyer who moves away can use it only by burdening survivors with the cost of transporting the body back from the place of death."

What's the Best Way to Choose a Cemetery?

Visit the cemetery first. The following points should be noted:

- Is it well maintained? If you are thinking of purchasing a perpetual upkeep service, note how well the graves that use this service are maintained.

- Ask yourself: Is this truly the place where I want my remains to lie?

- Is it quiet? Is it cramped? Is it *too cramped*?

- What are the cemetery regulations? What are the visiting hours?

- Is the plot you have picked actually available? (Various "bait-and-switch" methods have been used by cemetery owners from time to time, where a customer purchases a particularly attractive plot and then, after death, his heirs are informed that this purchased plot is no longer usable or obtainable—for whatever reason—but that another "just as nice" is available nearby. This is an illegal practice.)

- What have you heard about the management? What is the cemetery's reputation among those who have had relatives buried there?

- If a person plans to have her remains cremated, does the cemetery maintain a columbarium (a vault with niches for containing the ashes of the dead) or an "urn garden" area where ash-holding vessels are kept?

- If the cemetery is private, find out if it is a member of the National Association of Cemeteries or the Pre-Arrangement Interment Association of America. Both organizations demand a certain quality of service and ethical commitment from members.

Who Owns a Cemetery?

A cemetery can be owned in several ways: (1) private ownership, (2) national ownership (these are usually for military veterans only), (3) church ownership, or (4) ownership on a nonprofit basis by town or local organizations. Most cemeteries fall into the last category.

Who owns and who runs a cemetery is a significant factor to take into consideration. Private cemeteries tend to be more luxurious than public ones, and more expensive.

Are There Different Types of Cemeteries?

Two types: the traditional in-ground cemetery familiar across the landscape in every town and city, and the so-called "memorial park," where stone monuments are absent and where sites are marked with flat bronze plaques placed at the heads of each grave.

What about Mausoleums?

These are usually housed in a special section of the in-ground cemetery. Most cemeteries include a traditional monument park area together with aboveground crypts, indoor mausoleum buildings, outdoor mausoleum buildings, and underground vaults or crypts.

What Types of Maintenance Agreements Are Available from a Cemetery?

There are many possible plans. In some the price of perpetual care is included in the economics of the cemetery plot. This, of course, makes costs higher than if such a service is not included, sometimes 15 to 20 percent higher. But remember, heirs are billed on a yearly or even a monthly basis for upkeep of a grave if perpetual care is not taken. Over the long run this can end up costing more than perpetual care.

If perpetual care is purchased, the money as a rule is kept in a trust fund and the interest that accrues is used to pay for the upkeep of the grave site. The legal considerations surrounding this practice differ from state to state, however. One should inquire with the cemetery administration concerning how local laws work in this matter. Note, too, that perpetual care prices are lower for memorial parks, where the markers are flat and where duties such as lawn mowing and upkeep are most easily accomplished.

What Are the Costs Involved in Purchasing a Burial Plot?

They vary a good deal, depending on (1) whether the cemetery in question is church owned, publicly owned, privately owned, national, or otherwise; (2) whether it is in a metropolitan/suburban area or in a rural locale where prices are lower; (3) where in the community the cemetery is located; and (4) where in the cemetery the plot is situated.

With regard to the fourth point, the same cemetery may offer a deluxe burial area, where ageless oaks, uncrowded plots, and picturesque views abound. Then comes the midrange "parks," stately but less private. Finally come the "economy" plots, no-nonsense row-upon-row arrangements which are, as the salesperson tells you, "simple but dignified." In death, as in life, status reigns.

Costs at a cemetery include:

1. The price of the plot

2. The marker

3. Graveside services at the time of burial, such as opening and closing the grave

4. The cost of perpetual care of the grave (if it is not included in the price of the plot) or yearly upkeep charges

5. The metal or concrete grave liner into which the coffin is fitted at the time of interment.

The price of plots can run anywhere from $50 to $500 and up, with the median prices hovering somewhere in the range of $700 to $1000. (Vaults and mausoleums are considerably more expensive.) Opening and closing the grave at the time of interment runs several hundred dollars, and figure at least $500 to $600 more for the grave liner. Perpetual care is usually about 10 to 20 percent of the price of the plot. Markers vary in price from $250 to $50,000, depending on their size and elaborateness. In all, for a modest but decent cemetery plot, plus services and marker, one will pay at least $1200 to $1500, and, with even a small upgrading, quite a bit more.

Can a Body Be Moved from One Cemetery to Another?

State laws allowing, it can. But the process is surprisingly expensive and involves some rather advanced paperwork between the triangle of state, heirs, and cemeteries. It is a procedure not to be entered into without good cause.

If moving a body proves absolutely necessary, most local funeral homes can help make the arrangements. If they do not have facilities for exhumation, they will know who does.

Are There Regulations Governing What Kinds of Burial Monuments May Be Erected in a Cemetery?

Each cemetery handles this matter differently. In some town cemeteries the height and weight of funeral monuments are carefully regulated by municipal decree. In others the type of inscription and the materials the marker is made of is legislated by cemetery policy. Some cemeteries will not allow large statuary or unusual stones to mark the graves. They require that markers be identical and that they be symmetrically positioned throughout the burial property: this in the name of "simplicity" and "the democratic principle" (although looking at the row upon row of duplicate headstones in these Levittown-like necropolises the words "faceless conformity" and "anti-individuality" may come more readily to mind for some.) At the same time, outrageous or grotesque monuments can easily ruin the mood if not the entire esthetic of a burial ground, and restrictions of some kind are usually in order.

The memorial park features flat bronze plaques rather than tombstones. These cost between $250 and $400, considerably less than large granite or marble markers. Even very small stone monuments, however, are becoming prohibitively overpriced, and flat, markerless graves are increasingly popular. It is even possible, we might add, that in the years to come the sober, sun-bleached gravemarker which stands with its poignant inscription and weathered prayers, like something permanent in an impermanent world, will become extinct from our landscape altogether, and that citizens of the future will be interred in much the same way that they have lived—in anonymity.

Where Can Memorial Monuments Be Purchased?

From the cemetery, through the funeral home, or directly from the monument dealer.

There is usually at least one monument dealer near any cemetery. The telephone classified pages can be consulted under the headings "Monuments" and "Bronze Tablets." Buying directly from a manufacturer is usually cheaper than purchasing from a cemetery or funeral home, although the latter method entails less legwork for the customer.

What Should One Look for When Purchasing a Monument?

Materials, workmanship, dealer reputability, and guarantee.

Granite, being an igneous material formed of molten rock (as opposed to rocks formed from deposited layers of sediment, such as sandstone), is the most enduring of all monument materials. Marble weathers fairly well but does not hold an inscription as nicely as granite and tends to soften around the edges through the years. Sandstone is generally inferior. Slate dulls and chips, but it is fairly cheap. Bronze is beautiful and less expensive than stone, but it forms a greenish patina which some like and others do not, and it is not an easy substance to keep clean. Wood is an old standby but, of course, disintegrates in a few years. For this reason many cemeteries restrict its use (although the notion of durability as the *sine qua non* of grave markers is far from universal—in many places the very *nondurability* of such objects as wooden crosses is thought to carry its own symbolism).

Poorly cut stone can crack and weather easily, and unless the buyer procures a written guarantee against it, he has no recourse if it occurs. When examining monuments be aware that good stone does not show any crumbly edges, any seams, rust spots, discoloration, or suspicious-looking cracks, even very small ones. Well-hewn rock is clean and crisp at the cut lines, and the whole stone has a "feel" of quality about it. Do not assume, however, that unpolished stone is inferior. This is only a matter of taste. Contrary to opinion, a polished surface does not weather any better than a dull surface.

Often a monument dealer will push granite on the customer because, as the brochure informs you, it is both beautiful and durable. Sometimes granite monuments are the only ones displayed in the dealer's yard or show area, the implication being that they are the only markers available. But granite markers are more expensive than others; if your tastes run along different lines do not be talked into thinking it is the only material that lasts. Almost any piece of stone that catches one's eye on the landscape, after all, has already been on earth some several hundred million years.

About guarantees: A buyer should insist on an unconditional guarantee from the dealer and should make certain that the dealer has the wherewithal to back up this guarantee. Stones can split. They can crumble and topple off their bases. A reputable stone seller will repair defects or replace the entire stone, as part of the guarantee.

Best of all guarantees is "double protection." In essence, it means that if a stone is defective, both the cemetery administration and the owners of the stone are eligible to file for replacement or repair. From the cemetery's viewpoint a broken stone is an eyesore. From the standpoint of the bereaved a disfigured stone is a blot on the memory of the deceased.

Does a Grave Have to Have a Marker?

In most cemeteries some kind of marker is required. Temporary markers are kept on the grave until the permanent one is in place.

When Is the Marker Placed on the Grave?

There is usually no timetable. In memorial parks the marker is put in place more quickly because it can be quickly manufactured. A larger gravestone can take up to a year to order, cut, and deliver. Some people think that they must put the marker on the grave immediately after the person has been buried, but this is not ordinarily the case.

Can a Person Be Buried on His Own Land, or in a Chosen Plot of Land That Is Not Part of a Cemetery?

This depends on state law. Many states allow it, but not all. Inquire about this from local government agencies.

What about Burying the Deceased's Ashes on One's Own Property?

It is the same as above. Most states allow it. Frankly speaking, though, this is a private concern and there is usually little policing of such matters. Consult with local government for more information.

How Does One Arrange to Be Cremated?

Cremation—the disposal of human remains by burning—is arranged either beforehand by the person himself, or after death by his heirs.

Prearrangement takes place (1) when a person makes it known to his friends or relatives that he wishes to be cremated at death, (2) when he buys a pre-need funeral plan that includes cremation, or (3) when he presents his heirs with a signed document formalizing his last wishes.

When the time for the funeral arrives, the heirs inform the funeral director of the deceased's wishes and the director sets it up. Although cremation was once an unusual form of disposal in this country, it has become common over the last fifty years and is now a routine procedure for any funeral director to arrange.

Where Is a Body Usually Cremated?

Many cemeteries maintain their own cremation facilities. There are also independent crematory companies.

Is Cremation Done in Place of Having a Funeral?

Not necessarily. Cremation is simply a method of disposing of human remains. It operates independently of whether a funeral is held.

What Actually Happens to a Body When It Is Cremated

It is placed in a small rectangular furnace called a retort. The furnace is turned on and the temperatures are raised to extremely high heats. Residual smoke and gases are recirculated within the furnace in a special cycling mechanism so that objectionable odors do not escape into the environment. The body is burned for about an hour and a half until it is reduced to a granulated mass of bone and ash.

If Relatives Accompany a Body to a Crematorium, Must They Watch As It Is Placed into the Furnace?

Relatives are ordinarily barred from watching the burning of a body, although in some states a next-of-kin may be asked to witness the corpse being placed *into* the retort. Choice *is* usually given relatives as to whether they desire to watch the coffin of the deceased being brought to the "committal room" and pushed through the opening into the burning area.

For some people such a sight is the essence of morbidity. For others it serves to complete the process of disposition, in the manner of lowering a body into the grave. Funeral directors are expert in letting people set their own limits, and one will not be asked to witness or take part in an activity that repels them.

How Are the Ashes Returned?

In some cases they are returned in an urn and the urn is then placed in a columbarium at a cemetery. In other instances the relatives may keep the ashes at home in a special ceramic or bronze container, or bury them, scatter them at sea, over the mountains, whatever.

A word of warning: After a particularly inexpensive funeral with cremation, the ashes may be returned in a shockingly simple receptacle, sometimes as shockingly simple as a coffee can. This, obviously, can be dismaying. Furthermore, unless the crematorium calcinates the remains after burning—that is, pulverizes them into light ash—a lumpy residue of bone and sinew will remain and will make a hollow rattling sound inside the container that can horrify the unprepared. The can will be heavy as well, perhaps seven or eight pounds, and this is disquieting for those who assume the ashes of a cremated person are light and fluffy like wood ash. A thoughtful funeral director will warn the bereaved heirs of such concerns in advance.

Is Cremation Cheaper Than Cemetery Burial?

It depends on what type of cremation plan is purchased. Immediate disposition firms such as the Telophase and Neptune Society (see p. 308 for description and addresses) will pick up a body directly and cremate it with a minimum of red tape. Costs for everything are usually below $500.

More commonly, a funeral home will preside over the cremation and costs may run anywhere from $200 to $500. Add to these prices the usual hidden costs: transportation of the body to the crematorium, the coffin, the urn, space in the columbarium, and so on, and cremation can become as expensive as ground burial. Note, however, that cremation requires only a one-time output of cash. No future upkeep of the grave or purchase of a monument is necessary. In the long run cremation is cheaper—but not much.

Must a Coffin Be Purchased for the Body of a Person About to Be Cremated?

This issue is a sore spot with undertakers and has been the cause of much friction between their public representatives and consumer groups. The law in most states decrees that a body marked for cremation must be housed in *some* kind of container, but that this container need not be a regular in-ground-style coffin. The body can be kept, for example, in a special lightweight wooden box until disposal time, or even in a corrugated crate. Simple pine or fiberboard caskets are most common, anything that shields the cadaver and protects the public health.

There are, nonetheless, many instances of funeral homes strong-arming customers into purchasing expensive caskets for relatives about to be reduced to ashes, or suggesting (if not stating) that it is illegal *not* to be burned in a regular coffin. The essence of this entanglement stems from the legal ruling that a body must be transported to the crematorium in a "suitable container." What does this mean exactly? The funeral industry reads: a full-blown in-ground casket made of expensive woods or even bronze. Consumer groups read: any sturdy, sanitary receptacle that can comfortably bear the weight of a corpse.

After much embattled hassle through the years, the consumers' viewpoint has emerged victorious (the funeral industry's interests were not aided to any great extent when it was discovered that some unscrupulous funeral directors were shipping the body to the crematorium in a fancy casket, switching the casket at the last moment, returning it to their funeral parlor, and then reselling it). In a number of states it is now *illegal* for a body to be transported to a crematorium in a regular ground-style casket. Fiberboard or corrugated crates are the only containers that can be used for the purpose. Any efforts on the part of a funeral director to convince a customer that an in-ground casket is legally required for cremation is therefore both unethical and illegal.

Must a Body About to Be Cremated Also Be Embalmed?

In some states an odd law has it that a body cannot be cremated until 48 hours after death. Wherever this law prevails, as in Florida, for example, public sanitation rules that the body must be embalmed. In states where no such arbitrary dictum exists, a body marked for cremation need not be embalmed or otherwise chemically preserved.

Which Is Best, Cremation or In-Ground Burial?

Cremation is usually not as expensive as burial. It is faster and requires less paperwork and red tape. The heirs avoid having to deal with the cemetery administration, the grounds maintenance department at the cemetery, the monument manufacturer, and so on. Psychologically, both the dying person and his loved ones are spared the thought of decomposition, with all the morbid associations that such imagery conjures up. There is also a certain finality to cremation. Burial, in some people's minds, is messy and incomplete. Cremation has the cleanness of flame about it. For some it marks the end of life in a clearly delineated way, and helps mourners let go with greater grace and ease.

At the same time, fire is a violent medium, and the thought of having one's remains, or the remains of a loved one vanish so rapidly, convulsively, and entirely may be a source of anxiety. Others worry, against what their better sense may tell them, that the body in the flames is somehow feeling pain. In-ground burial is a more traditional and familiar means of disposition than cremation, and there is a certain security in knowing that one's last parts are returning to the elements, to ancient mother earth, and that they are somehow still *here* with us, even though lifeless and inert. Some religions (including orthodox Judaism, branches of the Eastern Catholic Church, the Mormon Church, Islam, and certain Christian fundamentalist sects) do not sanction cremation. This rule is based on scriptural interdictions or on the theological belief that destruction of the body interferes with the welfare of the soul.

In the end one must weigh the pros and cons of the question, many of which are emotional—or at least intangible—and decide for oneself which method seems most appropriate. It is easy, of course, to sluff off this unpleasant issue by declaring that "it doesn't matter" or that "all methods are the same in the end." But they aren't, at least not for the survivors. The particular method of burial chosen will cause distinct feelings and psychological reactions in the minds and hearts of those left behind. It pays to keep this fact in mind when coming to a decision.

At the Time of a Loved One's Death, What Are the Most Important Things the Survivors Must Do to Prepare for the Funeral and the Postdeath Activities? Where and How Does One Begin?

Hospitals will ordinarily not keep a deceased person's body very long after the hour of death, and there are many horror stories told of cadavers being preemptorily removed to funeral homes without relatives being advised, and of funeral homes then refusing to release the poor corpse until the heirs pay an assessed "storage" fee. It is therefore imperative that relatives and close friends of a dying person know what measures must be taken at the time of death, and that they be prepared to execute them with dispatch.

It should be plainly stated here that there is nothing morbid or unethical about advance planning for another's death. Repeat: There is nothing morbid or unethical about preparing oneself in advance for the death of a loved one. Some people believe that researching local funeral homes before the person has died or drawing up lists of what to do during the first twenty-four hours after death is ghoulish, or that it indicates an eagerness on the part of the heirs for the loved one to die sooner. But surely this is nonsense. If a person is dying, why pretend he's not? When death comes the experience will be a difficult one, perhaps the most difficult ever encountered. Why not cushion the shock by arming oneself ahead of time with the relevant contacts, the pertinent information, the knowledge of appropriate procedure, so that there will be less to perturb and confound one? Although the effort to preplan may be difficult now, the benefits of such actions will later be blazingly apparent.

So where does one begin?

First, by making up a checklist of things to be done during the first three days following a person's demise. Such a list will (1) help review the many possible contingencies that may arise during this time; (2) allow one to focus on what can be done *now*, ahead of time; and (3) help one to be mentally and emotionally prepared in advance.

Each person's checklist will be a bit different, of course, but there are basics. The following list, based on the one suggested by Ernest Morgan in *Manual of a Simple Burial*, (see bibliography) covers many of the significant concerns:

- Contact the funeral home of your choice. Decide on time and place of funeral. Decide if you (or according to the deceased's wishes) want a funeral or memorial service.

- Make a list of immediate family, close friends, and employer or business colleagues. Notify each by phone.

- If flowers are to be omitted, decide on appropriate memorial to which gifts may be made. (As a church, library, school or some charity.)

- Write obituary. Include age, place of birth, cause of death, occupation, college degrees, memberships held, military service, outstanding work, list of survivors in immediate family. Give time and place of services. Deliver in person to, or phone, local newspapers, send to any distant newspapers.

- Notify insurance companies, request claim forms.

- Prepare for get-together after funeral.

- Arrange for members of family or close friends to take turns answering door or phone, keeping a careful record of callers.

- Arrange appropriate child care.

- Coordinate the supplying of food for the next few days.

- Consider special needs of the household, such as cleaning, and so on, which might be done by friends.

- Arrange hospitality for visiting relatives.

- Select pallbearers and notify each of them. (Avoid men with heart or back difficulties, or make them honorary pallbearers.)

- Notify your lawyer and the executor of the deceased's will.

- Arrange for the disposal of flowers after funeral (they can be given to a hospital or a rest home).

- Prepare a list of distant persons to be notified by letter and/or printed notice, and decide which to send each.

- Prepare copy for printed notice if one is wanted.

- Prepare list of persons to receive acknowledgment of flowers, calls, etc. Send appropriate acknowledgments. (These can be written notes, printed acknowledgments, or some of each.)

- Check carefully all life and casualty insurance and death benefits, including Social Security, Railroad Retirement Act, credit union, trade union, fraternal, military, etc. Check also on income for survivors from these sources.

- Check promptly on all debts and installment payments. Some may carry insurance clauses that will cancel them. If there is to be a delay in meeting payments, consult with creditors and ask for more time before the payments are due.

- Call the religious leader of your choice if you desire him or her to officiate, and discuss the type of service you want.

- Arrange for transportation prior to, during, and after the funeral.

- Make arrangements for relatives arriving from a distant point.

- Arrange for purchase of flowers if they are desired or request that flower money be donated to deceased's favorite charity.

- Secure burial permits and death certificates (these are often necessary when filing a claim for benefits).

- Arrange for music at funeral service, if so desired.

How Does One Find a Good Funeral Home?

Assuming that arrangements have *not* been made beforehand, the first task facing the survivors is finding a good funeral home. Often feeling rushed and bewildered, inadequate and bereft, relatives of the deceased take the path of least resistance and choose the services of an undertaker at random, picking out the largest ad in the phone book or hiring a mortician simply because his office is nearby.

But more care of choice should be taken, even if the bereaved is in no mood for dealing with such difficult details. Funeral service in this country runs the gamut from excellent to egregious, and, as in any business which deals with emotionally vulnerable clients, unscrupulous practice abounds. A hasty choice made now can be paid for later both in monetary loss and emotional pain.

Best of all methods for choosing a funeral director is word-of-mouth recommendation from those whose advice you trust. Talk to people who have recently had a death in the family. Were they satisfied with the service they received from the funeral home? Whom do they recommend? Many older adults will have recommendations, as will friends and neighbors.

Sometimes doctors, nurses, or the hospital administration can be of help. Labor unions, civic organizations, fraternal societies, churches, and consumer groups may have suggestions. People of a specific ethnicity and religion often make use of particular funeral facilities. Inquire at your church or synagogue, or at your local club or community organization. If there is a memorial society in your area, they will be especially helpful. Their specialty is referrals. Perhaps a certain local mortician is highly thought of in civic and community organizations. This is a promising indication. If a funeral home is known to cooperate with a local memorial society, this is also a good sign. Many funeral directors are upright, sympathetic persons, and can be a genuine help in time of crisis. It is worth spending the effort to find a good one.

What Does the Funeral Home Actually Do?

As a rule, just about everything. At a typical American funeral the undertaker choreographs the whole elaborate ritual. His first chore is to remove the body of the deceased from the hospital or household. On the way he takes care of all legal permits, fills out the death certificate, contacts the church and chaplain, works out the logistics of the funeral service, including flowers, music, religious arrangements, pallbearers, schedule, seating placement, and so on. He oversees all preservation, dressing, restorative surgery and cosmetizing of the corpse, and prepares it for burial. He furnishes the coffin, phones the obituary into the local paper, sets up visitation rooms, prints memorial folders and tribute cards, assigns attendants and ushers for the various visitations and ceremonies, makes arrangements with the cemetery for burial or cremation, and provides limousines and oversees transportation of both the body and the guests.

Funeral costs are high, it is true, but it is also true that by performing a number of unpleasant duties that nobody else cares to perform, or knows how to perform, funeral directors earn their wages.

What Kind of Funeral Should a Person Choose If the Last Wishes of the Deceased Are Not Known?

Discuss the matter with friends and relatives. Does anyone recall the deceased having made any remarks, even humorous remarks, about the kind of funeral and interment she would have liked? What were the tastes and tendencies of the deceased? Would she have wanted a lavish funeral? Would she have enjoyed having many people attend or just a few close friends? Would she cherish flowers? Would she prefer that the money be donated to a charity?

Try mentally to put yourself in the deceased's place. Then decide: big funeral, small funeral, no funeral; cremation, burial; flowers, no flowers; whatever. Make your decision as best you can, based on your knowledge of the deceased, and then don't worry over the matter again.

What about Picking Out a Coffin?

If the deceased has not specified the kind of coffin she prefers, you must make the decision based both on what she *might* have liked and what you *can* afford. Most funeral directors have an elaborate selling dance worked out between themselves and the customer with the casket as the centerpole; and indeed the subtle strategies the director has been taught for merchandising these containers have become legend [these methods include: positioning showroom coffins in carefully designed arrangements to subliminally encourage the choice of the most expensive models; sales pitches that exploit customers' grief or play on their guilt; the use of certain light, color, and sound combinations to manipulate buying decisions; the refusal to put inexpensive caskets on display or the practice of downgrading lower-priced models; and so on—see the sections on funeral transactions in Jessica Mitford's scathing exposé of the funeral industry, *The American Way of Death* (Mitford, 1963.)].

There is no reason to go into detail concerning the particulars of these abuses, and in fairness to the profession, some undertakers are more temperate in their coffin salesmanship than others. Nonetheless, the coffin will probably be the most expensive item purchased by a customer, and most salespeople are loath to lose the opportunity to make the maximum profit.

Thus the first rule: Don't be bullied, brow-beaten, or tricked into purchasing a coffin you cannot afford. If the deceased wished to be buried in a simple pine box, it is your duty to see that her wishes are carried out, the pressures of the funeral director notwithstanding. If her wishes were not expressed, a less expensive coffin may still be more appropriate to your budget, and if this is the case, by all means stick to your guns. At the same time, larger, elaborate coffins are a security to some people and a boon to the funeral esthetic. If you or your family prefer this variety and can comfortably afford it, do not allow the antifuneral lobby to bully you out of obtaining one.

The second rule is as follows: As the customer you are entitled to receive an itemized list of services delivered by the mortuary. This list should include not only costs for the casket but for everything, down to the smallest services and items. You are entitled to this list, moreover, *before* you sign a contract, not after the funeral. Although for many years funeral homes were loath to provide this list, a recently passed Federal Trade Commission rule made itemization mandatory as of January 1984.

What guidelines should one follow as far as pricing goes? Many funeral homes provide customers with a *single* package price (or price estimate) for all their benefits rendered. These price offerings may come in several varieties. For example, customers may be quoted a "unit" price, which includes all coffin costs plus all delivered services. They may receive a "bi-unit" price, which includes a separate price for the coffin and another separate price for services. Or they may receive the "multi-unit" price, whereby all items and services are itemized. Rule three: The first two methods of pricing outlined above are unacceptable. They come as a lump sum and are not itemized, and hence do not provide customers with the chance to pick and choose *which* of these many goods and services they actually desire.

For example, the bi-unit price at one funeral house may include the cost of an organist to provide music, a flower arranger to deck the altar with sprays of orchids, and an attendant to check coats at the door for the guests. It then turns out that the family wishes a silent funeral, has ordered flowers omitted, and has no need of a coatcheck person, as the funeral is in the middle of July. Nonetheless, they must still pay the package price.

Although, as stated, there are many honest and upright people in the funeral business, the consumer should be warned that when negotiating for the purchase of funeral services, and a casket in particular, he is entering a country well known for its duplicity, half-truth, and outright fraud. Many funeral directors receive training in tactics of psychological manipulation and coercion, and a goodly number have no qualms about using ploys such as guilt provocation, inference of stinginess, disparagement of a customer's tastes, appeal to status, and so on, all to pull in a few extra dollars from the bereaved. State laws vary widely as to what kinds of pressure can be brought to bear on customers and as to how much information funeral homes must divulge about prices, sales techniques, available options, mandatory and nonmandatory items, and the consumers' rights in the face of all these. It thus pays to find out what your local funeral industry laws are, and also to bear in mind that when doing business in this peculiar area there is one slogan that endures: *Caveat emptor*—buyer beware.

Must a Body Be Embalmed?

This is another thorny issue. The answer is that in most states a corpse does *not* legally have to be embalmed, *except* in the following instances:

1. When the body is to be transported a long distance.
2. When the deceased has died from a highly contagious disease.
3. When an inordinately long period of time must elapse before burial.

What's the Point of Embalming?

The process of embalming has been much misrepresented and misunderstood through the years. Many think that it is a long-term preservation method, something akin to mummifi-cation or suspended animation, and that by draining the blood from the veins and refilling them with embalming fluid, the body will remain preserved for hundreds of years.

The truth is that embalming is simply a stop-gap measure that retards decay temporarily. This is especially true of the embalming done at most mortuaries today, where a less ex-pensive diluted potion of fluid is used instead of the full-strength solution popular some years ago. At best an embalmed body will stay quasi-intact for a few years, occasionally a decade or more, but this is very rare, and it can happen only when chem-ical and climactic conditions are perfect. As a rule, embalmed bodies decompose rapidly in the grave, sometimes within a month or less, and embalming serves only to keep the cadaver looking presentable for the funeral.

Can a Funeral Home Embalm a Body without Permission from the Heirs?

Presently, there is much confusion about whether a funeral home has the right to embalm without first receiving family authorization. Some states deem this practice illegal, others sanction it. *Do not, however, expect a funeral home to suggest the nonembalming option even when it does exist.* They get paid for the service (as much as $200), and can then display the remains in an open casket during the funeral, bringing in added revenues. It is encumbent on those who wish to bypass embalming pro-cedures to inform the funeral director *as quickly as possible about their wishes*, preferably before the body has been delivered to the funeral home. Put this decision in writing and keep a written copy on file.

For some people the avoidance of embalming is a religious issue. For others it is a matter of economic principle. In either case, the wishes of the family should be honored.

But Won't a Body Smell If It Is Not Embalmed?

Not if the funeral is conducted within a day or so after death. Even then, it must be kept at a funeral parlor with refrigeration facilities. If, however, the family wishes to wait the traditional three days and then put the body on view during the funeral, embalming will be necessary.

What Advance Arrangements Can Be Made If a Person Does Not Wish to Be Embalmed?

A person should do the following:

1. Inform all concerned parties of one's wishes in this matter.
2. Record the appropriate instructions in the will and in letters left for executors and supervising chaplain.
3. Locate a funeral home that will cooperate fully with these plans and will help make arrangements in advance.

How Can One Decide If a Body Should or Should Not Be Embalmed?

If the bereaved gain solace from temporary preservation, if the body is to be put on view at the funeral, and if three or four days are to pass between death and disposition, embalming is a necessity. If temporary preservation is not an issue, if the body is not to be placed in an open coffin, if the funeral or memorial service is to follow shortly after death, and if the survivors object to embalming on religious or other grounds, best not to embalm.

Should a Body Be Put on View at the Funeral?

Some people draw comfort from seeing a loved one for the last time. Some insist that seeing the body helps the mourning process. In some religions, it is a mandatory part of the burial ceremony to put the body on display.

Whatever is decided, remember that viewing costs represent an added expense. The body will have to be washed, dressed, and cosmeticized. It will have to be shaved if it is a man, the hair done if it is a woman, and so on. A room for viewing must be rented, and an attendant must be hired to stand at the door. Funerals charge by the hour, and viewing ceremonies sometimes do go on. Be sure to find out in advance what extra costs are involved.

Must a Body Have a Medical Autopsy Before It Is Buried?

If a person dies of unexpected, though natural causes, or if she dies from a rare or highly researched disease, the doctors may request an autopsy. This means that the body will be opened, the organs in question examined, and perhaps certain parts removed for study.

To conduct an autopsy in the case of natural death, the family must be consulted. Unless family permission is given, an autopsy may not legally take place.

What's the Point of an Autopsy?

It is primarily for purposes of medical research. In some instances it may also be of help to the deceased's descendants, as when an autopsy affords early detection of an hereditary disposition toward a certain disease. Occasionally, a family will be unsure why a patient died. They will order an autopsy to see if physician negligence had anything to do with the death, or if some kind of foul play was involved.

Technically speaking, while any person dying within 24 hours after arriving at a hospital is a "coroner's case," usually the coroner will bypass such a technicality unless he feels that the death is suspicious.

A coroner, or medical examiner, is an elected official. It is his job to investigate all unnatural or otherwise questionable deaths. He may, for example, be called if a person has died an accidental, unexplained, or bizarre death; if death occurred without a doctor present; or if there is suspicion of murder, violence, and foul play.

If a Coroner Is Called In and an Autopsy Requested, Must the Family of the Deceased Agree to It?

Yes, it is illegal to refuse a coroner the right to perform an autopsy.

Can a Funeral Director Help the Family of the Deceased Apply for Benefits?

Yes, this is one of his functions. A diligent undertaker will stay abreast of rules and policy changes in insurance and post-death benefits, and he will pass this information on to the survivors. In some instances, for a fee, he will also help the bereaved make out applications for these benefits, collect the proper papers, and file the claims with the Veterans' Administration, Social Security, or other parties of payment.

What Financial Benefits Exist besides Regular Insurance to Help a Family Pay for a Funeral?

Veterans of foreign wars are eligible for cash death benefits from the Veterans' Administration (V.A.) as long as all the discharge papers are in order. A burial allowance of up to $1100 will be paid if a veteran dies from a service-related disability, together with $300 plus transportation expenses if death occurs on V.A. hospital premises. When death does not occur on such premises, $300 will still be paid, together with the funeral payment benefit, in the case of a veteran who died on or after October 1981 and who had up to that time been receiving V.A. compensation or pension benefits (or who would be deemed to have been entitled to this payment if the evidence on file at the date of death supported a determination of entitlement). Burial will be provided in a national cemetery, provided that there is space available, and a marker will be supplied free of charge. In lieu of burial in a government cemetery a $150 plot allowance will in some instances be paid, together with an allowance for headstone and transportation costs. An American flag will be provided for use in the service. As well, some families may qualify for monthly benefits after the funeral. Consult with the nearest V.A. office on the particulars.

Social Security offers death benefits to the surviving spouse or to the survivors of any deceased person who has made regular Social Security payments. These benefits will not be offered automatically, however, but must be applied for. The usual sum paid at the time of death is a lump-sum payment of $225. Inquire at the local Social Security office for particulars. Also worth researching are union, Civil Service, or regular jobholders' benefits (occasionally, an employer will provide death benefits), and Worker's Compensation. Finally, the family should examine all insurance papers left by the deceased on the chance that a funeral or pre-need policy was purchased and then, for whatever reason, put away and forgotten.

Must a Person Leave a Will to Ensure That His Heirs Will Receive Their Inheritance?

If a person dies intestate, that is, without leaving a will (the person who leaves the will is called the *testator*), the state government takes over the estate, and after appointing their *own* executor, and after an interminable amount of time, they apportion it out to the heirs *in the manner they see fit*. Obviously, this is not an ideal situation, neither for the heirs nor for the testator himself, who may have had entirely different notions concerning who should get what. A will is a relatively simple legal document and it rarely costs more than a few hundred dollars to prepare. Having one drafted now can save a lot of people a great deal of frustration later.

Does Leaving a Will Reduce Tax Pressures on the Heirs?

There is both a federal and a state exemption offered to heirs if an estate is valued below a certain net worth. This exemption is imperiled if a will does not exist. There are also methods of passing on portions of an estate to heirs *during* one's lifetime so that at the time of death the final estate will be smaller and less taxable. This benefit, too, holds little water unless the terms are clearly spelled out in a legal document.

Who Should One Choose as an Executor for One's Will?

Basically, an executor's job is to administer a will after a person's death. His job may include any of the following:

- Assembling all important records
- Settling all the person's accounts outstanding and collecting all debts
- Filing the death certificate
- Guiding all donations to the proper recipients
- Watching over the finances of the funeral proceedings
- Having the will probated by the courts
- Filing estate tax returns
- Making sure that everyone gets what is legally coming to them

For performing these tasks an executor is paid a certain small percent of the inheritance money. The amount of this allowance is stipulated in the will itself.

In many states the law insists that unless it is otherwise stipulated in the will, an executor must be bonded, which means that he or she must post a certain amount of money against the value of the estate, to ensure that he or she will not misappropriate any funds from the estate while the will is being settled. This can be an expensive proposition in the case of a large estate and an unnecessary one if the executor is trusted. If you want to save the executor this trouble, be sure it is stated in the will that bonding is unnecessary.

The executor of your will should be a person you trust, a close relative, perhaps, or a longtime friend; a family lawyer; or a reliable institution such as a bank. The executor must be someone or some organization whose competence and common sense can be relied on. A "dotty" aunt or a "ditsy" brother-in-law may make endearing companions, but unless they have a sense of administrative savvy, it is better not to name them as guardians of your will.

What Are Some of the Moral and Legal Issues to Be Aware of concerning a Will?

A good lawyer will usually make sure that all aspects of a will are nailed down airtight. Nevertheless, it pays to be concerned with significant details. Some items of note concerning a will include:

- Make sure that once a will is prepared and signed, your lawyer has a photocopy, together with the executor and any-one else who will need it when the time comes. In fact, since the will should be easily findable at the time of death, it may be best to have the lawyer keep the original, while you and the executor(s) keep photocopies. Generally speaking, a law-yer's office is the safest place to store a will.

- If you have a valuable collection of anything in particular—antique furniture, rare books, ancient coins, collectibles—have the value professionally assessed so that your heirs know its worth should they wish to sell it.

- If it is necessary, leave a separate letter for the executor(s) informing him/them of the following pertinent information:

    - Where your important papers are kept (including the original of the will itself)
    - The location of hidden revenues, files, credit cards, automobile documents, insurance policies, receipts, tax papers, safe-deposit boxes, bank accounts, military discharge papers, Social Security and retirement papers, separate insurance for burial expenses, contracts for pre-need funeral or burial plan, mortgages and deeds, real estate papers, birth certificates, confirmation papers, marriage license, religious instructions, pensions, valued be-longings, and precious collections
    - Last wishes for funeral arrangements or memorial services
    - Papers pertaining to organ donation, if the deceased is a donor
    - A list of business associates to be contacted after death
    - Itemizations of any debts outstanding

- The original copy of the will should be clearly marked "Orig-inal" and kept in a location which is accessible at a moment's notice. (A safe or safe-deposit box is not a very smart place to stash the original copy if others do not know it is there, or if they do not have the combination.) All photocopies should be marked "Copy." If you move your residence or if you file the actual document in a new location, be sure to inform all parties involved. Make certain that those who hold photocopies also store them in a handy place.

• If you are moving your residence from one state to the next, bear in mind that state laws differ concerning inheritance. It is smart thinking to have a lawyer from your new state go over the old will and make sure that nothing needs to be amended.

• If a husband and wife maintain a similar will and one of the parties dies, the surviving mate should take quick steps to alter the will and name new beneficiaries.

• Make sure that a will includes provisions designating guardians for minor children.

• Be certain that all the signatures are on the will, and that these are in the rightful place and are accompanied by the proper dates.

• Be certain that no inappropriate notes, unidentified signatures, or unauthorized annotations are written anywhere on the will, as these may be considered part of the will at the time of probate and may cause complications.

• Be sure that no important person is overlooked on your bequest list. Sometimes a small but heartfelt gift will avoid hurt feelings on the part of relatives and friends.

• It is smart policy to review your will once every several years. In the rush of life it is easy to forget that an update may be required to comply with a new state law, or that a new executor is needed for whatever reason, or that a few paragraphs must be added to recognize the birth of a new child, and so on.

What If Someone Wishes to Change Her Will?

It is not a big undertaking to change a will. Every time you wish to add something a so-called codicil is prepared, before witnesses, and is appended to the will. Your lawyer will advise you on this procedure.

When Should a Codicil Be Added and When Should a Will Be Rewritten?

A codicil is added if you want to make a small amendment or add a brief point here and there. If major changes are required, the will should be redrafted.

What about Trust Funds? How Do They Work? Under What Circumstances Are They Advisable?

A trust fund is established so that money or securities can be held "in trust" for an heir over a certain amount of time. The holder of the trust is usually an individual or an institution such as a trust company or a bank.

The money from this trust is apportioned out to the heir over a period of time in the way the testator requests. Usually, a trust fund is drawn up as part of the original will.

The heir, for example, may be a minor who is slated to come into the proceeds from the trust fund at a certain age. Meanwhile the money in the fund earns him interest. Or the heir may receive only the interest from a trust fund up to a certain age, say 35, and after that receive the full principal. Or he may *never* be allowed to dip into the principal but may only receive the interest. The principal then passes on to his heirs and remains forever in trust within the family line. There are endless possible variations.

Trust funds are created to serve many purposes. They may pay for a child's education, cover a mate's medical bills, finance an heir's living expenses in perpetua, or even serve as an endowment for a group or organization. They offer many tax aids for the estate planner and help prevent family funds from being squandered. Details for setting up a trust can be gotten from banks, money managers, lawyers, and others.

Should the Property in a Will Be Put in the Name of Both Spouses?

There is not one but three kinds of joint ownership legally recognized in this country. These are:

1. *Joint tenancy.*   In this case both partners own property. If one dies, the other automatically inherits it.

2. *Tenancy by the entirety.*   This is similar to joint tenancy, except that the agreement exists *exclusively between husband and wife*, and *applies only to real estate holdings*. When one partner dies, the other receives the property.

3. *Tenancy in common.*   If a person dies, his or her property goes to whichever heirs are designated in his will, not necessarily to his mate or family. For example, if someone owns a house under tenancy in common with a friend, after that person's death that person's share is willed to anyone he chooses, his wife, say, or his children.

As a rule, husbands and wives make out joint wills. But joint ownership can be more troublesome than is commonly supposed, and *it is in no sense a substitute for a will*. Making out a joint will means that the estate is not eligible for the so-called marital deduction—see below; and further, each time the will is changed *both* parties must give their consent, even if they are estranged. There are, as well, considerations too detailed to go into here that make joint ownership questionable. The point is that while many people automatically assume that coownership is the wisest inheritance policy, there are often better ways to negotiate these tricky matters. Consult a lawyer for specific advice on this matter.

What Is a Marital Exemption?

In cases where property is not jointly owned, the marital exemption allows the surviving spouse—and only the surviving spouse—an exemption of 50 percent on the taxable estate. Whether or not it makes sense to use this deduction depends on the size of the estate in question. Again, one should get professional advice before taking any steps.

What Is Probate?

Probate in Latin means "to prove." In legal terms it means that the legality and validity of a will must be established before the assets can be distributed.

The scenario is this: After a death the executor files the will with the local courts and the courts decide whether everything is in order. If there is no sign of forgery or fraud or of insanity on the part of the testator, the court automatically probates the will and issues *letters testamentary* which empower the executor to handle all matters concerned with the will. With a simple will probate may take only a month. In complex cases the proceedings can shuffle on for years.

Must Everyone's Will Go through Probate?

In the past few years many states have simplified probate laws, and if an estate is small, it can often be avoided. However, although probate is often spoken of in negative terms, it is not always a liability. A lawyer can advise you on the particulars.

Must a Lawyer Make Out Your Will?

No, everyone has the right to make out his or her own will. The procedure is not terribly complicated when the estate is small, although there are definite pitfalls and one should approach this task warily. There are several books on the market which explain methods for drawing up your own will. The following will all prove helpful:

Kling, Samuel G., *Your Will and What to Do about It*. Chicago: Follett, 1974.

Schwartz, Robert J., *Write Your Own Will*. New York: Collier Books, 1961.

Dacey, Norman, *How to Avoid Probate*. New York: Crown, 1965.

Ashley, Paul B., *You and Your Will*. New York: McGraw-Hill, 1975.

13

Bereavement

There is no universal pattern. But there are tendencies which, with much variation, repeat among a majority of the bereaved.

Generally speaking, the first few days after death and during the time of the funeral, bereaved individuals are in a state of numbness and shock. Indeed, one of the valuable things about a funeral is that it provides activities to keep thoughts occupied and time filled.

Anyone who has been through it knows: The phone jangles on a regular basis, friends and family arrive with their condolences; there are insurance papers to locate, tax and inheritance matters to worry about, the undertaker to deal with, bills to be paid, possessions to be sorted, relatives to feed, children to be cared for, arrangements to be made. A general air of activity prevails.

Then comes the letdown. Stage two. The phone quiets down. Sometimes it seems to go dead. Friends who were so anxious to help during the time of the funeral now become strangely inaccessible; they are embarrassed, perhaps, or frightened that you might fall to pieces, who knows? But the silence is real, and the grieving person begins to face the fact that the loved one is *gone*, really gone, and that she, the bereaved, is alone. After the initial numbness wears off, as with an actual physical wound, the throbbing pain begins in earnest.

Stage two can last a long time. It is a period of disorientation, despair, bewilderment, unreasonable worry, fear for one's own survival. The bereaved may torture herself with "if only" messages, or "why bother anymore?" messages, or "I can't go on without him" messages. The thought of the dead person may become obsessive; a thousand times a day some silly association triggers a memory or some real everyday task no longer has to be done, and the mind runs wild.

Depression brings physical apathy. The bereaved feels drained of energy and impetus to do *anything*. It is difficult just to get out the door to work in the morning. It is difficult not to look for the dead person's face on the street, behind desks, through store windows, and especially in the eyes of friends and lovers. A lot of midnight crying follows, and a lot of dread of one's own death.

Then, after a cetain period of time, the bereaved begins to notice that the pain has abated—a little. She is able to think of the deceased without tears. She can accept the death with at least some sense of composure. Terrible lamentation turns into quiet sadness. Sleep patterns, appetite, energy, all make a gradual return, and forays into the outside world begin. This is the third stage—resignation and acceptance.

How Long Does the Second Stage of Mourning Last?

For a few people it can go on for years, although this is unusual. For most people after about a year there is a lessening of intensity. It depends on how close one was to the deceased, and how attached.

Do People Ever Really Recover from the Death of Someone Very Dear?

Yes, they do. Unless the grief becomes pathological or obsessive—we will discuss these possibilities below—it does abate. No matter how intense, no matter how many mornings one wakes up feeling as depressed as the day before, the time will come then the pain slacks off. Although it seems impossible now, things *will* change.

Of course, the sadness never disappears entirely, not if the person was much cherished. It is hard to imagine the parents of a dead child ever ceasing to feel sorrow for their loss. It is hard to imagine how the survivor of a happy marriage could ever stop missing the lost mate, no matter how many years they are separated by death. And perhaps this is as it should be. Most of us, however, do come to terms with bereavement pain and do reach an *accommodation* with grief. "Accommodation" is the key word. The pain never goes away entirely; it simply settles in a psychological place that becomes acceptable and perhaps even comfortable. As Michael Simpson puts it in *The Facts of Death* (Simpson, 1979, p. 249): "It is not a question of forgetting, but of regaining the capacity to remember peacefully."

What Part Does Denial Play in the Grief Process?

Huge emotional losses take a long time to sink into the unconscious. While intellectually a person may accept another's death without argument, below the psychic surface things move at a slower pace.

During the few weeks following a death, especially a sudden, unexpected death, close survivors may seem remarkably unaffected by the event. They may go about their business as always, speak of the deceased with no apparent remorse, work and play apparently without any sorrow. This does not necessarily mean that they are heartless, take note, but rather that unconsciously something inside them has not really taken in the reality of the situation. Then suddenly, six months later, the same person one day dissolves into a pool of tears over a seemingly insignificant incident. For weeks, months, even years he may remain in this turbulent state of mind, sometimes aware that the reaction is a delayed and subverted response to grief, sometimes not.

Other instances of denial are less subtle: A surviving spouse holds a long conversation with the deceased partner in front of strangers. She insists on speaking of the dead person in the present tense, or of informing others that the departed is "on a trip" or "has gone away for a while"—the word "death" cannot yet be pronounced. Or a mourner catches herself unconsciously starting breakfast for the dead person when she rises in the morning, or listening for his car in the driveway at night. In some extreme cases the bereaved may *literally* deny death, declaring, much to the consternation of everyone involved, that the dead person is alive as usual and will be back momentarily. This illusion may be reinforced by hallucinations or by dreams which are so remarkably vivid that survivors insist that the deceased *must* be alive somewhere and that it is all a terrible mistake.

Unwillingness to let go of the dead is demonstrated with particular vividness on a collective level, where a popular idol may be mourned among rumors that he is really in hiding, that he has changed his identity and is having a joke on the world. "Elvis Still Lives" or "Is Dag Hammarskjold Really Dead?" or "John Lennon Speaks to Friends from across the Grave" are all headlines that have crowned checkout counter tabloids through the decades. Following the shooting of President Kennedy there was a persistent rumor, avidly kept alive by the pulp press, that J.F.K. had not really been killed in Dallas at all but had been returned to Washington in vegetable condition, where his body is even now kept alive on a life-support machine.

Denial, in short, is a common reaction to any great loss. But since only a delusional person is likely to deny the fact of death outright, the process knows many deft and finely tuned subtleties.

Denial is a common reaction in one form or another for most people after the death of a loved one.

Is It Normal to Be Angry at the Deceased?

There is no relationship without its dark side. After death, these mixed emotions may surface, against one's wishes and sometimes beyond one's control, with anger and resentment leading the assault. "Why didn't so-and-so leave me better off?" a survivor finds herself thinking, or "So-and-so's not here to make a mess after taking a bath; what a relief!" Then follows the inevitable self-chastisements for thinking the unthinkable. "Of the dead, say nothing but good," a Latin proverb has it, and this is an attitude that runs deep in Western culture. So guilt follows anger follows guilt follows anger.

What Is the Best Way of Dealing with Anger toward the Dead?

Negative feelings toward the dead must be discussed. Otherwise, they fester. The best therapy for resentment is to realize that it is normal, that for certain of us it is inevitable, especially if the relationship was a rocky one, and that admitting one's anger is an integral part of the mourning process. One woman who had experienced a particularly tempestuous relationship with her husband found that after his death she dwelled more on the bitter memories than on the happy ones. In response she set aside a half-hour every day during which time she would lock herself in the bathroom and carry on long, passionate discussions with the deceased. During these dialogues she would accuse him, scream at him, dress him down, and then emerge from her cathartic session feeling better and more capable of recalling the positive things. Each person reaches his or her own accommodation.

If possible, find a sympathetic friend to speak with. These reactions should be aired. Although it is something of a taboo to talk derisively of dead persons, it is not a particularly strong taboo, and a little frankness often melts the ice, allowing others to vent their real feelings, too, and serving as a kind of purging mechanism for all involved.

Don't Mourners Also Tend to Get Unreasonably Angry at Other People—the Doctors, the Funeral Director, Relatives, and Others?

In times of crisis scapegoats become a premium item—the undertaker made a botch of the proceedings, the attending nurse "killed" the deceased with too many narcotics, the deceased's brother is a rat for not coming to the funeral. The whole world becomes culpable.

In the first months following a death, mourners are likely to indulge in irrational resentments and petty blamings. Displaced anger, that is, anger really meant for the deceased, or for oneself, or for both, may be deflected in peculiar tangents, with hurt feelings and severed friendships to show for it. Best to investigate these reactions. Who are they really aimed at? Is anyone really at fault? And if they are, will blaming them bring back the dead?

Might Not a Mourner Also Experience a Sense of Relief?

After the ordeal comes the letdown. Then feelings of unburdening and release. There is nothing wrong with these. The mourner has, as it were, earned them. Whether the relief comes from not having to drag off daily to the hospital any longer, or not being obliged to clean the loved one's soiled bed clothes, or even just not having to put up with the deceased's crankiness, such reactions are human and natural.

And Guilt Must Be Inevitable, Too?

If not inevitable, certainly common. It is hard to stop from thinking: "If I had only done such-and-so for the deceased while she was still alive." Now the opportunity for doing such-and-such is gone forever. Nothing can induce it to return. Poor me. Bad me.

Self-blaming is a no-win deal. No matter what miracles of nurturance the bereaved may have performed for the deceased, there will always be gaps in the record and hence room for self-doubts. The more a survivor broods on what might have been, the worse things get psychologically, until the person envelops herself in a cocoon of recriminations. Occasionally, survivors will even blame themselves for having actually *caused* the death—by not being by the person's bedside at the right hour, by not insisting that the dietician withhold salt from the diet. Guilt-mongering internal dialogues are self-perpetuating. Guilt is one of the most common and most insidious side effects of grief.

Doesn't Guilt Show Itself in Hidden Ways, for Instance, in a Tendency to Idealize the Deceased?

In the period immediately following death the bereaved tends to think about the deceased continually, talk about her constantly, until her image becomes subtly transformed from real to super-real. This process is known as *idealization,* and its end product is a false all-positive portrait of the deceased.

But since this idolization is artificial, or at least incomplete, there are possible complications. Disguised as respect and admiration, idealization may be the survivor's unconscious method of paying off guilt. That is, the higher the survivor raises the deceased up on a pedestal, the more the survivor reproaches himself. "Why wasn't I worthy of such a perfect person?" the bereaved wonders again and again. "I am no good. She was all good." It is a seesaw effect.

Idealization, further, can involve the mourner in the strange game of identification and imitation. Without realizing it, the survivor starts to mimic certain of the dead person's habits and opinions. Even physical mannerisms are copied. Everything about the deceased becomes worthy of emulation, and in extreme cases friends will note with alarm that the survivor tends literally to take on the dead person's personna.

Idealization in some form is a natural reaction to the death of a loved one and is, within bounds, a normal one. Like many aspects of the mourning process, it becomes dangerous only when exaggerated and prolonged.

What about Depression During the Mourning Period?

Depression, as we have stated elsewhere, does not necessarily mean the blues or feeling down in the dumps. It is a psychophysical response to loss which often manifests as a series of physical symptoms such as insomnia, impotence, midnight sweats, anxiety attacks, lack of appetite, and physical inertia. All of these symptoms can come without the accompaniment of dejection per se. One does not necessarily have to be "down" to be depressed.

Furthermore, depression can become a substitute for grief rather than a complement. By this we mean that grief and depression are by no means the same, that one is a natural reaction and the other—can be—a disease.

What is the difference? Although grief may bring on somatic changes such as those described above, these symptoms do not usually last for long periods of time, certainly no longer than a year. People in a state of grief are bereft and deeply saddened. But they are not zombie-like or inert or in unbroken despair, at least not for long periods of time. Depressed people often are.

This is a generalization, of course. Nonetheless, if after a long period of mourning a person still seems mired in hopelessness, and if the pall shows no signs of lifting, indications may be that the natural self-healing process of grief has been aborted and has given way to a more serious and more prolonged depressive illness.

Is Anxiety a Common Symptom of Bereavement?

Anxiety attacks may be a sign that something has gone wrong with the mourning process, that in some way it has been subverted or repressed.

It is not unusual, for instance, to find that people who bottle up their grief experience sudden heart palpitations, seizures of irrational fear, an inability to catch their breath, a tendency to frequent swallowing, and that they undergo these symptoms many months or sometimes many years after the death. Such a response may be a reaction to repressed grief that was never aired. It may also be a reflex of one's own death fears, tripped off by the death of someone close.

Anxiety attacks are not necessarily a sign for alarm among the bereaved if they take place within the first year of mourning, and if (1) they do not happen too frequently, (2) they do not continue to occur regularly over a long period of time, and (3) they do not become so intense that they cripple normal functioning.

So in Short, It Can Be Said That There Are Many Different Feelings a Bereaved Person Is Likely to Go through during the Mourning Period? And That the Particular Emotions One Is Likely to Experience Are Determined on a Personal Basis by Each Person's Temperament and Personality?

To quote Earl Grollman (Grollman, 1974. p. xiv): "Some people will refuse to think about death at all; others will think about nothing else. Some will vehemently protest; others will quietly resign themselves to the reality. Some will curse God; others will console themselves in a future world-to-come. Some will be disorganized; others will effectively reshape their lives. Some will cry hysterically; others will remain outwardly impassive and emotionless; while still others may even laugh. Some will deify the deceased; others will be angry at the dead person for leaving them alone and abandoned. Some will blame themselves for the death; others will project the guilt upon the physician, the clergyman, or another member of the family. Reactions to death are varied and contradictory; they are neither prescribed nor are they predictable."

Occasionally, in the Midst of Feeling Great Sadness for the Death of a Loved One, There Will Come a Sensation of Pleasure or Even a Kind of Glee That the Person is Dead. How Does One Deal with Such a Thing?

Ambivalence is a major motif of mourning. Just as we are ambivalent about those we love in life, so this attitude carries through to those we love in death. How could it not? It is just that in death there is a taboo against admitting what we so freely thought and felt about a person while she was alive.

The fact remains that one of the goals of grief work is to come to terms with negative feelings concerning the deceased: to admit one's negative attitudes is to take a step toward becoming free of them. "I am a man," goes the ancient saying. "Nothing that is human is alien to me."

Do the Bereaved Tend to Go through Stages That Parallel Those of the Dying Person?

Yes, and these can take place both before and after the death of a loved one. That is, those close to a dying person will pass through some form of denial as soon as they learn the person has a terminal disease—"It can't be so, it can't be true that my husband is dying." Then anger—at oneself, at the dying person, at the doctor, at the angels. And also bargaining ("Just give him a little more time, God") and depression ("I can't go on without him if he dies"). And finally acceptance.

After death the same stages present themselves also, although often in random patterns. Denial is there, as we have seen, and certainly anger and depression, and sometimes even bargaining. But in the end, most people arrive at acceptance. Indeed, the five steps on which Kübler-Ross founded her theories describe the standard sequence of responses that one may have to *any* great loss.

In What Ways Does the Mourning Process Differ If the Deceased Has Died a Sudden or Violent Death?

Sudden death is easiest for the person who dies, hardest for the survivors. Sudden death means that survivors have had no time to participate in any of the psychological predeath rites of passage that steel the soul against the inevitable, rites such as those discussed in the previous question and throughout—denial, depression, anger, and so on. Thus unprepared, the victim's family is vulnerable and psychologically unarmored. Their grief tends to be violent and extreme. Sometimes they require special help.

How Do People Usually Behave after Receiving News of Sudden Death?

In times of sudden death survivors react in two general ways: with stoic silence or with hysteria. The first instance calls for no immediate aid other than giving the person permission to let out his feelings, if he so wishes. Hysterics are more needful. Allow them to scream and cry and get out the choked emotions, even if their behavior is extreme; experience shows that after a couple of hours most people come to grips with the problem and take care of what must be taken care of. Do *not* order an hysterical person to "Get hold of yourself!" or "Try to calm down a bit!" at least not immediately after they have received the news. Such statements are really just reprimands barely disguised. They only stoke the flames and add guilt to an already bitter cup.

It is wise to keep mourners under surveillance if they are extremely distraught and to make sure that they are constantly accompanied by a friend, a relative, a social worker, or a chaplain. Doctors should be on hand to answer questions. The bereaved will want to know all about what happened: Did the deceased feel pain? Was he conscious? How long did it take him to die? Is his body mutilated? What parts have been disfigured? Who witnessed the accident? Was somebody with him when he died? Whose fault was it? If these questions go unanswered now they are likely to haunt survivors far into the future; the imagination can conjure images of horror that far surpass anything known in real life.

Further, survivors may behave irrationally. They may make embarrassing accusations, they may blame the doctor or some uninvolved party for the person's death. They may threaten to sue the hospital, or the pharmaceutical company, or the town ambulance corps. They may even make physical threats. Remember, these people are in a state of deep shock. They are not fully responsible for their behavior. This is a time for patience.

Involve the bereaved in postdeath activities. If the patient has been seriously injured and the family is waiting it out, keep them informed. Let them feel they are part of things. Certainly, do not lie to them about the condition of the patient or about the fact that the situation is critical.

Survivors may sometimes be in a condition of profound shock much like that experienced by survivors of natural disasters such as earthquakes and floods. Various motor-neurological slowdowns occasionally are noted, together with speech problems, temporary paralysis, and even amnesia. Survivors are in a state of high suggestibility and may become exaggeratedly dependent on others around them.

There is not a great deal that can be done at this point for these victims of fate other than being there for them, helping them through the logistics of postdeath activities and serving as a ready listener should they wish to talk. If counseling or psychiatric help is to be provided, many believe that it should not be forthcoming for at least a month or two following the death, after the bereaved has had time to take in the tragedy and begin the adjustments.

Should the Bereaved Family See the Body of the Deceased If It Has Been Disfigured?

The family should learn all they can in advance about how badly damaged the body really is. If they then still wish a viewing, they must mentally prepare themselves for a difficult sight. The question comes down to this: Will the solace viewers receive from seeing the body of a loved one countermand the grisly memory picture of the body they will be forced to carry with them for the rest of their lives? This is a very personal choice, one that should be considered from the practical question of *how* mangled the body is—in many cases nurses can clean up a corpse so that it is generally presentable—as well as how capable each family member is of dealing with such a confrontation.

What about Drugs to Calm the Bereaved?

Many think that the best approach a mourner can take during the postdeath period is to meet grief head-on, give vent to pent-up anxieties, anger, dismay, relief, self-doubt; and to directly experience—or "experience out" as some psychologists like to say—the pain.

No doubt it would be difficult to accomplish such a feat if drugged. On the other hand, the fact is that at times psychic pain becomes just too great, especially in the beginning. Then the easy way out may be the only way. A good doctor or psychiatrist will know what antidepressants and sedatives are appropriate for this situation and how best to oversee the dosage. Narcotic prescriptions can be especially helpful for insomnia or to calm the grating manic energy some people experience in the first weeks following a loved one's death. Each case must be considered separately. Those who make absolute rules on issues of drug use and who use guilt-provoking language to carry their point—"It is *wrong* for a mourner to take *stupefying drugs!*" "Tranquilizers *ruin* a person's chances of recovering from grief!"—are as out of step as those whose reflex it is to turn automatically to these chemical panaceas during every emotional crisis.

What Are the Indications That a Person's Mourning is Becoming Unhealthy or Even Pathological?

Practically any bizarre physical or emotional reaction is possible during the mourning period. This includes the most grotesque and uncharacteristic behavior imaginable—a normally gentle person becomes violent; a demure virgin starts to chase men; a conventional executive goes bohemian. When such outlandish behavior appears people start to worry.

Should they? Are abnormally intense reactions to death just a passing stage? Will such personality changes be permanent?

The question boils down to this: What separates a normal grief reaction from an abnormal one? The following list gives some indications:

1. If the reaction manifests in a violent way, either toward oneself or toward others, this is a danger sign.

2. If the reaction continues for a long period of time without any indication of abatement or change, something is unresolved.

3. If the reaction is so intense that it impairs the person's normal functioning for an extended time period, this calls for outside help.

In other words, while many strange changes may occur in the mourner both on a physical and a psychological plane, they are only cause for serious worry if they are destructive and if they go on too long.

What Are Some of the More Common Abnormal Reactions to Grief?

There are many of these. They may include:

1.   Unusual denial. The survivor refuses to accept the fact that the person is dead. She may get angry at others who talk of the deceased in past terms or who dare suggest that he will not return. Sometimes she consults mediums or believes that she is communicating with the spirits of the dead in her dreams.

2.   Numbness. Heavily bereaved persons often become zombie-like or shell-shocked. They seem in a daze. Although it is not unusual for survivors to behave this way during the funeral and shortly thereafter (Jackie Kennedy was a famous example of this at the funeral of her husband), if it continues for a long time afterward it can be a sign of pathology.

3.   Irrational fears. The survivor becomes phobic about ordinary things. He is suddenly afraid to drive the car, to take an elevator. Although such fears may seem far removed from death per se, at bottom the phobia and the terror can be directly related.

4.   The compulsive thought. The aggrieved person cannot stop thinking about the deceased. He feels compelled to incessantly touch some object that belonged to her. He ruminates over the details of her death and seems unable to control his thoughts. They inevitably return to the memory of the person or to thoughts of his own death.

5.   Unrelieved sorrow. A healthy mourning process describes a parabolic graph: The line goes up, rounds off at the peak, and then slowly descends toward normalcy. If no such rhythm occurs and if the pain remains uninterruptedly intense, something may be blocked.

6.   Delayed grief. The person who feels nothing at the time of death often experiences somatic and psychological reactions at a later time. Sometimes these reactions do not seem to be connected. Suddenly one is overcome with an unnamed terror or a migraine headache. Neither experience *seems* to have anything to do with grief. But it may.

7.   Extreme sense of hopelessness. Despair is a common aftereffect of death, especially if the survivor was particularly close or dependent on the deceased. When this despair will not go away, or when it begins to show itself as a desire for self-destruction, this is a real flag of danger. One should seek help.

8.   Fantasies and hallucinations. Occasionally, a person will see the ghosts of the departed, converse with them in dreams, or hear their voices, often in odd places like the office or the supermarket. Some describe sensing the "presence" of the dead person, or feeling that the person's spirit is somehow watching. Although such a confrontation can be disorienting, it is not unusual, especially in the first months following a death. In fact, supernatural encounters with the dead are far more common than is generally believed, mainly because people are embarrassed to speak of them.

Whether or not these visits are objectively valid—and who are we to know for certain?—the point is that they are sometimes a great comfort to those who have experienced them. They should not be belittled or explained away "scientifically." Chances are the person won't believe you anyway. At the same time, if the apparitions are malicious or oppressive, if they madden the bereaved rather than provide strength, and if they have the earmarks of paranoia or psychosis about them, it is wise to seek help. Often it is better to let go of the departed entirely rather than to keep them captive in one's own visionary prison.

What about Physical Problems Resulting from Mourning?

Broadly speaking, if a person tends to have a repressed, controlling personality, the aftereffect of mourning is likely to be somatic. If a person has a loose ego structure and inclines toward hysteria or depression, the illness is apt to be psychic.

Physical side effects of mourning can include a number of possible ailments, ranging from headache attacks to asthma, fatigue, indigestion, constipation, impotency, skin rashes, shortness of breath, dizziness, weight loss, fainting spells, palpitations, change in menstrual patterns, tightness in the chest, loss of appetite, nausea, and prostate problems. More serious diseases can also be linked to bereavement, especially when the bereavement is intense. There is, for example, an unusually high percentage of people who develop cancer during the first year of mourning, as well as rheumatism, heart trouble, kidney malfunction, and various other heavy-duty ailments.

Does This Mean That Grief Is a Disease?

There is no doubt that the postdeath period is a kind of danger zone as far as physical and mental health are concerned. In ways both understood and not understood the health becomes more vulnerable than in normal times, especially if a person is already sickly. Mourners tend to become ill more easily and recover with less speed.

What Can a Mourner Do to Protect Herself against Physical Side Effects?

It is sound policy for a person who is grieving to seek frequent medical checkups; to get extra sleep, rest, and exercise; to eat well; to surround herself with loving, supportive people who are good for the soul; and to be as emotionally gentle on herself as possible. How one treats oneself during this time *does* matter. The grieving person *is* more physically fragile than usual.

Does Bereavement Affect the Sex Drive?

During a crisis situation sex is the first biological drive to shut down. The same process takes place when one is psychologically stressed or when one is passing through a difficult period of change. Don't panic. The need and desire for physical intimacy will come back. Any great loss can induce a reduction of the sexual drive. In almost all cases the condition is temporary.

Is It Possible to Die from Grief?

Although the storybooks are filled with tales of lovers slain by separation from their loved one, grief per se cannot kill. The so-called "broken heart syndrome" is primarily a description of the fact that the health of the sorrow-stricken can be weakened by intense emotional anxiety, and that illness and even death can become a greater likelihood. Apparently, there are isolated cases of healthy people dying on the spot when suddenly informed of a loved one's death, but such reports are so rare that they really do not figure into the practical picture.

Don't Some People Try to Speed Up the Mourning Process or Avoid It with Escapism?

Grief runs its own peculiar cycle. Because this process is a slow one, people often become impatient and try to return to normalcy as quickly as possible, picking up where they left off with friends, relatives, lovers, and business associates. They may also try to numb themselves with alcohol, partying, sex, work, and mindless amusements.

None of these diversions make a loss hurt the less, not in the long run, and a person who indulges in them too liberally may end up feeling more alienated than before. It is better not to rush grief or to suppress it with escapism. It does not work anyway. One can feel sadness even through a stupor. Let the sadness dissipate at its own speed.

Some People Think It Is "Weak" or "Unmanly" to Show Their Real Feelings of Bereavement.

Tears are a healthy response to pain, especially the great pain of death. If a person feels that he or she must maintain a steel-like facade in the face of it, all a bystander can do is let the person know verbally and nonverbally that it is all right to be sad and that it is acceptable to show that sadness. From then on the person is on her own.

Friends of the Bereaved Will Sometimes Stop Calling or Break Off the Relationship. Why Is This?

Probably because the bereaved reminds the friends of their own death, because being with the bereaved is too gloomy, or because the friends are worried about knowing what to say, or how to behave, or whether to mention "it." Often, in fact, it turns out that a particular friend may have stopped calling not out of dislike or disloyalty but simply because he was embarrassed at his own inability to handle a difficult situation.

A variation on this theme is the friend whose "help" is really just a means of controlling and curtailing the expression of strong emotions. "The idea of helping is often a euphemism for controlling the expression of feelings," writes David Peretz (in Schoenberg et al., 1970, p. 18). "The need to escape these feelings often leads to the failure to realize that what the bereaved person needs may be presence alone, without words. The ambiguous responses that bereaved individuals give in answer to what they want makes it possible to select that with which the relative or friend is most comfortable. If help is offered, it may take the form of encouragement of occupational therapies rather than of expression of grief. This leaves the bereaved isolated and alone at a time when the knowledge that there are those who care and are prepared to share painful feelings is crucial."

What Positive Steps Can a Bereaved Person Take to Work through Grief?

1. It is helpful for most persons to give visible expression to grief. Keeping feelings pent up can lead to side effects, both mental and physical. Find someone to talk it all over with. Get it out. Do not worry if you find yourself telling anyone who will listen the same story, over and over. If it helps, why not? Your

main job now is to work through the grief in whatever way you can.

2. Be sure to carry out any promises made to the deceased before death, especially those which were especially important to him. Not attending to such agreements can eat at one's conscience.

3. Seek variety and new impressions. Getting a pet brings joy into a gloomy house, especially if children are present. So does a new paint job for one's room, a new piece of furniture, a new group of shrubs for the garden, new curtains for one's apartment. A trip may be in order, although not until all immediate postdeath matters are taken care of as a source of worry. When you are up to it, new friends, new hobbies, visits to fondly remembered places, learning to meditate, taking an exercise class, sawing wood, cooking special dishes, making models, programming a computer, planting a lawn, taking a class in something you have always wanted to study, doing spring cleaning, going swimming, nature walks, photography, learning to type, getting a massage, taking a skiing trip, participating in sports, gardening, camping, working with a craft, renovating one's apartment, joining a local club or civic organization, all can be therapeutic. *Small things do help.*

4. If you feel you cannot make it on your own, by all means seek help. Every community has religious, social, and psychological services available. They can be of much value, so take advantage of them. Silent suffering brings more suffering, not less.

5. Go back to work as soon as possible. Although this may seem like the most difficult prospect imaginable, keeping busy is a key to successful mourning.

6. Refrain from making any major decisions during the period of intense mourning. Postpone any major domestic moves, job changes, divorces, marriages, financial decisions—anything. Although it may not be apparent, one's judgment tends to be hazy and even irrational during this time. Wait at least a year

before you decide on anything drastic. A year and a half would be better.

7. Join a bereavement group or bereavement workshop. There are many of these throughout the country and they really do work. A list of the available societies is given on pages 259–263.

8. Like sex, death is a subject much repressed. Especially after one has gone through the lugubrious exercises of the funeral, the wake, the visitation, the interment, the cremation, the mourning, the memorials—help! Finally, there comes a time when all this solemnity grows so large it seems about to pop. What better, more salutary way to pop it than with the great anxiety-reliever par excellence, laughter—at oneself, at things you recall about the deceased, at whatever is funny. Mourning, remember, does not preclude a little laughter now and then to clear the air.

What Are the Signs That One Has Successfully Worked through His Grief?

You will start to feel better. There will be a sense of completeness, as if some kind of dues have been paid off. The sadness will not disappear entirely, of course, but it will become integrated into one's consciousness as the rocks and the trees are integrated into the body of the earth. Many of the strange sensations and even physical reactions will abate. Gradually. Some morning you will wake up and just know that things are different. Energy returns, and with it the will to go back to the world, to move among the living, to be alive oneself—to live—to be a sentient creature in this strange place at this strange time, now, right now, to return, to be among us—to be alive.

References
and Books
of General
Interest

Aitken-Swan, J., "Reactions of Cancer Patients on Being Told Their Diagnosis." *British Medical Journal,* (1959), 779–783.

Anderson, J., A. Cartwright, and L. Hockey, *Life before Death.* London: Routledge & Kegan Paul, 1973.

Aries, Philippe, *Western Attitudes toward Death.* Baltimore: Johns Hopkins University Press, 1974. A concise series of four essays profiling the various postures that Western man has taken toward his own mortality from the Middle Ages to the present, traced through the fine arts, history, tomb building, literature, religion, and so on.

Bakan, David, *Disease, Pain and Sacrifice: Toward a Psychology of Suffering.* Chicago: University of Chicago Press, 1968.

Becker, Ernest, *The Denial of Death.* New York: Free Press, 1973. A Pulitzer-prize-winning study of death denial taken from both a psychoanalytic (principally Freudian) and philosophical perspective. Heavy reading, but full of fruitful insights.

Bennett, A.E. (ed.), *Communication between Doctors and Patients*. London: Oxford University Press, 1976.

Berkow, Robert (ed.), *The Merck Manual*. Rahway, New Jersey: Merck, Sharp and Dohme Research Laboratories, 1977.

Boase, T. S. R., *Death in the Middle Ages*. New York: McGraw-Hill, 1972. Fascinating study of a time in history when humanity was truly obsessed with death. Included in this highly pictorial study are chapters on the Last Judgment, death in battle and in art, the Christian "art of dying," the dance of death, morbidity and death, and the black plague.

Bowers, Margaretta K., Edgar Jackson, James Knight, and Lawrence LeShan, *Counseling the Dying*. New York: Harper & Row, 1964. Slender volume filled with worthy essays on working with the dying patient, psychotherapy for the dying, how the living feel about the dying, and religious considerations in counseling.

Bowlby, John, *Loss: Sadness and Depression*. New York: Basic Books, 1980. Erudite psychological examination of human reactions to loss.

Bluebond-Langner, Myra, "Meanings of Death to Children." In Herman Feifel (ed.), *New Meanings of Death*. New York: McGraw-Hill, 1977. A classic, often-quoted study.

Brandreth, Gyles, *871 Famous Last Words*. New York: Bell, 1979. The first parts of this book present a fascinating collection of last utterances, some of them profound, some pitiable or ludicrous, almost none without interest of some kind. The dying speakers in question range from Lorenzo de Medici to Rudolph Valentino to Boris Pasternak to Dutch Schultz.

Brantner, "Death and the Self." In Betty Green and Donald Irish (eds.), *Death Education: Preparation for Living*. Cambridge, Mass.: Schenkman, 1971.

Browning, Mary H., and E. Lewis, *The Dying Patient: A Nursing Perspective*. New York: American Journal of Nursing Company, 1972. A textbook for nurses, but good enough to stand on its own for anyone interested in understanding the problems of death from the viewpoint of health professionals in general and nurses in particular.

Carey, Raymond G., "Living until Death: A Program of Service and Research for the Terminally Ill." In Elisabeth Kübler-Ross, *Death, the Final Stage of Growth*. Englewood Cliffs, N.J.: Prentice-Hall, 1975. "The author describes a study of terminally ill patients. The aim is to discover what factors predict who will best cope with dying and what can be done by helping professionals to make life more meaningful for dying patients."

Choron, Jacques, *Death and Western Thought*. New York: Collier Books, 1963. A kind of warm-up for *Death and Modern Man* (see below). Deals specifically with how various writers and philosophers (Socrates, the New Testament, Descartes, Epicurus, Schopenhauer, Whitehead, etc.) have explained the problem of human extinction.

Choron, Jacques, *Death and Modern Man*. New York: Collier Books, 1964.

Explores contemporary and historical human fear of death through such avenues as the search for immortality, varieties of death fear, hard and easy deaths of famous people, morbid death fear, and versions of immortality. A fascinating, objective (if slightly aloof) historical analysis of the ways humanity has attempted to find answers for the unanswerable.

Daudet, A. *Suffering*. New Haven: Yale University Press, 1934. A classic study on the subject.

Davies, D.M. (ed.), *Textbook of Adverse Drug Reactions*. New York: Oxford University Press, 1972.

Dempsey, David, *The Way We Die*. New York: McGraw-Hill, 1977. A highly intelligent and incisive study of attitudes, manners, legal questions, moral dilemmas and shifting fashions concerning death among members of the medical profession, the funeral industry, and the public at large. Lucidly written and full of thoughtful insights.

Donnelly, Katherine Fair, *Recovering from the Loss of a Child*. New York: Macmillan, 1982. Some helpful advice here and there if you read it carefully.

Duda, Deborah, *A Guide to Dying at Home*. Santa Fe, N. Mex.: John Muir, 1982. Excellent primer for home care.

Dumont, R.G., and D.C. Foss. *The American View of Death: Acceptance or Denial?* Cambridge, Mass.: Schenkman, 1972.

Eissler, K., *The Psychiatrist and the Dying Patient*. New York: International Universities Press, 1955. A classic study of death from the perspective of the mental health professional. The first half of the book is a series of essays discussing cultural and psychoanalytic theories of death, the second half contains carefully detailed case studies. This book is of special interest to the professional; laypersons may find it too technical, although the effort to get through it will reveal many interesting insights.

Exton-Smith, A.N., "Terminal Illness in the Aged." *Lancet*, 2 (1961).

Feifel, Herman (ed.), *The Meaning of Death*. New York, McGraw-Hill, 1959. One of the first and best collections of essays ever assembled on the subject of death. Includes classic studies such as "The Soul and Death" by Carl Jung, "The Child's View of Death" by Maria H. Nagy, "Treatment of the Dying Person" by Gerald J. Aronson, and "Time and Death in Adolescence" by Robert Kastenbaum.

Feifel, Herman (ed.), *New Meanings of Death*. New York: McGraw-Hill, 1977. A follow-up to Feifel's *The Meaning of Death* (see above). More of the same high-level essays on the subject, although by the time this book was printed much more had been published on death than when the first in the "Meanings" series came out.

Feifel, Herman, et al., "Physicians Consider Death." *Proceedings of the 76th Annual Convention, American Psychological Association*, 1968.

Fichter, Joseph, *Social Relations in the Urban Parish*. Chicago: University of Chicago Press, 1954.

Freud, Sigmund, "Thoughts for the Times on War and Death." In *Collected Papers*, Vol. 4. London: Hogarth, 1915. An often-quoted essay, revealing some of Freud's private feelings about death.

Fruehling, James (ed.), *Sourcebook on Death and Dying*. Chicago: Marquis, 1982. A giant compendium of essays, surveys, statistics, reprints, studies, and articles taken from numerous sources, compiled in the fashion of all the Marquis Professional Publications. Lots of significant reading here, but the book is expensive. Get it from the library if possible.

Funerals: Consumers' Last Rights by the editors of *Consumer Reports*. New York: Pantheon Books, 1977. Extremely helpful, no-axe-to-grind handbook designed for the reader who must face funerals, cremation, burial, dealing with morticians, pre-need plans, postdeath expenses, cemeteries, memorial societies, embalming practices, and so on. Well worth reading *before* the topic becomes a present issue.

Furman, E., *A Child's Parent Dies: Studies in Childhood Bereavement*. New Haven: Yale University Press, 1974.

Garfield, Charles A. (ed.), *Psychosocial Care of the Dying Patient*. New York: McGraw-Hill, 1978. Good series of essays. Subjects include terminal patient care, families facing life-threatening illnesses, doctor–dying patient relationships, psychological needs of the dying and their families, counseling the patient's family, care of the dying, and assorted issues in the field of death and dying.

Gillespie, W., "Some Regressive Phenomena in Old Age." *British Journal of Medical Psychology*, 36 (1963).

Glaser, Barney G. and Anselm L. Strauss, *Awareness of Dying*. Chicago: Aldine, 1965. A classic, ground-breaking study of death denial among health care professionals. One of the first books to confront this loaded subject head-on.

Gonda, Thomas A., "Pain and Addiction in Terminal Illness." In Bernard Schoenberg, Arthur Carr, David Peretz, and Austin H. Kutscher (eds.), *Loss and Grief: Psychological Management in Medical Practice*. New York: Columbia University Press, 1970.

Goodman, Lisl M., *Death and the Creative Life*. New York: Springer, 1981. A fascinating and at times surprising study of how scientists and artists deal with the reality of their own deaths.

Graedon, Joe, *The Peoples' Pharmacy*. New York: Avon Books, 1976.

Grollman, Earl, *Explaining Death to Children*. Boston: Beacon Press, 1967. One of the best works on the subject. Like all of Grollman's books it is full of warm, reflective, informed advice.

Grollman, Earl, *Concerning Death: A Practical Guide for the Living*. Boston: Beacon Press, 1974. Excellent guide for the dying person, the person's family, and the bereaved. Covers all aspects of the death cycle, from diagnosis to burial. Written mostly in question-and-answer form.

Grollman, Earl, *Living When a Loved One Has Died*. Boston: Beacon Press,

1977. A series of notes to the bereaved, full of hope, useful guidance, and frank common sense.

Herzog, E., Psyche and Death. Translated by E. Rolfe and B. Cox. London: Hodder and Stoughton, 1966.

Hinton, John, Dying. Baltimore: Penguin Books, 1967. Short English classic. Readable and relevant.

Hutschnecker, Arnold D., "Personality Factors in Dying Patients." In Herman Feifel (ed.), The Meaning of Death. New York: McGraw-Hill, 1959.

Jacobson, Edmund, Anxiety and Tension Control. Philadelphia: Lippincott, 1964. Famous study of a physician's method for relieving anxiety through stretching and tightening exercises. Basically a how-to book, easily read and easily practiced. The exercises really work.

Jepson, Gordon, "A Study of the Relationships between Religious Involvement, Religious Affiliation, Sex and Definitions of Death." M.A. thesis, University of Maine, Orono, 1967.

Kalish, R. A., "The Onset of the Dying Process." Omega 1 (1970), 57–69.

Kasper, August, "The Doctor and Death." In Herman Feifel (ed.), The Meaning of Death. New York: McGraw-Hill, 1959.

Kavanaugh, Robert E., Facing Death. Baltimore: Penguin Books, 1974. Few people have ever written with such empathy or unsentimentalized sincerity on this subject as Kavanaugh. Highly recommended, for both the person facing death or anyone interested in the subject.

Kübler-Ross, Elisabeth, On Death and Dying. New York: Macmillan, 1969. The classic book by the most famous proponent of death reform in this country. Highly recommended.

Kübler-Ross, Elisabeth, Questions and Answers on Death and Dying. New York: Collier Books, 1974. Short series of questions and answers, taken verbatim from many of Kübler-Ross's lectures and seminars. Covers some offbeat and rarely considered aspects of death. Also reviews some of Kübler-Ross's original work, as presented in On Death and Dying (see above). Excellent.

Kübler-Ross, Elisabeth, Death, the Final Stage of Growth. Englewood Cliffs, N.J.: Prentice-Hall, 1975. Collected essays edited by the most visible personality in the field of death and dying. Most of the articles are of considerable value, especially Kübler-Ross's own moving contribution, "Death as Part of My Own Personal Life."

Kübler-Ross, Elisabeth, To Live Until We Say Goodbye. Englewood Cliffs, N.J.: Prentice-Hall, 1978.

Kübler-Ross, Elisabeth, Living with Death and Dying. New York: Macmillan, 1981. Like all Kübler-Ross's books, recommended.

Lepp, Ignace, Death and Its Mysteries. New York: Macmillan, 1968. Study of death from a historical-religious viewpoint. Includes chapters on fear of death, suicide, death and love, the meaning of death, and images of the afterlife.

LeShan, Eda, *Learning to Say Goodbye*. New York: Macmillan, 1976.

Lief, Harold (ed.), *Medical Aspects of Sexuality*. Baltimore: Williams & Wilkins, 1975.

Lingeman, Richard, *Drugs from A to Z*. New York: McGraw-Hill, 1974.

Long, James W., *The Essential Guide to Prescription Drugs*. New York: Harper and Row, 1982.

Lorrance, Arleen, *Why Me?* New York: Rawson, 1977.

Martinson, I. M., *Home Care for the Dying Child: Professional and Family Perspectives*. New York: Appleton-Century-Crofts, 1976. Much sound advice for the person facing this distressing and difficult situation.

McMahon, Arthur, Jr., and Paul Rhudick, "Reminiscing in the Aged: An Adapted Response." In Sidney Levins and Ralph Kanaha (eds.), *Psychodynamic Studies on Aging*. New York: International Universities Press, 1967.

Mitford, Jessica, *The American Way of Death*. Greenwich, Conn.: Crest Books, 1963. Best study ever done on abuses in the American funeral industry. Full of ironic humor and authentic horror, this book did much to launch funeral reform in the United States.

Mount, B., "Death and Dying—Attitudes in a Teaching Hospital." *Urology*, no. 4 (1974), 741–748.

Nagy, Maria, "The Child's Theories concerning Death." *Journal of Genetic Psychology*, 73 (1948), 3–27. One of the first and best case studies done on children's attitudes toward their own death.

Nierenberg, Judith, and Florence Janovic, *The Hospital Experience: A Complete Guide to Understanding and Participating in Your Own Care*. Indianapolis/New York: 1979. Excellent warning and self-help manual for anyone facing imminent hospitalization.

Oken, D., "What to Tell Cancer Patients." *Journal of the American Medical Association*, 75 (1974), 1120–1128.

Pattison, E. Mansell (ed.), *The Experience of Dying*. Englewood Cliffs, N.J.: Prentice-Hall, 1977. Readable series of essays, not the least relevant of them being Mansell's own contributions in the first part of the book.

Pearson, Leonard, *Death and Dying: Current Issues in the Treatment of the Dying Person*. Cleveland: The Press of Case Western Reserve University, 1969. Collection of essays by top writers in the field, including Robert Kastenbaum, Cicely Saunders, Richard Kalish, and Anselm Strauss.

Quint, Jeanne C., *The Nurse and the Dying Patient*. New York: Macmillan, 1969. Specifically for nurses, although of some relevance to interested laypersons. Subjects include dealing with dying patients, nurse identity, conversations with dying patients, and first encounters with death.

Rosenthal, Hattie R., "The Fear of Death as an Indispensable Factor in Psychotherapy." In Hendrik M. Ruitenbeek (ed.), *Death Interpretations*. New York: Dell, 1969.

Rossman, Parker, *Hospice*. New York: Fawcett (Columbine Books), 1977.

Ruitenbeek, Hendrik M. (ed.), *Death Interpretations*. New York: Delta Books, 1969. Interesting selection of essays on all aspects of death and dying.

Saunders, Cicely, "The Last Stages of Life." In M. Browning and E. Lewis (eds.), *The Dying Patient: A Nursing Perspective*. New York: American Journal of Nursing Company, 1972. Specifically on the hospice system and how it works.

Schilder, Paul, and David Wechsler, "The Attitudes of Children towards Death." *Journal of Genetic Psychology*, 45 (1934), 406–451.

Schoenberg, Bernard, Arthur Carr, David Peretz, and Austin H. Kutscher (eds.), *Loss and Grief*. New York: Columbia University Press, 1970. Important series of essays on all aspects of loss and bereavement.

Schoenberg, Bernard, et al. (eds.), *Anticipatory Grief*. New York: Columbia University Press, 1974.

Shipley, Roger, *The Consumer's Guide to Death, Dying and Bereavement*. Palm Springs, Calif.: ETC, 1982. Excellent source book for information on navigating the funeral industry, plus sections on death preparation, helping the living after your death, obligations following the funeral, and euthanasia.

Schneidman, Edwin S., "Orientations towards Death." In R. W. White, *Study of Lives*. New York: Atherton Press, 1963.

Schneidman, Edwin S., *Deaths of Man*. Baltimore: Penguin Books, 1974. A literary, historical, psychological, and warmly poetic extended essay dealing with certain clinical aspects of death, with the ways in which the aftermath of death influences the family, and above all with the notion of how a sick person may die an "appropriate death." Also discusses the ways in which the threat of "megadeath"—that is, the constant threat of total annihilation via nuclear weapons—affects humanity at large.

Schneidman, Edwin S. (ed.), *Death: Current Perspectives*. Palo Alto, Calif.: Mayfield, 1980. A large, extensive tome of essays on the subject of thanatology, edited by one of the foremost authorities in the field. Includes articles on death as a social disease, the demography of death, the determination of death, psychological aspects of death, death and dignity, life after death, and suicide.

Simpson, Michael A., *The Facts of Death*. Englewood Cliffs, N.J.: Prentice-Hall, 1979. Readable, friendly, comprehensive, and human. Simpson seems to cover all the bases, remaining unimpeachably professional even while he writes from a personal point of view.

Smith, Kathleen, *The Stages of Sorrow*. Totowa, N.J.: Biblio Distribution Center, 1978.

Tas, J., "Psychical Disorders among Inmates of Concentration Camps and Repatriates." *Psychiatric Quarterly*, 25 (1951), 679.

Tatelbaum, Judy, *The Courage to Grieve*. New York: Lippincott/Crowell, 1980. A sincere self-help book.

Vail, Elaine, *A Personal Guide to Living with Loss*. New York: Wiley, 1982.

Formularistic and sentimental here and there, but generally helpful for anyone attempting to recover from the death of a loved one.

Vernon, Glen, *Sociology of Death*. New York: Ronald Press, 1970. Replete with both common and offbeat sociological information on death and its immediate ramifications. Academic, yet highly readable, and at times fascinating.

Waechter, E. H., "Children's Awareness of Fatal Illness." *American Journal of Nursing*, 71 (1971), 1168–1172.

Wass, H., "How Children Understand Death." *Thanatos*, 1, no. 4 (1976), 18–22.

Weisman, Avery D., *On Dying and Denying*. New York: Behavioral Publications, 1972. One of the most penetrating and best-written books in the field by one of death's most eloquent interpreters. Subjects include denial plus problems of thanatology in general. A great book.

Weisman, Avery D., and Thomas Hackett, "Predilection to Death." *Psychosomatic Medicine*, 23 (1961), 232–256.

Weisman, Avery D., and Robert Kastenbaum, *The Physiological Autopsy*. New York: Community Mental Health Monograph 4, 1968.

White, Laurens P., "Death and the Physician." In Herman Feifel (ed.), *New Meanings of Death*. New York: McGraw-Hill, 1977.

Wilcox, S.G., and M. Sutton, *Understanding Death and Dying: An Interdisciplinary Approach*. Port Washington, N.Y.: Alfred, 1977.

Index

Memorial Societies *(cont.)*:
  cooperating society, 303
  way of joining, 305
Memories of deceased of children, 187–189
Mental-emotional equation in pain, 100
Mental health professionals on hospital
  staff, 251
Mental retardation and withholding heroic
  means, 140
Middle knowledge, 8–9
Minority religious group and religious
  counselor visits, 243
Modeling and purposeful death, 286
Monument:
  guarantee with purchase of, 315–316
  kinds of, permitted in cemetery, 314
  materials of, 315–316
  place of purchase of, 314–315
  workmanship of, 315–316
Mood enhancers, use of, 53–54
Mourner:
  anger of, at scapegoats, 345
  drugs to calm, 351–352
  feelings of, 348–349
  friends of, stop calling or break off
    relationship, 357
  protection of, against physical side
    effects, 355
  sense of relief of, 345
  working through grief by, 357–359
Mourning:
  length of second stage of, 341
  physical problems from, 354–355
  process of: and escapism, 356
    after sudden or violent death, 349–351
  with sick person, 122–123
  unhealthy or pathological, 352–353
Musical instrument and purposeful death,
  286
Mutual pretense, 9–10
Myth and death, 167–168

Neurosis and fear of death, 90
Neurovegatative symptoms, 98
New goals for dying person, 118
Nonjudgmentalness, 120
Nonverbal communication, 26
  about death to children, 166
  and patient with preparatory depression,
    52–53
Nurse:
  and learning truth about diagnosis, 13
  personality conflicts of patient with, 145
  visiting (*see* Visiting nurse)
Nursing techniques taught to family
  members in home care, 227
Nurturance, art of, 28
Nutrition and home care, 228

Open awareness, 3, 14
  being forced on patient, 17
  inadvisability of, 19
Open-minded patient and chance for
  remission and recovery, 28
Oppression, overwhelming, in dying
  person, 72
Optimism:
  and chance for remission and recovery,
    28
  and survival rate in concentration camp,
    57
Order not to resuscitate, 138
Organ:
  donated, acceptance of, 300
  donation of: costs involved, 301
    to medical science, 295–296, 300
  transplantation of, religious objection to,
    301

Pain:
  alleviation of, 94–95
  anger as reaction to, 35
  and anxiety, 96–98
  control of, for person dying at home,
    100
  dealing with, 93–110
  and depression, 98–99
  and embarrassing ailment, 101
  escape from, by denial, 22
  fear of, 86, 93–94
  increase of, as disease progresses,
    100
  kind of, 16
    nausea and difficulty in swallowing,
      100
    suffocation and choking, 100
  and longing to die, 81
  measurement of, 94
  medication for, 100–103, 105–110
    control of, 104
    dosage adjustment of, 107–108
    upon request, 101–102
    side effects of, 108–109
  methods for relief of, 96
  prediction of, 101
  relief of, and alcohol, 109–110
  and remaining alert, 109
  response of different national, ethnic,
    and racial members to, 102–103
  and self-induced relaxation, 104
Painkilling drugs, addictiveness of, 107
Painting and purposeful death, 286
Palliative care unit in hospice, 270
Panic and dying, 111
Parents:
  actions of, with child after death of close
    relative, 171–174